THE
PAUL HAMLYN
LIBRARY
---•---
DONATED BY
THE PAUL HAMLYN
FOUNDATION
TO THE
BRITISH MUSEUM
---•---
opened December 2000

WITHDRAWN

Leon Trotsky (right) with his secretary Erwin Wolf, in a photograph taken in Norway, 1936.

THE CRISIS OF THE FRENCH SECTION [1935-36]

LEON TROTSKY

PATHFINDER

NEW YORK   LONDON   MONTREAL   SYDNEY

Copyright © 1977 by Pathfinder Press
All rights reserved

ISBN 0-87348-520-3 paper; ISBN 0-87348-519-X cloth
Library of Congress Catalog Card Number 77-81289
Manufactured in the United States of America

First edition, 1977
Second printing, 1996
Edited by Naomi Allen and George Breitman

Pathfinder
410 West Street, New York, NY 10014, U.S.A.
Fax: (212) 727-0150
CompuServe: 73321,414 • Internet: pathfinder@igc.apc.org

PATHFINDER DISTRIBUTORS AROUND THE WORLD:
Australia (and Asia and the Pacific):
    Pathfinder, 19 Terry St., Surry Hills, Sydney, N.S.W. 2010
    Postal address: P.O. Box K879, Haymarket, N.S.W. 2000
Canada:
    Pathfinder, 4581 rue St-Denis, Montreal, Quebec, H2J 2L4
Iceland:
    Pathfinder, Klapparstíg 26, 2d floor, 101 Reykjavík
    Postal address: P. Box 233, 121 Reykjavík
New Zealand:
    Pathfinder, La Gonda Arcade, 203 Karangahape Road, Auckland
    Postal address: P.O. Box 8730, Auckland
Sweden:
    Pathfinder, Vikingagatan 10, S-113 42, Stockholm
United Kingdom (and Europe, Africa except South Africa,
    and Middle East): Pathfinder, 47 The Cut, London, SE1 8LL
United States (and Caribbean, Latin America, and South Africa):
    Pathfinder, 410 West Street, New York, NY 10014

Table of Contents

Part Two
Split (November 1935-March 1936)

Part Three
Reunification and New Split (June-July 1936)

Introduction

Why, when so many important books are begging to be read, should anyone read a book about an internal dispute in a small French revolutionary organization more than forty years ago? For the same reason that people continue to benefit from reading Lenin's *One Step Forward, Two Steps Back,* which is about an internal dispute in the Russian Social Democratic Labor Party almost seventy-five years ago. Because useful lessons for today about Marxist politics and the nature of revolutionary parties can be learned from events of the past as they were seen at the time by great Marxist fighters and teachers. History does not repeat itself exactly, and it would be futile to search in this book for tailor-made solutions to current problems. But readers can find here concrete examples of the method Trotsky used in the 1930s when he was trying to train cadres able to build a party that could lead a socialist revolution.

The French section mentioned in the title was the Bolshevik-Leninist Group (GBL) in the Socialist Party (SFIO, the French section of the Second International). The GBL's members had joined the SFIO in 1934 in order to win over leftward-moving members of the SFIO to the program of the International Communist League (ICL), which was working to create a Fourth International in opposition to the Second and Third Internationals. Information about the French section of the ICL, its entry into the SFIO, and the political conditions of the period will be found in the editorial prologue entitled "Trotsky and the French Section Before July 1935."

Trotsky, the leader of the ICL, had been living in France as an exile since 1933. Although he was greatly restricted in his public political activity (the government had ordered him to leave France in April 1934, but he remained until mid-1935 because no other government would admit him before then) he followed French politics very closely and served as the chief political adviser of the GBL. In fact, he was the first to propose that his followers enter the SFIO.

In June 1935 Trotsky moved to Norway. Just before he left, he wrote in a letter that the GBL had accomplished about all it could in the SFIO and that it should reorient itself toward an independent existence and the formation of a new revolutionary party. A day or two later Léon Blum and other leaders of the SFIO, speaking at a national congress of the party in Mulhouse, indicated that they would have no compunction in expelling the GBL if it became an obstacle to their plans for a coalition with the Stalinists, and before the end of July expulsions of GBL members began.

That was what precipitated the crisis of the French section: disagreements among the GBL leaders over how to respond to the expulsions and to Trotsky's insistence on an independent course. Some, who thought it was premature to conclude the SFIO episode, wanted to make concessions to the SFIO leadership in the hope of averting the expulsion of the whole group. Others felt that while the expulsion of the whole GBL was probably inevitable, it should be drawn out as much as possible in order to gain more time to win over SFIO left-wingers who had not joined the GBL. Still others wavered between these positions and Trotsky's, which at first was not well understood or widely supported in the GBL leadership. The situation was further complicated by the fact that the GBL leaders were divided into three factions, two of which had been vying for hegemony in the section for five or six years.

Selection of a policy to meet the crisis could not be found at a purely tactical level, although some participants undoubtedly had illusions on this score. Trotsky stressed issues of principle and strategy, to which tactics had to be adjusted or subordinated. The questions that were posed included:

What was the nature of the epoch? How could the coming world war be opposed, and how could it be prepared for if it could not be prevented? How could the French masses be mobilized against the very real threat of fascism? How could the workers be won away from class collaborationism in the form of the new People's Front supported by the Stalinists and Social Democrats? What should be done to respond to the new turn to the right by the Communist International at its Seventh World Congress? How could the revolutionary nucleus in the SFIO become a force strong enough to play a decisive part in the coming social explosion (the huge sitdown strike wave in May-June 1936)? How could centrist elements still inside the SFIO be won over to the revolutionary Marxist program? Was the Fourth International only a propaganda slogan or had the time come for action to bring it into being? What, in fact, is a revolutionary party? Is it a collection of factions or tendencies each of which is free to go its own way whenever it fails to win a majority? Can a faction justify violating the discipline of a revolutionary party because it has tactical differences? And that was not all—even the nature of the revolutionary newspaper became a subject of contention.

The crisis led to a split in the French section and the split led to the loss of many new members and the estrangement of potential recruits. Attempts to heal the split were made in 1936, but they failed. In disarray and under government repression, the French section was not able to play much of a role in the great strike struggles of 1936. The dissipation of the early gains made by the SFIO entry was probably a factor in the decision by delegates to an international conference called by the ICL in July 1936 not to establish the Fourth International then, as Trotsky had urged, but to postpone it (until 1938, as it turned out). The split plagued the French section until nearly the end of World War II, when a reunification was finally achieved. A summary of the consequences of the crisis will be found in the editorial epilogue entitled "Trotsky and the French Section After July 1936."

An important part of this book is Appendix A, which translates a pamphlet entitled *L'Organe de masse* (The Mass Paper), published in June 1936 by the International Secretariat of the ICL. Its author was Erwin Wolf, writing under the pseudonym "Nicolle Braun." Wolf, a citizen of Czechoslovakia born in 1902, was a member of the International Secretariat in Paris when Trotsky moved to Norway, and he kept Trotsky informed and supplied with documents about the developing French crisis until September 1935, when he joined Trotsky as his secretary. There is a certain amount of repetition between Trotsky's texts and Wolf's, but it is not excessive; and we have retained all of the Wolf pamphlet intact, except for the introduction written by Trotsky (which will be found in its chronological place in Part Three of the book) because the pamphlet, written for the ICL as a whole, contains much explanatory material which Trotsky did not bother to include in the letters written for the French section. Wolf's pamphlet was written perhaps at Trotsky's suggestion, and certainly with his help, at a time when the French factions were exploring a reunification and when Trotsky feared that the lessons of the crisis might be pushed aside and forgotten. That Trotsky thought the pamphlet had lessons useful for sections other than the French was demonstrated by his March 15, 1937, letter suggesting that the leaders of the American section translate and publish it in English (see *Writings of Leon Trotsky [1936-37]*). Wolf was expelled from Norway when the government interned Trotsky in September 1936, and he was assassinated by the GPU in 1937 while he was carrying out an assignment in Spain.

Appendix B is a short retrospective comment on the French crisis by Pierre Frank, one of the central participants in the 1935-36 events and the only French leader of that period still active in the leadership of the Fourth International. He has no responsibility for anything else in this volume.

Trotsky's letters and articles in this book begin in July 1935, a few weeks after his arrival in Norway, and extend to July 1936, a few weeks before the opening of the sensational Moscow trial of Zinoviev and Kamenev, which monopolized his attention for the next eight months. Most of these letters have never been printed in English before, and some are published here for the first time in any language. For reasons connected with Trotsky's insecure legal status as an exile, most were written under pseudonyms or were unsigned. The date preceding each selection indicates when it was completed; if that is not known, the date when it was first published is given.

This book does not contain everything Trotsky wrote on the French crisis while he was in Norway; other material is in the closed section of Trotsky's archives at Harvard, which remains inaccessible until 1980. In addition, individuals undoubtedly possess the full texts of letters that are represented here only by published excerpts.

The editors have provided extensive prefaces to each of the book's three parts, as well as occasional notes when they are essential to clarifying the meaning of a passage. A comprehensive glossary of names of persons, organizations, and newspapers begins on p. 269.

Acknowledgments about the sources of articles and translations from the French originals will be found on the first page of each article. Special thanks are due the following individuals for assistance in preparing this volume: Pierre Frank and Jean van Heijenoort, for providing information and answering interminable questions; Pierre Broué, for helping to locate copies of the texts; Nat London, for research and assistance in producing needed primary and secondary sources; Tamara Deutscher, for making available some of Leon Sedov's papers belonging to the late Isaac Deutscher and pertaining to the subject of this book;

David Keil, for his translation of *L'Organe de masse;* the Harvard College Library, for permission to examine manuscripts in the open section of the Trotsky archives; the Library of Social History in New York, for permission to examine and publish letters from the archives of the late James P. Cannon; and Louis Sinclair, for the help afforded by his *Leon Trotsky: A Bibliography* (Hoover Institution Press, 1972). Needless to say, any errors of fact or interpretation in the prefatory material and in the notes are the responsibility of the editors alone.

The Editors
February 1977

Prologue:
Trotsky and the French Section
Before July 1935

Trotsky became a Leninist in 1917 and remained one to his death in 1940—which is another way of saying that he thought the construction of an internationalist Marxist party, firm in principle and flexible in tactics, was the key to the proletarian revolution in every country. The only party of this type in the 1920s, in his opinion, was the Third (Communist) International and its affiliated national sections, and when the Comintern began to depart from the principles of revolutionary internationalism and proletarian democracy, Trotsky's initial response was to try to reform it, not to replace it with a new party. In collaboration with Lenin he initiated the opposition to the bureaucratization of the Communist Party in the Soviet Union in 1923, and through the Left Opposition (Bolshevik-Leninists) he continued this fight after Lenin's death. Expelled by the Stalinist faction from the CP in 1927, banished to Alma Ata in 1928, deported to Turkey in 1929, he founded the International Left Opposition (ILO) in 1930 as a faction of the Comintern, dedicated to its reform and regeneration. But in 1933 the Comintern's policies were not only responsible for Hitler's easy triumph in Germany and the crushing of the whole working class movement in that country, but were defended and reaffirmed by the Moscow-dominated leadership after Hitler came to power. When no fundamental lessons were drawn from the debacle, the ILO decided that the Comintern had degenerated to the point where it could no longer be reformed, and set to work gathering the forces for a new (Fourth) International.

This was a truly gigantic task. The ILO, which was now renamed the International Communist League (ICL), was a tiny organization, with no mass following, which existed in only a dozen or so countries. Most of its sections in 1933 had no more than a few hundred members; the number of its supporters in the Soviet Union was much bigger, but severe repression made it impossible for them to function as an organization; only the

Greek and Spanish sections claimed more than a thousand members, and they were both to split from the ICL by 1935. In comparison with the size of the Comintern and the Second International, the ICL was a drop in the bucket.

Trotsky had been in a small minority in the past, and being in one again did not deter him from trying to do what he thought was necessary. The first efforts at regrouping revolutionary forces had relatively promising results. In August 1933, shortly after he moved from Turkey to France, Trotsky persuaded the representatives of three independent organizations—the Socialist Workers Party of Germany (SAP), the Independent Socialist Party of Holland (OSP), and the Revolutionary Socialist Party of Holland (RSP)—to cosign with the Bolshevik-Leninists "The Declaration of Four," which proclaimed the need to build a new International and pledged joint activity to that end. But within a few months the SAP had changed its mind and the OSP had wavered, so the coordinating committee they had set up fell apart. The RSP joined the ICL but on the whole little organizational headway had been made by 1934.

But repercussions from the crushing defeat of the working class in Germany were spreading throughout Europe and creating new political conditions. On one side the fascists and reactionaries everywhere were emboldened by Hitler's victory; on the other class-conscious workers began to discuss the lessons of Germany and seek ways of averting a fascist takeover in their own countries. Ferment was especially notable in the Social Democratic parties of the Second International, where left wings critical of the traditional reformism and opportunism of their leaders began to appear and grow. Then in February 1934 the French royalists, fascists, and other ultraright forces staged a bloody attack on the Chamber of Deputies in Paris, forcing the downfall of the bourgeois Radical Socialist premier Daladier and the installation of a conservative cabinet headed by Doumergue. But this thrust from the right was immediately countered by a thrust from the left: a one-day general strike organized by the Socialist and Communist parties and the two major labor federations, engaging in the first massive workers' united front in many years, and serving notice that the French workers had learned some of the lessons of Germany. Strong sentiment to extend and expand the united front spread rapidly, even inside the CP, whose leaders, on orders from Moscow, had prevented serious joint action by the workers' organizations for more than five years. In July 1934, the SFIO signed a formal united front pact with the CP. And both the traditional workers' parties began to grow: The

SFIO had around 100,000 members before the February events, and the CP at the most 30,000. By the end of 1936 each party claimed a membership of over 200,000.

Trotsky believed that France had become the key to the international situation, as Germany had been before 1933; that is, that the class struggle there was the focus of European and world politics, where decisive class battles were about to erupt and where the forces working for the Fourth International faced their biggest opportunities and tests. But he also was keenly aware of the fact that the growing united front sentiment, which soon led to discussion of a possible merger of the SFIO and the CP, would probably result in greater isolation for the ICL's French section. Seeking a way to prevent this, he reached the conclusion that a bold step was needed: the French section should join ("enter") one of the two workers' parties in order to break down organizational barriers that kept it from influencing and winning over the leftward-moving workers inside the new united front. "The Koran says that the mountain came to the prophet," Trotsky wrote. "Marxism counsels the prophet to go to the mountain." And he also concluded that the SFIO was a better place to go than the CP because the CP was much more heavily bureaucratized while the SFIO boasted about its internal democracy, had recently expelled its most reactionary right wing (the Neo-Socialists), and had publicly called on revolutionary workers and groups outside of the SFIO to join it. So in June 1934, at the time the SFIO and CP leaders were preparing to sign their pact, Trotsky urged the French section to join the SFIO.

Here we must go back briefly to the origins of the French section. When Trotsky arrived in Turkey in 1929 there were several groups in France that considered themselves Left Oppositionists or sympathizers. Most of their leaders had been expelled from or had quit the CP in various disputes between 1924 and 1929, but they had little in common outside of dissatisfaction with Comintern policy, and they were incapable of working together. With Trotsky's help a functioning Left Oppositionist group was brought together to found a weekly paper, *La Vérité,* in August 1929, and to become the Communist League, French section of the ILO, in April 1930. The only well-known leader of the League and the only one with extensive experience in the workers' movement was Alfred Rosmer (1877-1964), who was a revolutionary syndicalist before World War I, a member of the Comintern executive committee in Lenin's time, and a central leader of the CP before his expulsion in 1924. But Rosmer did not last long, withdrawing without explanation from the League and the International Secretariat of the ILO in November 1930.

The other leaders were all young and had the advantage of having come to Marxism early, but they were relatively inexperienced and their training had been influenced by the bureaucratized, clique-ridden CP and its youth organization. The membership hovered between one hundred and two hundred in the early years; its composition was largely petty bourgeois, with a disproportionate number of émigrés who were not well acquainted with French conditions. As a self-designated faction of the CP, their attention was necessarily focused on the CP and its periphery, which reinforced tendencies among them to function as a narrow circle with sectarian, inward-turned habits and ways of working. Despite these limitations, they did a fairly good job at their main task, which was the production of Left Opposition propaganda exposing the errors and crimes of Stalinism and defending the program and perspectives of Leninism. *La Vérité* and their theoretical magazine, *La Lutte de classes,* were among the best publications of the ILO, and the French leaders also cooperated with the International Secretariat in publishing an important internal international bulletin.

From Turkey Trotsky attentively followed the development of the French section, praised its positive qualities, and expressed hopes for its future. But he also was severely critical of its shortcomings: its organizational laxness and passivity, its closed-circle mentality, and above all the dead-end factionalism of its leaders. Of the latter he told one of the French leaders around 1930 or 1931, "You know, I've never seen faction fights like yours. With us [Russians], there were many of them. It wasn't always sweet, oh no. But ferocious rows like yours, no, I've never seen that. It's extraordinary. How is it possible? It must be straightened out" (*Trotsky vivant,* by Pierre Naville, 1962).

But it wasn't straightened out. From its start the French section went through one crisis after another, in part provoked by the unfavorable objective situation which it faced, but also induced, or at least sharpened, by the bitter hostility between the leaders of the two main tendencies in the section, Raymond Molinier and Pierre Naville.

Molinier, born in 1904 into a family that ran a small bank in Paris, joined the Young Communist League when he was sixteen and became a cofounder of *La Vérité* when he was twenty-five. Some political opponents charged that he was an unscrupulous businessman and adventurer who did not belong in the revolutionary movement; his reputation was also clouded by a business bankruptcy and allegations that he had pleaded insanity to escape imprisonment for desertion as an army conscript in the 1920s. Rosmer and Naville thought Molinier was unfit to be a leader of the French section and tried to have him removed from the leadership of its Paris region in 1930, but the members rejected this move. So did Trotsky, who had met Molinier in Turkey in 1929 and had formed a favorable impression of him as an activist displaying great energy, initiative, and dedication to the cause. (Trotsky also thought that some Left Oppositionists had inherited from the Comintern tendencies to abuse such measures as expulsions and splits and threats of expulsions and splits.) Molinier's principal collaborator in the League leadership was Pierre Frank, born in 1905, who joined the CP when he was twenty. After becoming a chemical engineer, he was active in a CGTU chemical products union. He joined the Left Opposition when he was twenty-four, helped found the French section, served on the International Secretariat during the early thirties, and was a secretary of Trotsky, 1932-33.

Pierre Naville, born in 1904, joined the Young Communist League at twenty-one and the CP a year later. He was in charge of the CP's student youth work, a writer and cofounder of a surrealist journal as well as editor of a Communist student magazine. A supporter of the Left Opposition, Naville met Trotsky in Moscow at the end of 1927 and was expelled from the CP in 1928. After visiting Trotsky in Turkey in 1929, he became a founder of *La Vérité* and of the Communist League, edited *La Lutte de classes,* and served on the International Secretariat through most of the thirties. Trotsky valued his literary gifts and propagandist talents but sometimes criticized him for political passivity and conservatism and a tendency to make the record with abstract pronouncements instead of actively intervening in political openings. Naville's closest co-worker in the League leadership was Gérard Rosenthal (pen name Francis Gérard), born in 1903, also a writer, surrealist, and cofounder of *La Vérité,* who became a lawyer and Trotsky's legal representative in several important French court cases.

Although Trotsky usually supported the Molinier tendency in the French section's internal disputes, this was because of his agreement with it on specific issues and not at all because of any "favoritism" toward Molinier, as was sometimes charged. That was demonstrated irrefutably in September 1933, two months after Trotsky's arrival in France and one month after the decision to work for a new International, when he wrote a scathing criticism of the French leadership as a whole. "Almost

from the very beginning of the existence of the French League,"
he said, "its inner life represented a series of crises that never
reached the level of principles, but distinguished themselves by
extreme bitterness and poisoned the atmosphere of the organization, repelling serious workers despite their sympathy for the
ideas of the Opposition." The orientation to a new International
required and permitted a clean break from the narrow life of the
past and a correction of the leaders' serious shortcomings,
especially their failure to provide "constant and timely information to all the members" and their "passive tolerance" of alien,
disruptive, and degenerate elements in the organization. The new
orientation posed a vital test for the French section, he said: "No
matter what the origin of the [past] discontentment, conflicts,
personal friction, etc., may have been, all the old disagreements
must of necessity group themselves now around the basic
alternative: *forward* to a wide arena of the Fourth International
or *backward* to small circles stewing in their own juice " ("It Is
Time to Stop," in *Writings of Leon Trotsky [1933-34]*).

The proposal to enter the SFIO came as a shock to many
members and leaders of the ICL and elicited a good deal of
resistance, outside France as well as inside. To formalistic minds
it seemed to be in glaring contradiction to the call for a new
International and new revolutionary national parties and in
violation of the principle that the revolutionary party must
remain independent under all conditions; some rejected it as a
betrayal of principle ("capitulation to the Second International!"),
others opposed it on tactical grounds. Trotsky patiently explained
that independence was a principle for revolutionary parties but
that this principle could not apply to small nuclei like the sections
of the ICL which were trying to create revolutionary parties but
had not yet created them; and he recalled that some national
sections of the Communist International, notably the French,
were founded as the result of revolutionary work inside left wings
of the Social Democracy. Programmatic superiority by itself was
not enough to make the Fourth International a reality, he said;
tactical flexibility to take advantage of favorable opportunities
while they existed was also necessary if the ICL forces were to
break out of their isolation. A supplementary factor in Trotsky's
reasoning was that an entry experience would provide a healthy
antidote to the sectarianism of the French section.

A majority of the international movement eventually accepted
Trotsky's approach. In France, Molinier supported the entry
proposal from the start; Frank supported it after some hesitation;

Naville opposed it, largely on tactical grounds but with great vehemence. After a two-month discussion marked by considerable heat, during which a split was averted only through the intervention of the IS, the French section held a national conference in Paris at the end of August 1934 where a decisive majority voted to dissolve the Communist League and join the SFIO. The total membership reported at the conference was little more than a hundred. In September they joined the SFIO, where they immediately established the GBL as a faction, with *La Vérité* as their paper. Naville voted against the entry, refused to abide by the conference decisions, and tried for a short time to speak publicly in the name of the dissolved League's Central Committee. For this the new Central Committee voted to expel him. The French section's small youth group also joined the Young Socialists (JS), the SFIO youth affiliate which claimed 11,000 members, among whom the young Bolshevik-Leninists had been doing fraction work for almost a year.

Trotsky had conceded that the entry entailed certain dangers, especially from the opportunist pressures to which the Bolshevik-Leninists would be subjected in the SFIO milieu, but he felt that these could be counteracted by international support and leadership from the ICL and other sections. To provide such leadership, as well as to pass international judgment on the "French turn," as it came to be known in the literature of the movement, a plenum of the ICL was held in Paris in October 1934; this was the highest body of the ICL between international conferences and consisted of the International Secretariat and representatives of the major national sections that could attend. Among those participating was James P. Cannon of the Communist League of America, a veteran of the Comintern who was highly respected by the European sections, and had come at Trotsky's insistent urging. The plenum adopted a resolution, "The Present Situation in the Labor Movement and the Tasks of the Bolshevik-Leninists," which answered the various objections to the French turn made by Naville, the German Bauer, the Belgian Vereecken, the American Oehler, etc., commended the GBL on the first steps it had taken in the SFIO, and called on the Naville group to join the GBL on the basis of a common discipline (see *Documents of the Fourth International: The Formative Years [1933-40]*).

The latter decision so infuriated Molinier that he announced his resignation from the plenum before it ended. Two weeks later he wrote a bitter letter to Trotsky, then living under close police scrutiny in a mountain village near Grenoble, complaining about the "secret diplomacy carried out here by your representative Cannon in order to bring Naville back to our League, despite himself" (*La Crise des Bolcheviks-Léninistes*, 1939). Cannon had met privately with Naville and other opponents of the turn to remind them that revolutionaries usually do not split over tactical differences. Trotsky, it seemed, wanted to keep Naville in the section's leadership in 1934 (as he had wanted to keep Molinier in it in 1930)—to the chagrin of Molinier, who had hoped that the section would now be permanently rid of Naville and thus more amenable to the uncontested leadership of the Molinier group. Naville's group joined the SFIO but refused to join the GBL. Publishing *La Lutte de classes* as its own journal, it operated independently inside the SFIO, although on some occasions it cooperated with the GBL. In any case it is clear that serious differences between Molinier and Trotsky began not in 1935 but at least one and maybe two years before then.

During the first nine months that the Bolshevik-Leninists were active in the SFIO, the major international developments influencing their work were an uprising led by the Spanish Socialist Party in Asturias, crushed in October 1934; the start of mass purges in the Soviet Union following the assassination of Kirov in December 1934; a Nazi victory in the Saar referendum, when a majority of the voters chose to become part of Hitler's Reich in January 1935; and—above all—the signing of a Franco-Soviet nonaggression pact in May 1935, in return for which Stalin publicly approved the rearmament plans of French imperialism. The immediate repercussions of this pact in France were the CP's switch from antiwar to rabidly social-patriotic policies, which convinced sections of the French bourgeoisie that collaboration with the Stalinists could be useful, and the spreading conviction in all layers of society that another world war was in the making.

This was a time of deepening class polarization in France. The radicalization of the workers continued, from which the SFIO and the CP benefited; in the May 1935 municipal elections both made gains at the expense of the Radical Socialists, the major bourgeois party. In October 1934 the Stalinists extended a hand of friendship to the Radical Socialists, and thereafter they worked hard to prove that it was not a workers' (anticapitalist) united front they were interested in, but something different: a class-collaborationist alliance between the workers' parties and the Radical Socialists and other bourgeois-democratic parties. This alliance, which had to be based on a bourgeois program because otherwise the bourgeois parties would not participate, was formed in 1935 as the People's Front, its initial committee being established by the Radical Socialists, the SFIO, and the CP in June, just as Trotsky reached Norway. Meanwhile the conservative coalitions that ran the government in 1935 lost ground as they pushed ahead with unpopular measures, such as a law extending the term of military conscription from one year to two in March. When Laval became premier in June, after negotiating the Franco-Soviet pact with Stalin, he soon decided that issuing edicts ("decree-laws") was a safer way to promote his austerity program (for nonmilitary expenditures) than seeking the passage of legislation in the parliament. The fascist bands (Croix de Feu, etc.) probably reached their maximum strength in 1935 or early 1936.

On the whole, conditions were favorable for the growth of the GBL, at least in the short run, and it did expand its numbers and influence significantly; by the summer of 1935, its membership reached 300. Their main impact was on the various centrist groups that made up the SFIO's loose left wing and on new members joining the SFIO in this period. Their chief concentration was in the Seine (Paris) department of the SFIO but they also began to make headway in other areas, including in the North and Southeast.

The important Seine Federation of the SFIO was controlled by the *Bataille Socialiste* group, which in turn was divided into two tendencies, one led by Jean Zyromsky, who leaned toward the Stalinists, the other by Marceau Pivert, who favored a more independent policy. The GBL made contact with these forces, worked out common projects against the party right wing, and pushed both *Bataille Socialiste* tendencies to the left. Its propaganda for the creation of a popular militia in every district to fight the fascists was particularly effective with the forces led by Pivert. Together with them the GBL members succeeded in organizing an SFIO defense guard, called the TPPS (Toujours Prêts Pour Servir, Always Ready to Serve), which protected workers' meetings and literature sales against fascist attacks and provocations. Sometimes they were able to make blocs with the left centrists around common resolutions for action at SFIO meetings against the Blum-Faure right-wing leadership; at other times they introduced their own resolutions independently of the *Bataille Socialiste* forces. At a Seine Federation assembly in May 1935, the GBL got 805 votes out of 5,400. At another in June, their vote had risen to 1,037 (against 1,570 for Blum-Faure and 2,370 for *Bataille Socialiste*). (There was of course a distinction between joining the GBL and voting for one of its resolutions, but the trend was up in both respects.) Pivert undoubtedly reflected the GBL's influence when he said "The struggle against Trotskyism in this period is the mark of a reactionary outlook in the ranks of the working class." Membership in the SFIO also gave the Bolshevik-Leninists openings for more extensive and varied work in the trade unions than before, and although it was on a modest scale this began to have a favorable effect on their social composition.

In the Young Socialists the Bolshevik-Leninists made bigger gains. They established close working relations with the left wing leading the Seine Alliance and through it began publishing a paper, *Révolution,* which claimed sales of 80,000 copies per issue in August 1935 as against 30,000 for the official national JS paper. This left bloc had around one-third of the delegates at the national JS congress in July.

The SFIO's thirty-second national congress took place June 9-12 in Mulhouse, under the sign of the recent Franco-Soviet pact and the decision of the SFIO and CP bureaucracies to join with the Radical Socialists in setting up the first formal People's Front committee. Two-thirds of the delegates supported the Blum-Faure wing, which saw no profit in spelling out the implications of the People's Front. But the voice of revolutionary Marxism was heard at an SFIO congress for the first time since 1920 as the GBL, together with the Naville group, compelled the congress to debate or at least listen to its positions on "national defense," the need for the Fourth International, etc. The French press took note of the disputes at the congress to observe that the obstreperous Bolshevik-Leninists were now a factor in the nation's politics. The vote on the main political resolution was 2,025 for Blum-Faure, 777 for *Bataille Socialiste,* 105 for the GBL. Blum's warning that the GBL would be ousted if it obstructed collaboration with the Stalinists was not taken seriously by the GBL leaders, who seemed indifferent to the heavy pressure that the Stalinist bureaucrats were exerting on their Social Democratic counterparts to purge the "Trotskyists." At the congress the GBL was given representation on the SFIO's national administrative committee (CAP): Jean Rous was elected to the CAP, with Pierre Frank as an alternate. (Rous, a lawyer, born in 1908 in Catalonia, was a former SFIO member who joined the Communist League in 1932. Elected an alternate member of the Central Committee at the 1934 national conference, he became national secretary of the GBL, the chief representative of the non-Molinier tendency in its leadership, and a member of the IS until World War II. Trotsky collaborated with Rous—most of the letters to the French section in this book were addressed to him—but he felt Rous lacked decisiveness in meeting the crisis of the section and let Molinier get away with too much.)

The Mulhouse congress was just opening and Trotsky had not yet heard about its proceedings as he prepared to leave France for Norway. Independently of the congress, he felt that the SFIO episode was virtually finished and wrote a letter recommending that the section make a shift in its orientation away from the SFIO and toward the construction of a new revolutionary party ("A New Turn Is Necessary," June 10, 1935, in *Writings 34-35*; major excerpts are also included in Appendix A, p. 177). En route, he stopped in Paris a couple of days where he met with comrades who had not gone to Mulhouse, some of whom seemed to have illusions about a long perspective inside the SFIO. He tried to convince them they were wrong, and before leaving Paris wrote a letter calling for a speedy reunification of the GBL with the Naville group.

Trotsky's "new turn" was undoubtedly based in part on a shrewd reading of French political reality and the probable effects of the coming together of the two big workers' bureaucracies in collaboration with the capitalist class. But it was also undoubtedly based (1) on the new international climate following the Franco-Soviet pact and the widespread feeling in the summer of 1935, when the Italian fascist government was openly preparing an invasion of Ethiopia, that another world war might break out suddenly; and (2) on Trotsky's consequent conviction that a new stimulus had to be given to the creation of the Fourth International.

Despite growth in some areas, the ICL had not recorded much progress since 1934. In 1934 the American section merged with the American Workers Party to form the Workers Party of the United States, but the WPUS, while sympathetic to the ICL, did not join it at first. Early in 1935 the Dutch section merged with the larger OSP to form the Revolutionary Socialist Workers Party (RSAP), which did affiliate with the ICL but also affiliated with the London or London-Amsterdam Bureau (International Bureau of Revolutionary Socialist Parties). The London Bureau was a loose grouping of centrist parties belonging to neither the Second nor the Third International; its ideological leadership was supplied by the SAP, which had become violently anti–Fourth International by 1935. The Greek section left the ICL in 1934 and the Spanish section broke away in 1935 to merge with another group and organize a new centrist party, the Workers Party of

Marxist Unification (POUM). Both the former Greek section and the POUM joined the London-Amsterdam Bureau.

The French turn had not been conceived of as a worldwide tactic, but it soon became clear that favorable openings existed inside the Social Democracy in other countries. Trotsky was bitter against the leaders of the Spanish section who rejected the entry tactic for Spain in 1934, when the Socialist Youth were calling for a new International, and held them responsible for the subsequent swallowing up of the Socialist Youth by the Spanish Stalinists. Once the ice was broken and the French section started making gains in the SFIO, other sections adopted an entry tactic too: the Belgian, the Swiss, the Polish. In 1936 the WPUS was to enter the American Socialist Party. In some of these cases the ICL sections were to make healthy gains through the entry tactic, but in the meantime, temporarily restricted by their membership in the Social Democratic parties, they were unable to conduct much public work on behalf of the Fourth International (although they were able to win new adherents inside the Social Democratic parties).

In the spring of 1935, Trotsky and the International Secretariat decided it was time to resume the organizational work for the Fourth International which had begun in 1933 and then had been interrupted or subordinated by the applications of the French turn. The first step they chose was an "Open Letter for the Fourth International," to bring up to date the ideas formulated in 1933 in the "Declaration of Four" and to be signed by whatever organizations agreed. Trotsky wrote the first draft of the Open Letter while he was still in France and then it was circulated. The WPUS concurred in June, but added some conditions: it wanted the SAP to be given a month to sign, if it wished, and it wanted some additions made to the text. The Dutch section was also slow in adding its signature. There is evidence that at least some leaders of the French section, concerned chiefly with the effects it might have on their position inside the SFIO, were not very enthusiastic about Trotsky's proposal that they should sign the Open Letter in the name of the GBL. Finally, in July, when it became clear to everyone that the SAP had no intention of signing the Open Letter, it was published. The initial signers were the RSAP, the WPUS, the IS of the ICL, the GBL in the SFIO, and the Workers Party of Canada (see *Writings 35-36* for the final text). Trotsky was disturbed by the GBL's apparent lack of interest in the Open Letter and the low-key manner in which it was treated in *La Vérité*. This was to become one of the differences leading to the French crisis.

Preface to Part One

Trotsky's letters in this book begin in July 1935, a few weeks after he reached Norway.

His call for a quick fusion of the GBL and Naville's group had almost immediate results. The two agreed on a reunification congress, which was not held until September, but in the meantime started acting like a single organization. It soon became clear that the leadership was divided into three tendencies, with the two led by Rous and Naville usually agreeing and composing a majority of the Central Committee against the one led by Molinier.

Trotsky noted with concern that the Central Committee was discussing plans to launch a "mass" newspaper in place of *La Vérité;* he detected in this a possible tendency to dilute the GBL's program at precisely the time when it should be advanced fully and with the utmost vigor. On August 1 the Central Committee voted unanimously to start a mass paper, but each of the factions interpreted the motion differently, and action to implement it was not taken for several months, during which the GBL's status in the SFIO underwent many changes. Despite confusion and modified positions, it was plain that all three groups in the leadership thought of a mass paper as one that presented less than the GBL's full positions, which Trotsky characterized as a centrist paper. This became one of the focal issues debated in the section (letters of July 3, July 26, and September 13 [to Van]).

The People's Front was born on a patriotic holiday, July 14. A huge demonstration, headed by Daladier, Blum, Thorez, and the officials of the two major trade union federations, marched in the streets of Paris, waving both the red flag and the French tricolor and singing both the "Marseillaise" and the "Internationale." Mass enthusiasm and euphoria infected the workers. On the left only the Bolshevik-Leninists were not swept away into support of or adaptation to the People's Front; but they too felt the pressure all around them. Trotsky was quick to supply them with slogans differentiating them from the class collaborationists: Oust the bourgeois politicians from the People's Front, for a Socialist-

Communist government, for a workers' and farmers' government (letters of July 11 and July 25). These demands, based on the strategy of the working class united front, also proved important for the GBL's relations with the SFIO centrists, who did not want to come into conflict with the class collaborationists, and for elements in the GBL itself who did not want to clash with the SFIO centrists. By October, Trotsky was convinced that some Bolshevik-Leninists were weak on People's Frontism and his writings on the subject undoubtedly were aimed at them as well as at the centrists (letter of October 3).

On July 25 the Seventh World Congress of the Communist International began in Moscow. The People's Front policy first introduced in France was endorsed and laid down as the line to be followed by all the sections of the Comintern. Also approved were the moves previously started in France and other countries for unification ("organic unity") of the Social Democratic and Stalinist parties and Internationals. The international scope and weight of the pressures it was under in France contributed to the tenseness of the situation in which the GBL soon found itself.

The Comintern congress had barely begun when the SFIO leaders made the first moves to rid themselves of the GBL. At a national congress of the Young Socialists, held in Lille July 28-29, their representatives introduced and passed a motion dissolving the GBL as a tendency in the JS and expelling thirteen leaders of the JS left wing. The accused were charged with having "placed themselves on record for affiliation to the Fourth International," with "systematic denigration and violation of the [SFIO] theoretical line," and with repeatedly attacking the best SFIO and JS militants in order to promote "the well-established intention to split the Socialist organization." Expelled were eight Bolshevik-Leninists, and five "indigenous" Seine Alliance leaders, including their secretary, Fred Zeller. The vote was 3,667 for expulsion, 1,534 against, 331 abstaining.

The expulsions had the advantage, in Trotsky's view, of clarifying things, of demonstrating that the SFIO chapter was indeed coming to an end. They had not occurred impulsively but as a result of a sober decision by the top SFIO bureaucrats, which meant they would soon be followed by expulsions in the SFIO too. Trotsky hoped that the expulsions would settle the question of the new turn for the GBL and urged its leaders to seize the opportunity for an ideological offensive that would utilize the symbolism of the expulsions—the youth are the first victims of the new wave of social patriotism as they will be the first victims in the coming war itself, etc. (letters of July 30 and August 1).

But Trotsky's view was not shared by many of the French leaders. In the youth, David Rousset argued that the expulsions could be reversed as constitutionally illegal if the GBL conducted a vigorous offensive for readmission; he also proposed that publication of the Open Letter be postponed as untimely. Yvan Craipeau was ready to consider dissolving the GBL faction in the JS if it would help the fight for readmission. After Mulhouse, Pierre Frank wrote in the GBL's June internal bulletin that it would be "criminal" to think of leaving the SFIO; of the Lille expulsions, which he called a "provocation aimed at running us out of the SFIO," Frank wrote: "On the whole, that changes nothing in the perspective."

While disagreement persisted over the perspective, accord was reached on a campaign to appeal the expulsions, which Trotsky favored as a tactic supplementing, but subordinate to, the orientation to a new party. The left centrists led by Zeller and the Bolshevik-Leninist youth decided to continue publishing *Révolution* and to maintain a youth organization, whose main base was in the Paris area and which was referred to both as the JS Seine Alliance and the JSR (Revolutionary Socialist Youth). For the next five months they carried on a campaign for reinstatement which received encouraging support in the SFIO and JS ranks until October, when an SFIO committee headed by Blum formally refused to overrule the expulsions.

Zeller and his comrades were supporters of Pivert's tendency in the SFIO, and their expulsion could be seen as a tacit warning from the bureaucrats to Pivert, who issued an open letter to the expelled which under the circumstances had to concern the Bolshevik-Leninists as well as the Zellerites. The letter was a classical centrist performance. On the one hand, Pivert protested the expulsion of all thirteen, urged them to appeal to the party for reinstatement, and assured them they would prevail if they relied on the party's democratic traditions. On the other hand, he gave the Bolshevik-Leninists a little lecture on their "psychological error" in having chosen that name, advising them to abandon that label if it stood in the way of reinstatement. He also disparaged their adherence to the idea of a Fourth International since in his opinion it was sufficient to hope for a better International, "with or without changing the number."

It would be hard to say whom this statement helped more in the long run—the GBL or the Blum bureaucracy. In either case, it needed an answer. None of the GBL leaders wanted to write one, however, according to Erwin Wolf, then a member of the International Secretariat in Paris, and the reply was written by Trotsky in Norway (article of August 7). Also, according to Wolf, it was the last time Pivert was publicly criticized in the GBL press for several months. This was not because the GBL leaders were unaware of Pivert's weaknesses and derelictions but because they still hoped, whatever they said or wrote formally, that their stay in the SFIO could be prolonged, and they saw an alliance with Pivert—if possible, through a unified tendency with him—as the best way of achieving this. While Trotsky was publicly rebuking Pivert early in August for not yet having "cut the umbilical cord that binds him to the small world of the Blums and the Zyromskys," Molinier was meeting privately with Pivert as the GBL's representative to discuss closer relations. In August and September these two were also engaged in a friendly correspondence.

Early in August the internal SFIO and JS disputes were lit up by sudden explosions of the class struggle in Brest, Toulon, and other port cities. In July, shortly after the huge People's Front demonstration in Paris, Laval had issued decree-laws aimed at cutting the budget, social services, and workers' living standards, and in August the government extended these cutbacks to new areas. The CP, the SFIO, and the union leaders protested but did not call for any action that might irritate their Radical Socialist partners in the People's Front who were supporters of the Laval cabinet. So the resistance to the decree-laws was largely spontaneous—and exceptionally militant. The government responded with heavy violence, the seamen and other workers fought back with audacity and heroism. Five workers were shot to death and hundreds were injured before the insurgent strikers were put down. Trotsky saw in these events the harbinger of the great strike struggles that were to sweep France less than a year later and he did not fail to cite them as an additional argument for a new course by the GBL (letter of August 11).

The final text of the Open Letter for the Fourth International, cosigned by the GBL, was approved for publication July 10, but it was not published in France until August 23 (letter of August 10). The postponement was for political reasons, not technical ones. Rous reported to Trotsky August 17 that both Molinierists and Navillists on the Central Committee were dubious about making propaganda for the Fourth International a key issue at a united front conference against the war preparations. Naville reported to Trotsky August 27 that some partisans of the mass paper idea were talking about abandoning *La Vérité* in favor of a "broad" paper to be published by the "new unified tendency" they were hoping to create with the Pivertists.

The whole discussion about perspectives took on a new concreteness August 28 when the CAP met and voted to outlaw *La Vérité* as a paper that could be distributed by party members. It also asked the next National Council of the party to take disciplinary measures against the publishers of the paper, who were guilty of "outrageous attacks on fine party comrades" and of associating themselves "with an attempt to create a Fourth International."

The GBL Central Committee quickly adopted a resolution, drafted by Naville, calling for an all-out two-pronged campaign: to mobilize maximum resistance in the SFIO against the CAP attack, and to "prepare for independence." It warned against illusions that a showdown could be averted through maneuvers and stressed that "the dominant question is that of organizing the new party." That seemed to be a definitive settlement of the GBL's perspectives, except that some of those who voted for it in the Central Committee did not really believe expulsions were inevitable or soon changed their minds. The result was that the internal dispute continued, often in masked forms, and the leadership followed through on only the first part of the promised campaign. No issue of *La Vérité* was published during the following crucial four weeks, and when it did appear the bureaucracy's attack was handled very defensively, and on a back page.

Pivert did not share the CAP's reasons for getting rid of *La Vérité* but, as he wrote Molinier on September 3, he too thought it should be discontinued. (He also advised Molinier that it was necessary to remain in the SFIO "at any price" and to "abandon this impossible attitude of being affiliated to two Internationals at the same time.") A week later Molinier was arguing in the GBL Central Committee that the paper should be discontinued for tactical reasons. Others thought the GBL should offer a deal to the CAP: it would give up the paper if the CAP would forego expulsions and agree on some other way that the GBL could express its views. Using Pivert's position to make his points against both Pivert and the GBL waverers, Trotsky explained the logic of capitulation on the right to publish *La Vérité* and to advocate the Fourth International, and showed that acceptance of this logic was the first step toward political suicide (letters of September 13). He also warned against the danger of forgetting the subordinate place of tactics (toward the CAP, toward the Pivertists) and letting them determine the political line (independence) (second letter of September 16).

The only kind of deals that interested the CAP were with the bourgeoisie and the Stalinists, not with the GBL. On September 13, thirteen GBL members, including its central leaders, were informed by mail that a motion had been made to expel them for slandering comrades and assisting *La Vérité*'s campaign in favor of a Fourth International. On September 19, the SFIO's National Disputes Commission "confirmed" the expulsion motion and sent it to the CAP for further action. That was how things stood when the GBL national conference took place in Paris on September 21-22.

The conference voted unanimously in support of the Central Committee's position that preparations for a new party were the central task but, as before, such unanimity concealed basic differences and postponed their settlement. The Rous-Naville tendencies were in the majority. Molinier spoke about the importance of remaining in the SFIO because the time for an independent party had not yet come, but seeing that his tendency was in a minority he did not present a countermotion and abstained in the vote. The only serious division in the voting came over the "mass paper" question: a motion to make *Révolution* a mass paper and to turn *La Vérité* into a GBL factional journal got 131 votes, while a motion (by Rous) to concentrate on transforming *La Vérité* into the GBL's mass weekly, with lesser support being given to *Révolution* as the paper of the JS left bloc, got 118 votes.

On October 1 the CAP approved the expulsion of the thirteen Bolshevik-Leninist leaders, an action which was not final until reviewed by the SFIO National Council. But a far more damaging blow had been dealt the GBL in the preceding week, immediately after its conference. That was when Pivert, separating himself from *Bataille Socialiste*, began to put together a new centrist tendency in the SFIO, which was presented to the public on September 30 under the name of the Revolutionary Left (GR). It was damaging, first of all, because the GBL leaders were unsure of themselves and divided over how to react. And it was damaging, also, because the new Pivert group, while opposing the GBL expulsions and borrowing parts of the GBL program, adopted as its cardinal principle the need to remain inside the SFIO at all costs. The effect was to undercut the GBL's fight against the expulsions: if it was possible for the GR to have oppositional views and remain inside the SFIO, why couldn't the GBL do the same? Responsibility for the expulsions was thus shifted from the CAP, which tolerated the GR for the time being, to the GBL, especially so long as it would not swear that it wanted to remain in the SFIO at all costs.

Floundering, the GBL seemed incapable of deciding whether to fight the GR or fuse with it, and its tactics confused not only the SFIO left-wingers but its own members. In the GBL's Political Bureau, Rous voted for a motion by Molinier which Naville claimed would open the door to a quiet fusion with the GR, but once again a motion by Naville was adopted unanimously. Despite his conciliatory views, the Central Committee sent Molinier as its representative to a preparatory meeting of the GR, where he expressed the GBL's desire to remain in the SFIO as long as possible and to participate in the new Pivert group. The issue of *La Vérité* that appeared at the end of September finally took up the CAP's expulsion drive in public, but in the kind of defensive fashion that would appeal to the Pivertists, and contained no criticism of Pivert whatever. *Révolution*, which a majority of the GBL conference had voted to turn into a mass paper, hailed the new tendency: "Long live the Revolutionary Left!" After the formation of the GR, *La Vérité* began to downplay the need for a new party or present it in abstract terms, and references to the Fourth International virtually vanished.

The GBL was so ardent in its attentions to the GR that the Pivertists decided on October 3 to sound it out for a common examination of a platform and possible fusion, or at least fraternal collaboration. (Pivert may have gotten from Molinier an exaggerated picture of the GBL's eagerness for a fusion on almost any basis.) The GBL responded favorably to the idea of immediate joint activity and discussion of a platform for fusion, but pointed out in a comradely tone that the GR platform was unfortunately silent on such questions as the International and the arming of the masses. It also suggested that in the meantime the GR, the GBL, and the JS publish a joint weekly paper, an idea that did not appeal to the GR leaders. The Pivertists soon decided that a fusion would have few advantages for them, but the Bolshevik-Leninists persevered. At the end of October they drew up a resolution (Motion C) to be presented at a Seine Federation congress of the SFIO early in November, and they asked the GR to cosponsor it. Motion C was formulated in a way that the GBL thought would be acceptable to the GR (no mention of the need for a new party or of the Fourth International). The

GR rejected the offer and presented its own motion, despite the GBL's sad plaint that Motion C contained nothing that GR members had "not accepted or could not accept." Pivert clarified the relations still further after the congress when he "annulled" the membership in the GR of all who had voted for Motion C. But the GBL remained mired in its tactical maneuvers and hopes, unable to move on the promised campaign for a new party.

At the end of October Zeller paid a visit to Trotsky, who had just completed a six-week stay in an Oslo hospital. Trotsky won Zeller over to the GBL and Zeller returned to France early in November determined to win the JS over to the Fourth International. He was not much helped in this task by the disarray and factionalism he found in the GBL leadership. On November 17 the SFIO National Council approved the expulsion of the thirteen Bolshevik-Leninists. This settled the matter according to the party statutes, unless an appeal were made to the next national congress, but the Blum bureaucracy decided that it could disarm critics of the expulsions by dropping hints at the National Council that the expulsions might be withdrawn if the accused would demonstrate their loyalty to the party. They had already pledged not to engage in "insults" and to continue abiding by discipline in action, so something beyond that was wanted. Incredibly the Central Committee voted nine to four (Molinier and Rous vs. Naville) to submit to the National Council a strong loyalty statement, expressing the GBL's readiness to accept changes in the SFIO's statutes limiting the rights of tendencies in the party, provided only that they apply to all tendencies in the party. Of course, the GR was pleased with the tone and content of this statement. Rous's justification of his vote—that it was a shrewd maneuver because it would bind the GR to solidarity with the expelled—demonstrated how preoccupation with the GR was blinding the GBL leadership to more important questions. The SFIO bureaucracy of course did not accept the Central Committee's concessions, the main effect of which was to undermine the GBL's credibility and to confirm GR prejudices against leaving the SFIO under any circumstances.

When the GBL leaders, acting through Molinier and Rous, tried to impose similar concessions on the Bolshevik-Leninist youth at a special congress of the Seine Alliance, held while the National Council was in session, they were met by an actual rebellion. Several of the youth leaders openly defied GBL discipline and some of them announced their resignations from the GBL (soon retracted). On most of the points Molinier and Rous had to retreat, although a centrist-type motion on the International was passed. Molinier later pointed to these violations of discipline to justify his own conduct, but the spectacle as a whole did not add anything to the GBL's prestige.

In November as well as in July Molinier believed that there were many left-wingers in and around the SFIO who still could be won over to Bolshevik-Leninism through skillful maneuvers and regroupments and that Trotsky's approach prevented this. There is no reason to question the sincerity of these beliefs. But a majority of the GBL leadership, prodded by Trotsky, rejected them—not always firmly, not always in a consistent way, but most of the time. Molinier had a contemptuous attitude toward his opponents in the Central Committee, whom he viewed as intellectual dilettantes and sectarian hairsplitters incapable of providing genuine revolutionary leadership or of resisting Trotsky when his advice was wrong; indeed, they were weak and indecisive toward violations of GBL discipline in general, did not know how to handle "vanguardist" excesses among some of the youth leaders, and often showed themselves to be incapable of controlling Molinier and making him abide by majority decisions.

The crisis of the French section deepened because Molinier felt driven to disregard the Central Committee majority when possible, to circumvent its decisions, and even to use against it the type of maneuvers he had learned to use against opponents in the SFIO. His ability to pursue a semi-independent course was enhanced by the Central Committee majority's habit of entrusting to him (because of his energy and initiative) responsibility for carrying out decisions they knew he did not agree with and by the fact that he enjoyed the confidence of a large part of the "old" (pre-entry) adult members. The sometimes vacillating policies of the Central Committee majority reinforced his belief that his course was correct and would prevail if he persisted enough to produce tangible, practical results (which would also ultimately give him a majority in the Central Committee).

Since neither the GBL nor the new GR was ready for a merger, Molinier cast about for ways of demonstrating that a unified tendency was possible and desirable, even if it began at a local and informal level. In the fluid and uncertain situation that existed around the time the GR was founded, members of various tendencies were getting together to discuss what should be done, not just in the SFIO but in the class struggle as well. Molinier had no trouble convincing the Central Committee that GBL members should participate in such bodies during the transition toward a new party. And so on October 10, Bolshevik-Leninists, Pivertists, and other left-wingers acting as individuals formed the first Revolutionary Action Group (GAR) in Paris's nineteenth arrondissement (district); the plan was to create such bodies in other districts, and some were created. The concept of the GARs was rather fuzzy: people should join, despite their political differences and their different political affiliations, to promote revolutionary action for common objectives in struggles against war, fascism, etc., but what kind of action—propagandist action or some other kind—was not clearly specified. In the normal course of events the GARs surely would have faded away quickly once the SFIO's internal situation was settled, except that Molinier was anxious to preserve them as a model for the larger unified tendency he had in mind and as a possible power base for his own faction in the GBL. He therefore felt it necessary to construct a theory about the GARs that would justify their continuation and extension. Theory was not Molinier's strong point, and the theory he hit on was notable for its elasticity. Sometimes the GARs were seen as embryos of the new revolutionary party, at other times they became embryos of soviets, or soviet-type formations. Ever since the People's Front had been formed in the summer, Trotsky had been hammering away at the idea that the French section should counterpose "committees of action" to the People's Front; Trotsky held, and the GBL agreed with him, that such committees, created in strikes and other mass struggles in the factories and the streets, could develop into the French equivalent of soviets and the revolutionary alternative to People's Front class collaborationism (letters of September 7 and November 13 and the undated letters of November). Molinier's caricature—that a few hundred radicals could at will set up their own soviet-type bodies, independently of the masses—was guaranteed to become a source of dispute in the GBL crisis.

The GARs were not enough for Molinier's purposes, however; he was obsessed even more with the idea of a mass paper that would blaze the path to a broad revolutionary regroupment by avoiding narrow, sectarian, and abstract positions that the Pivertists, for example, were not ready for (letters of November 21 and 25). He tried for several months to get GBL authorization for the projected paper and in effect he did get it, at least for a time and in part, as the Central Committee majority wavered back and forth. But he never got the complete authorization he wanted.

which would have put in his hands the power to determine what kind of mass paper it would be. Finally, in November, his patience ran out and he decided to go ahead and present the GBL with an accomplished fact. Previously, he had stretched GBL discipline; now he deliberately broke it by publishing an unauthorized paper. Perhaps he thought the Central Committee would accept the indiscipline rather than risk a split, and perhaps the Central Committee would have accepted it without Trotsky's intervention. In any case, the whole future of the French section was now put into jeopardy.

As the GBL leadership stumbled back and forth, Trotsky grew increasingly apprehensive about the outcome in France, but he was unwilling, before the end of November, to conclude that differences over principle were involved as well as differences over stupid and self-defeating tactics. As long as that was the case he confined himself in his letters to pointing out the mistakes he saw, and in his public articles to discussing the issues where he thought the GBL was going astray, without polemicizing by name against the organization or its leaders. Thus even his public article on committees of action at the end of Part One (November 26) must be read as, among other things, an attempt to counter incorrect formulations being expressed by the GBL in its press or by Molinier inside the GBL. But the GBL's failure to publish *any* serious criticism of Pivert struck him as inexplicable on a purely tactical level (letter of November 25 and undated letter to Zeller of November). Neither *La Vérité* nor *Révolution* printed the introduction Trotsky dictated for a pamphlet written by Zeller after he came over to the Fourth International (article of November 7); the only possible reason was the introduction's critical remarks about Pivertism. Trotsky was on the verge of drawing some pessimistic conclusions about the ability of the French section to resist hostile class pressures when Molinier made his move in November.

PART ONE
EXIT FROM THE SFIO
(July-November 1935)

A False Idea
July 3, 1935

The idea of counterposing to *La Vérité* a mass paper that arises from the will of one group or another like a *deus ex machina* is absolutely false. I have observed similar attempts several times in Russia and elsewhere: they led either to failure or to the camouflaged formation of a new faction.

From *L'Organe de masse*. Signed "Crux." An excerpt from a letter to Jean Rous.

Bourgeois Politicians
and the People's Front
July 11, 1935

For the moment, the People's Front is a fact (not for long). Our slogan must be something like: "Bourgeois politicians out of the People's Front! The popular masses have nothing to learn from the capitulator Daladier! Down with the Radical betrayers of the popular masses," etc., etc. All the possible variants. Perhaps a formulation like this could be used: "To turn the People's Front against the bourgeoisie, it is necessary to get the bourgeoisie out of the People's Front."

From *Bulletin Intérieur*, GBL, no. 9, December 1935. Translated by Naomi Allen.

Conflicting Slogans
July 22, 1935

The experiment of the reformist and Stalinist government lies ahead. The experiment of the Radical government is accomplished. To identify or even to associate the two slogans—"For a Socialist-Communist government (government of the united front), workers' and peasants' government," etc., and "For a government of the People's Front, including the Radicals"— would be absolutely fatal.

From *Bulletin Intérieur*, GBL, no. 9, December 1935. Translated by Naomi Allen.

How to Transform La Vérité
July 26, 1935

. . . I want to dwell especially on the question of a "mass paper." I do not at all consider this question to be "secondary"— quite the contrary. It is because I see all of its gravity that I cannot indulge in facile solutions. To create a mass paper apart from *La Vérité* would be a criminal adventure; you will quickly compromise both papers and end up at the same time with two factions. You must try to transform *La Vérité* into a mass paper *without depriving it of its character as the paper of a tendency.* That is the only possible solution.

From *L'Organe de masse.* Signed "Crux." An excerpt from a letter to Naville.

The Expulsion of the French Youth
July 30, 1935

Dear Comrade Rous:

We have just received a telegram from Van on the expulsion of the youth. What an act! A new chapter is beginning.

In my last letter to you I spoke, in passing, of the possibility of creating the independent revolutionary party in the very near future. I expressed myself somewhat vaguely in order to feel out the ground, and in order not to provoke a premature discussion. Now the ice is broken—not by us, but it is definitely broken. We can condense the discussion. Clearly, it involves a new party.

They maneuvered with the date of the congress of the Comintern so as to have it coincide with the expulsion of the youth. That must be the great motive of the congress, revenge for the defeats in China, Germany, Austria, etc.[1] It is the revenge of organic unity.

Why have they begun with the youth? The *political* explanation: because their heads are at stake. The plot of Blum-Lebas-Cachin-Thorez-Stalin has as its objective to sell the French youth to French imperialism. On the basis of this explanation a national campaign must be launched. The national conference must be held under this aegis.

By that I do not mean to say that the adults must *leave* the party. Oh no! We must not make their job easier for them. But we are naturally all in agreement that the struggle against the expulsions, eventually for the reinstatement of the youth, must have an extremely aggressive character: *We accuse!* We can draw up posters with this headline: "We accuse the leaders of the French party of preparing to betray the French youth." Our attack must in no case be impeded by considerations of party legality. In order to strengthen the lefts in the *Bataille* group, in order to sow confusion in the camp of the majority, and especially in order to reduce to a minimum the hesitations among our sympathizers, we must speak out in a self-assured, firm, and vehement tone.

In assessing the situation as a whole, I am quite optimistic.

From *International Information Bulletin*, Workers Party, no. 2, September 7, 1935. A letter to Jean Rous.

Antimilitarism and antipatriotism are important traditions of the French working class. Just recall for a moment prewar revolutionary syndicalism and the Hervéism which complemented it. The slogan which stood uppermost was antipatriotism and antimilitarism. Jaurès had to humble himself before the trade unions and promise "not to intervene" precisely because the party was compromised by patriotism. After the war, France was the only country where the Comintern won the majority of the SP by accusing it of social patriotism. Now the Stalinists are making common cause with the reformists on the basis of patriotism, and Jouhaux embraces Monmousseau. *We are the only representatives of the great traditions of revolutionary antipatriotism of the French proletariat.* By this very act of expulsion, the traitors have given us an excellent opportunity. We can still become a great force before the year is out.

At the first opportunity, the expelled youth must present their candidate for whatever election comes up, perhaps Fred Zeller, if he is firm. The first election campaign directed against French imperialism and its Radical lackeys, and the lackeys of these lackeys, the reformists and the Stalinists, can open unexpected opportunities for us. We must not await the expulsion of the adults for a similar attempt. Above all, no time must be lost.

Discussions with other groups, especially with the teachers, the New Age, and even with St-Denis, are inevitable.[2] But these negotiations must not for a single instant impede our action. Only through action will we be able to draw all the activists behind us. The negotiations with St-Denis, if held, must be directed against the Doriot-Laval-Hitler bloc. No deals with Doriot on this question—this is of capital importance.

If Zeller is firm and ready to come along with us, it is necessary, for example, not to rush the fusion. Chances are that the initiative for the negotiations will come from him and not involve us openly. If the Spartacus group is momentarily hesitant, so much the better. That would mean a new ferment.

But all these questions are secondary. What is decisive is our own attitude, internal cohesion, an unshakable will to overcome all obstacles. We must speak out clearly: before the next legislative elections we must appear before the country as an independent party, as the only party which has no fatherland.

They will very probably begin expelling the adults not in Paris, but in the provinces: it appears that they are preparing expulsions in Isère. In this instance, Alexis Bardin will be our first candidate. In any case I repeat once again: no trickery, no diplomacy; on the *fundamental* question, vigorous attack.

P.S.—It is not excluded that the Stalinists will deceive the Socialists after having won the expulsion of our comrades as the condition for organic unity; and that after thus having cut off the lefts from the SP, they will drag out the affair indefinitely so their "Socialist brothers" will disintegrate, and finally they will turn their backs on them. This is also a possible variant.

Crux [Trotsky]

Our Cohabitation with the Reformists
August 1, 1935

Our cohabitation with the reformists could not last forever. They themselves took the initiative for the split. Good; that saves us the trouble of doing it ourselves. I certainly hope that the expulsion will not frighten anyone in our ranks, but that it will, instead, stimulate them. It would be absolutely wrong to want to complain and to show our wisdom after the fact: "With a more reasonable, more careful attitude it might have been possible," etc. No, that would be wrong, completely wrong.

With a less combative attitude we would never have produced the necessary effect. The only guarantee we have of success is our vigorous action. On the other hand, these successes could not fail to provoke a split. The reformists do not want us to devour them. That's all. I view the situation and the prospects with great optimism. I wrote to Paris about my point of view, and I am sure that we shall agree on the conclusions to draw from it and on the tasks ahead.

The workers who think—and the other ones, through them— must understand from now on that:

—In order to make an alliance with the bourgeois Radicals, they must separate themselves from the Bolshevik-Leninists.

—In order to make docile cannon fodder of the youth, it is necessary first to drive out the Bolshevik-Leninists.

—In order the better to fool the workers, the Stalinists and the

From *Bulletin Intérieur*, GBL, no. 9, December 1935. Translated by Mary Gordon.

reformists have to get rid of those annoying witnesses, the Bolshevik-Leninists.

National unity is valuable for the bourgeoisie only if it maintains private property intact. Working class unity is acceptable in the eyes of the reformists and Stalinists only if it remains in the framework of national defense.

Such are the rude facts which, in the course of the coming months, must assemble the revolutionary elite of the French proletariat around us.

"Labels" and "Numbers"
(On Marceau Pivert's Letter to the Expelled Young Socialist Comrades)
August 7, 1935

The letter of Marceau Pivert on the expulsions of the leaders of the revolutionary youth of the Seine, despite its laudable aim, reveals some incorrect ideas, whose development can lead to serious errors. The true task of a Marxist is to warn the young comrades against these errors.

Pivert himself accuses our comrades of committing a great "psychological error" by assuming the name Bolshevik-Leninist. Since "original Bolshevism," according to Pivert, denies the democratic structure of the party, equality (?) for all tendencies, etc., by their very name the Bolshevik-Leninists give the bureaucracy of the party a weapon against them. In other words, the "psychological error" consists in an inadequate adaptation to the psychology of . . . the bureaucracy of the party.

This opinion of Pivert represents a very serious "political error," and even a series of errors. It is not true that "original Bolshevism" denies the democratic structure of the party. I advance the absolutely contrary affirmation: there was not and there is not a more democratic party than that of Lenin. It depended only on the advanced workers. It did not know the hidden, masked, but no less fatal dictatorship—the bourgeois "friends" of the proletariat, the careerist parliamentarians, the

---

From *New Militant*, September 7, 1935. Marceau Pivert's letter of July 30 to the expelled Young Socialists was printed on the same page.

drawing-room journalists, the whole parasitic coterie—which permits the ranks of the party to speak "freely" and democratically, but tenaciously holds on to the apparatus and in the final analysis does anything it pleases. This kind of "democracy" in the party is nothing but a replica of the bourgeois democratic state, which also allows the people to speak "freely" but leaves the real power to a handful of capitalists.

Pivert commits a very great political error by idealizing and embellishing the hypocritical and fraudulent "democracy" of the SFIO, which curbs and paralyzes the revolutionary education of the workers, drowning out their voice by the chorus of municipal councilors, parliamentarians, etc., who are imbued to the marrow of their bones with egoistic petty-bourgeois interests and reactionary prejudices. The task of the revolutionist—even if the march of events obliges him to work in the same organization with the reformists, those political exploiters of the proletariat— consists not in taking the attitude of a disciple and of pretending to maintain friendship toward the agents of the bourgeoisie, but of opposing as clearly, as harshly, as unremittingly as possible the opportunists, the patriots, the absolutely bourgeois "Socialists," before the reformist masses. In the final analysis, those who will choose and decide will not be the Blums and the Zyromskys but the masses, the millions of exploited. The party must be built on and for them.

The misfortune of Pivert is that until now he has not cut the umbilical cord that binds him to the small world of the Blums and the Zyromskys. On every new occasion he looks at his "friends" and feels their pulse with anxiety. It is this policy— false, illusory, unrealistic—which he offers to the Bolshevik-Leninists. They must, you see, renounce their own name. Why? Does the name frighten the workers? On the contrary. If the so-called "Communists," despite all the betrayals and all the crimes which they have perpetrated, retain an important section of the proletariat under their banner, it is only because they present themselves to the masses as the bearers of the traditions of the October revolution. The workers do not fear either Bolshevism or Leninism. They ask only (and they are right): Are these real or false Bolsheviks? The task of consistent proletarian revolutionists is not to renounce the name "Bolshevik," but to show their Bolshevism in action to the masses, that is, the spirit of absolute devotion to the cause of the oppressed.

But why then—insists Pivert—cling to a label (?) instead of "following the teachings which it implies?" Now, does not Pivert

himself wear the "label" Socialist? In the field of politics as in all
other fields of human activity, it is impossible to proceed without
"labels," that is, without denominations and appellations that
are as precise as possible. The name "Socialist" is not only
inadequate but absolutely deceptive, for everyone in France who
has a mind to calls himself a "Socialist." By their name, the
Bolshevik-Leninists say to each and all that their theory is
"Marxism"; that it is not the denatured and prostituted
"Marxism" of the reformists (like Paul Faure, J. Longuet,
Séverac, etc.) but the true Marxism restored by Lenin and applied
by him to the fundamental questions of the epoch of imperialism;
that they base themselves on the experiences of October,
developed in the decisions of the first four congresses of the
Communist International; that they are in solidarity with the
theoretical and practical work accomplished by the "Left
Opposition" of the Communist International (1923-32); finally,
that they stand under the banner of the Fourth International.

In politics, the "name" is the "banner." Those who renounce
today a revolutionary name for the benefit of Blum and Company
will tomorrow just as easily renounce the red flag for the tricolor.

Pivert proclaims the right of every Socialist to hope for a better
International—"with or without changing the number." This
slightly misplaced irony about the "number" (entirely—alas—in
the spirit of the philistines of the SAP) represents a political error
of the same type as the irony on the "label." Politically, the
question is posed as follows: Can the world proletariat struggle
successfully against war, fascism, capitalism, under the leadership of reformists or Stalinists (that is to say, Soviet diplomacy)?
We reply: it cannot. The Second and the Third Internationals are
outlived and have become obstacles on the revolutionary road. It
is impossible to "reform" them, because the whole composition of
their leadership is radically hostile to the tasks and the methods
of the proletarian revolution. Those who up until now have not
understood the collapse of the two Internationals cannot raise the
banner of the new International.

"With or without changing the number"? This phrase is devoid
of meaning. It is not by accident that the three old Internationals
were thus numbered. Every "number" signified a distinct epoch,
program, and method of action. The new International must not
be the sum of the two corpses, as the old social patriot Zyromsky
dreams, surprised in his unexpected recognition of the "defense of
the USSR," but the living "negation" of these corpses and at the
same time the "continuation" of the historic work accomplished

by the preceding Internationals. In other words: it is a question of the *Fourth International*. The "number" here signifies a perspective and a distinct program, that is, a "banner." Let the philistines wax ironic on the above. We must not imitate them.

The aversion for "labels" and "numbers" in politics is as dangerous as the aversion for precise definitions in science. In one case as in the other we have before us an infallible symptom of lack of clarity in ideas themselves. To invoke the "masses" serves in this case only to cover one's own hesitations. The worker who believes in Vandervelde or Stalin will undoubtedly be an opponent of the Fourth International. The worker who has understood that the Second and Third Internationals are dead for the cause of the revolution will immediately place himself under our banner. That is precisely why it is criminal to hide this banner under the table.

Pivert is deceiving himself when he thinks that Bolshevism is incompatible with the existence of factions. The principle of Bolshevik organization is "democratic centralism," assured by complete freedom of criticism and of groupings, together with steel discipline in action. The history of the party is at the same time the history of the internal struggle of ideas, groupings, factions. It is true that in the spring of 1921, in a time of terrible crisis, of famine, of cold, the Tenth Congress of the Bolshevik Party, which at that time was seventeen years old, suppressed factions; but this measure was considered exceptional and temporary, and was applied by the Central Committee with the greatest degree of prudence and flexibility. The real annihilation of factions began only with the victory of the bureaucracy over the proletarian vanguard and rapidly led to the virtual death of the party.

The Fourth International will not tolerate mechanical "monolithism" in its ranks. On the contrary, one of its most important tasks is to regenerate on a new, higher historical plane the "revolutionary democracy of the proletarian vanguard." The Bolshevik-Leninists consider themselves a faction of the International which is being built. They are completely ready to work hand in hand with other truly revolutionary factions. But they categorically refuse to adapt their policy to the psychology of opportunist cliques and to renounce their own banner.

No Concessions on the International
August 10, 1935

I am a little disturbed that *La Vérité* has not published the Open Letter. It seems some comrades find that this document doesn't interest "the masses"; they thus accept the SAP's arguments. . . .

You are in the process of preparing for a bloc with Marceau Pivert. I am far from being opposed to it. . . . But this bloc demands an absolutely intransigent attitude on your part on the question of the Fourth International. The slightest concession on this point would be fatal to the further development of our section. . . .

The secret of success now consists in not allowing yourselves to be taken unawares. On the contrary, without the knowledge of the enemy a vehement offensive must be carefully prepared that will take the adversary by surprise.

From *L'Organe de masse.* Signed "Crux." An excerpt from a letter to Jean Rous.

After the Toulon Events
August 11, 1935

To the French Bolshevik-Leninists

The revolutionary events at Toulon, le Havre, and Brest, of which we have received the details here after an unavoidable delay of two or three days, are of capital importance—and can be of decisive importance.

The objective situation in France is revolutionary. This fact has been denied by the reformists, and particularly by the Stalinists, who have tried to conceal their miserable policy behind an alleged lack of fighting spirit among the masses. We have always affirmed that rebelliousness is growing among the laboring

---

From *International Information Bulletin,* Workers Party, no. 2, September 7, 1935.

masses and that it is precisely the organizations of the workers—
the parties and trade unions—which are preventing them from
finding an outlet for their will to struggle. This has now been
proved to the hilt. The sailors are perhaps more explosive than
the others, but they represent a section of the working people and
their vigorous action is entirely symptomatic of the mood of the
masses.

A strong revolutionary organization would immediately call
upon the working class of the whole country to support the sailors
in revolt. There is not the least doubt that the masses would reply
with a vigorous general strike. The rest would depend upon the
strategy of both sides and the relation of forces, which would
unfold in the course of the struggle.

L'Humanité accuses Laval of having provoked the conflict to
divide the People's Front. It sees a divisive maneuver in the
explosion of the class struggle. The People's Front is based upon
a negation of the class struggle, for which it substitutes fictions:
"antifascism," "republic," "democracy," etc. The explosion at
Toulon is a shattering negation of the People's Front and a
magnificent confirmation of our analysis and our perspective.

The election in Clermont-Ferrand is an important step along
the path of the decomposition of the Radical Party. The events at
Toulon, etc., must enormously accelerate the decomposition of
Radicalism, parliamentarism, and "democracy." The fascists will
inevitably profit from this. On the other hand, the rebellion of the
sailors is a sign of the accelerated rhythm of the revolutionary
movement. It is on this basis that we must now direct our
campaign against the reformists and the Stalinists and also
against the hesitations of our centrist allies and semi-allies. All
considerations of form, internal discipline, etc., must give way
before considerations of direct action among and at the head of
the masses. Our participation in the SFIO has produced results
invisible only to the blind. But none among us has ever
considered that our opportunities inside the SFIO were unlimited
and that we would remain linked to this party indefinitely. The
declarations of the [expelled] youth in favor of discipline, etc., are
useful to demonstrate to the inexperienced the bad faith of the
reformists and the Stalinists and to unmask the intrigues of the
SAPists who are also at this time trying to sabotage the action.
But all statutory maneuvers must now after the first flashes of
the revolution be subordinated to an implacable offensive on the
basis of revolutionary strategy. It is necessary to denounce Blum,
Cachin, Jouhaux, Monmousseau, for betraying the masses in

revolt in order to retain the favor of the Radicals, i.e., of the bourgeoisie against whom the workers are rebelling.

We must say to ourselves: The transitory period of adaptation to the regime of the SFIO is drawing to its natural end. We must orient ourselves in practice toward the *revolutionary party* with the shortest possible delay, opening up the period of independent activity among the masses.

The Perspective of Soviets
September 7, 1935

The slogan "Radicals out [of the People's Front]!" remains correct, but it is insufficient, because you do not indicate how to get them out. The means, however, were indicated by the Seventh Congress of the Comintern. The resolution on fascism recommends the creation, wherever possible, of large bodies, elected by the popular masses (Dimitrov's resolution, chapter 2, paragraph 3). Our slogan for a certain period has been the slogan "United front," "Workers' alliance," etc. Now the same role must be played by the slogan for the creation of bodies representative of the masses of the united front (the perspective of soviets). We must declare openly: We are not in accord with the content of Dimitrov's proposal, because it calls for class collaboration, the policy of the Kuomintang. But in that proposal there is one paragraph that is quite correct, progressive, and extremely important.

From *Bulletin Intérieur*, GBL, no. 9, December 1935. Signed "Crux." Translated by Naomi Allen.

No Evasions on the Independent Party
September 13, 1935

Is it or is it not necessary to speak openly about the perspective of an independent party? How can it be avoided? You would certainly like to remain in the SFIO to the limit of its possibilities. You would really like to remain in and work with the unified party, provided that the fusion takes place. You would not play an insignificant role in the battles of this party. All of that is clear. You can and should repeat it once again and a hundred times over. At the same time you say that both bureaucracies are against it and perhaps cannot even allow it, in view of their obligations to Stalin on the one hand, and Daladier and Company on the other. We denounce their intention to split and announce that from now on we shall pursue our uncompromising struggle against social patriotism of every stripe, both inside and outside of the unified party. We say openly to our friends: Defend your place in the SFIO zealously, but be prepared for independent struggle if it is forced on us—and it looks as though that will be the case. *How can we avoid saying that openly?*

The Spartacists' notion that it is necessary to remain inside the SFIO *at any cost* is treachery. The reformists say, we will do everything within the framework of bourgeois legality. But bourgeois legality allows "everything" except the most important things. Blum's legality is nothing but an adjunct to and a reflection of bourgeois legality. It allows you to do, or rather to say, "everything" except those things that would effectively oppose imperialist patriotism. Marxists take advantage of legality (both legalities, the legality of the state as well as that of Blum) to the fullest extent, without ever relinquishing their reason for existence: the class struggle—the real one, not the imaginary one. Those who say "we will forego telling the masses the truth about the latest social-patriotic treachery so as not to be expelled from the party led by the social patriots" become the witting accomplices of these traitors. By claiming to speak in the name of Marxism they reveal what contemptible scoundrels they are.

From *Bulletin Intérieur*, GBL, no. 8 (undated). Signed "Crux." Translated by Naomi Allen. An excerpt from a letter to Jean Rous.

The Path to Political Suicide
September 13, 1935

It is possible that the two bureaucracies, with the aid of the two governments, will succeed for a certain period in making our existence quite precarious. With the approach of war the situation of revolutionists can be neither easy nor pleasant. Lenin and Liebknecht began by "isolating themselves" from the mass organizations. Neither M[arceau] P[ivert] nor anyone else will be able to come up with any other method. Do what must be done, come what may.

Marceau Pivert calls for the discontinuation of *La Vérité,* as if that measure could appease the gods. And *Lutte de classes* as well? And *Révolution?* And the leaflets? Those wretches of Spartacus show more consistency by abandoning *Révolution.* But by doing so they will succeed only in whetting the appetite of Blum and Zyromsky. You will find no better defense against the offensive unleashed by the social patriots than to openly denounce social patriotism. Before they throttle you they seek to deprive you of your means of defense. To consent to that is to commit political suicide.

In 1914 all these struggles began after the outbreak of the war. Today the opposing camps, having learned from experience, commence hostilities on the eve of the war. This gives the revolutionaries a big advantage. They must exploit it to the fullest possible extent. Whoever adopts a policy of political abdication in a period of preparation will be isolated and expelled just the same once the war begins. It is possible to cheat in small matters but not in large ones.

From *Bulletin Intérieur,* GBL, no. 8 (undated). Signed "Crux." Translated by Naomi Allen.

SFIO Discipline and the Fourth International
Published 1935

The question of the Fourth International must be formulated precisely; that is, here too it is necessary to state matters as they are. You belong to the international group for the Fourth International. But what is the significance of that formation at the present time? It is a coalition of organizations and tendencies whose purpose is to propagandize for the Fourth International. No less, but no more either. There is no administrative body capable of imposing its discipline on any part of this international group regarding any question whatsoever. This means that the group "for the Fourth" can in no way encroach upon the internal discipline of the SFIO. The only question at issue is whether or not one has the right to carry on propaganda within the SFIO around the need to prepare a new International, in view of the revolutionary bankruptcy of the two old ones. That is the only question.

From *Bulletin Intérieur*, GBL, no. 8 (undated). Signed "Crux." Translated by Naomi Allen.

Pivert's Relation to Blum and Zyromsky
September 16, 1935

The more I consider it, the more I am persuaded that Pivert's latest article is a wretched and ignoble retreat before the pressure of social patriotism. In reality, he already has carried out the same function in relation to Léon Blum that Zyromsky carried out before him. . . .

You are not yet proclaiming the new party, but you are in effect preparing the groundwork for it. A serious break in the CP or a Pivertist split from the SFIO,[3] or even an important local development, like Doriot's open betrayal, could serve our purposes if we present ourselves all at once as a new party.

From *L'Organe de masse*. Signed "Crux."

Our Political Line and Our Tactics
September 16, 1935

I have spoken many times in the past weeks about the situation in France. If my suggestions sometimes lack the necessary precision, that is because I cannot observe developments close up, and important elements of the whole picture fail to appear. But I will try to summarize my point of view in a few lines once again.

There is the question of our *political line.* It must be directed toward *independence,* which is dictated by the whole situation, above all by the conscious will of our enemies (the imperialists, the reformists, the Stalinists, the centrists, the SAPists, etc.). But there is the *tactical* and *pedagogical* question. This has its own rights and obligations which—in the final analysis, of course—are subordinate to our political line. We can and should use every means that is likely to convince the hesitant, the poorly informed, the inexperienced, of the ill will of our enemies. But these measures and these procedures must not fetter our will to action and our fundamental intransigence. We ourselves must fully understand the secondary character of the statutory struggle, of the formal concessions, etc., despite all their conjunctural importance. If there is a serious division over some important concessions, it is better to give them up, because in such cases there is always the risk of losing more than you gain. Nine-tenths of our forces, at the very least, for the political offensive, for mass work, etc. . . . One-tenth, at the very most, for the statutory struggle and the purely pedagogical measures.

From *L'Organe de masse.* Signed "Crux."

A Dangerous Symptom in Our Ranks
October 3, 1935

To the International Secretariat

Dear Comrades:

From various sides comes the news that there are SAPist tendencies concerning the People's Front policy in our ranks, too, at least among some individuals and small groups of comrades. This fact seems to me of decisive importance. To permit ambiguity or evasions on this matter would mean exposing ourselves to extreme political demoralization.

When some comrades complain about the "sharp tone" of our criticism of the SAP, the older comrades, at least, can't help but remember the history of the discussions between the Marxists and the revisionists. Marxists have always been accused of using the wrong tone. Not so much by the revisionists themselves as by vacillating elements who wanted to blur the discussion in order to soften the sharp angles and avoid posing problems precisely. It goes without saying that sometimes the tone of an article may be too blunt, and it is everyone's right and duty to call that to the attention of both the author and the editor. But those elements who speak always and nearly exclusively about the tone prove that it is the substance that in fact bothers them, whether they can or will realize it. A discussion about the tone and the permissible degree of severity is, moreover, quite sterile. It will be much more fruitful when it reaches political ground, which is actually where the problems of the People's Front and social patriotism belong in the first place.

It is understandable that during the first weeks some hesitation appeared even in our ranks; the situation was complicated, and the People's Front was a new phenomenon for many of us and consequently a new problem. But the fact that some comrades show themselves to be People's Front politicians even now, after rather significant experience with the People's Front and after

From *Bulletin Intérieur,* ICL, no. 4, November 1935, where it was dated November 4, 1935. The correct date was provided by the German original at the Harvard archive. Translated for this volume from the French by Russell Block.

the important articles printed in our press, seems to me an extremely dangerous symptom. On this matter, we must raise a sharp protest before it is too late, because what is at stake here is neither more nor less than the line of demarcation between Bolshevism and Menshevism.

Some say that to demand the expulsion of the Radicals from the People's Front would be wrong: the masses must first go through experience with the Radicals; that is why it would supposedly be much better to demand that the People's Front take power; only its bankruptcy will supposedly convince the masses to accept our ideas, etc. This way of thinking is Menshevik from beginning to end.

1. "The popular masses must go through experience with the Radicals." All right. But why should the working class organizations take part in it? The Radicals can also demonstrate their bankruptcy without the People's Front. The People's Front does not expose but covers up this bankruptcy.

2. The Socialists have been participating in People's Fronts with the Radicals for years. Starting with nothing, they passed through nothing and got nowhere. The crisis forced them to a break (which is far from complete) with the Radicals. This break brought about a split inside the Socialist Party (with the Neo-Socialists). We hope that these facts have some weight. They are precisely the result of the working masses' disillusionment over the Socialists' collaboration with the Radicals. This disillusionment sums up a whole historical period. The pressure of the masses has forced the Socialists to form a bloc with the Communists, and the idea of the People's Front, that is, of restoring the alliance with the Radicals, was raised not by the "masses" but by Moscow. Only the authority of the united leaderships (Socialists and Communists) has made the renewal of the coalition with the Radicals halfway palatable to the working class. If we, the revolutionary wing, say to the working class: "Radicals out of the People's Front!" we express the result of their historical experience and we reflect the thinking of their vanguard.

3. "The masses must convince themselves." We by no means stand in their way. We only want to be sure that the petty bourgeoisie doesn't acquire its new "convictions" at the expense of the working class. And what would these convictions be? If the People's Front continues to vegetate, achieves governmental power, and fails, then the experience of the masses will lead them to this one great lesson: the Radicals, the Socialists, and the

Communists are all the same sorts of scoundrels; it was no accident that they joined forces to betray us. We must turn our back on them and seek justice from the fascists.

4. They forget that the whole crisis of the parliamentary regime originates in the crisis of confidence of the masses in the Radicals, and that the working class organizations have sacrificed themselves, like good samaritans, to try to repair the reputation of the long-since discredited Radical Party. It would be pure treason for our party not to issue the most severe warnings and not to raise the demand: "Radicals out of the People's Front!"

5. But the Stalinists do not stop with the Radicals. They already have won the admission of the Neo-Socialists. The split with the Neo-Socialists was a step forward. This step forward has been liquidated. They have accepted the party of Briand, Paul-Boncour, etc., into the People's Front. And, as if this were not enough, they are now trying to win Flandin's party to the People's Front. To be sure, there are a lot of petty bourgeois who vote for Flandin. Is that a good enough reason to make a *common front* with him? For it is not a matter of the masses' experience, which they will have without us, against us, and under the blows of our criticisms, but rather of a *common front*—that is, political collaboration—with the class enemy. That was what the Menshevik philosophy consisted of in 1905, and above all in 1917, in Russia; that was the Stalinist policy toward the Kuomintang in China, etc. Those traitors will always try to mask their own disloyal policy of aid to the bourgeoisie with the "need of the masses for experience."

6. We can really sigh with relief now that the SAP has finally stopped reproducing our analysis and our slogans, in a somewhat diluted form, and is making an effort to show its own political colors. Around the questions of the war, the Seventh World Congress, and the People's Front (Spartacus), they have now shown their hand. Let naive souls believe that our "sectarianism" and our "overly severe criticism" has driven them away from the Fourth International. You lie, gentlemen, we shall answer: you are common pacifists (for disarmament); you are second-rate Brandlerites (your attitude toward the Seventh World Congress); you are Mensheviks (your position on political fraternization with the bourgeoisie—"People's Front"). If all the good comrades in our ranks understand the depth of our differences, then they will also have to understand that the *tone* of the polemic must correspond to the sharpness of the differences. Otherwise, the workers would believe that it is a matter of secondary differences

within the same family. Marxism comports itself here in an irreconcilable manner toward right-leaning centrism. This means a fight to the finish, without considerations of tact.

7. Some comrades accuse our French section of being "rash": they supposedly have provoked the reformists with exaggerated criticism or untimely slogans, etc. Those objections are false and rotten to the core, and are only a reflection of SAPist guile. It is not a problem of "tone" or of "rashness," which are of secondary importance, but of *national defense*. The whole plan of Léon Blum and Company is not to let this question be raised for discussion at all, so that they will be able, at the last minute, to spring a surprise on their own party. Stalin's crude declaration to Laval did not look good in this gambit. The congress of the Comintern, using the little jesuit Ercoli, has succeeded in retreating to the line put forward by Léon Blum in this matter.[4] The resolution says nothing to the masses. But it leaves the hands of the leaders free to deceive the masses. Léon Blum showed himself superior to Stalin in the methods of social patriotism. But Léon Blum could not stand anyone stepping on his toes, that is, he could not stand having the question of national defense raised over and over again in the party. But that is just what the Bolshevik-Leninists do. That is what they consider their essential task, and rightly so. Therein lies their real "rashness" and "tactlessness." Whoever has not understood this crucial point may get distracted by superficial things and chance gossip. At a time when the French comrades are under heavy attack from the reformists and Stalinists, when they are ignominiously betrayed by the SAPists and the Pivertists, our duty is to help them as much as we can. Whoever repeats the SAPist arguments, despite his best intentions, lines up with all the agents of social patriotism.

I suppose that some comrades will also find the "tone" of this letter too sharp, not fraternal enough, etc. I have already resigned myself to it. But let them not neglect the substance of my arguments. If my arguments are wrong, I beg that they be answered in the sharpest way. I promise never to complain about the polemical tone, because the essence is always more important than the form.

Crux [Trotsky]

Third-Rate Aides of Imperialism
October 26, 1935

Dear Comrade van Driesten:

I am sure that you, as well as the other Dutch comrades, are following the situation in France with the greatest attention. It is important as a whole, as well as in its details. By the whole, I mean the formation of the People's Front, which has become a "model" for the entire Comintern. By the details, I mean the maneuvers of the Stalinists and the reformists to isolate our friends, the opponents of the sacred union, before they fall into the hands of the authorities as enemies of the state.

For the internal struggle of the Dutch youth, the attitude of the French Spartacus group, inspired exclusively by the ideas of the SAP, is of the greatest importance. This living example shows quite well how false and superficial is the idea that there are, on the one hand, the utopians, who are trying to pull the Fourth International out of a hat, and, on the other, the realists, who, while they too are for the new International, take reality into account and adapt to the stages of development of the masses.

To reduce the argument to the purely formal question of the "proclamation" or "nonproclamation" of the Fourth International is to ignore the theoretical and political basis of the matter. The Spartacus group has *capitulated politically* to the SFIO bureaucracy, just as Marceau Pivert, the French cousin of Schwab, has. Only a few weeks ago Marceau Pivert wrote, word for word: "The fight against 'Trotskyism' in this period is the mark of a reactionary outlook in the ranks of the working class." Now he uses the columns of *Le Populaire* to denounce our "sectarianism" and to crawl on his belly before Léon Blum.

Obviously, the Spartacus group as well as Marceau Pivert stress the need for "unity." Not to be separated from the masses? Our French section, in taking the rather daring step of entering the SFIO—a step that has proven quite correct—has shown that we understand the importance of having close contact with the masses. But it is necessary to understand well that those who capitulate before their own imperialism will most often do it while

---

From *Bulletin Intérieur*, ICL, no. 4, November 1935. A letter to Theo van Driesten, a member of the ICL's Dutch section. Translated by David Keil.

invoking the need to preserve the unity of the working class, especially in case of war.

The Spartacus group, Marceau Pivert, and the others are naturally "against our own country's imperialism" no less than the Bolshevik-Leninists; but unlike the latter they do not want to be isolated from the masses, and therefore they continue to be concerned about "unity." This is also more or less the attitude of the new official leadership of the Seine Youth (Chochoy and the others). I fear also that similar attitudes are to be found among many leading comrades of the Belgian Young Socialist Guards. "We, the youth, are ready to transform the imperialist war into a civil war, but on the condition that Uncle Léon Blum (or Uncle Emile Vandervelde) permits it." With this attitude one reserves for oneself the agreeable privilege of putting forth "international-ist" speeches and articles at party conferences and in the internal discussion bulletins while at the same time continuing to be the base of support for the "unity" which serves Messrs. Léon Blum and Emile Vandervelde, that is, in the last analysis, the French and Belgian imperialists. By this I naturally do not mean that one must today or tomorrow leave the reformist party on one's own initiative. Nor are our French friends doing this. But where the bureaucracy, which understands its interests and those of its bosses quite well, forces on us the alternative of submitting to social-patriotic, i.e., imperialist, discipline, and renouncing the right to bring revolutionary ideas to the masses, we should— precisely for the sake of the masses—refuse to obey the social-patriotic servants of imperialism. At the very instant that Fred Zeller took this step together with our people, the French SAPists shamefully betrayed the honest revolutionary wing.

What is at issue is not at all the "abstract," "theoretical" question of the Fourth International (the social-patriotic profi-teers don't care at all about theories and abstractions) but the vital question of our epoch: with imperialism or against it?

By their attitude, the French Spartacus supporters make themselves third-rate aides of imperialism. Take, for example, the articles in the miserable sheet *Neue Front* on the Seventh World Congress or on the People's Front government: at bottom they salute the reformist degeneration of the CI and accept their new coalition program. These articles alone prove that the SAP is not separated from the Second or from the Third International in their present form by truly irreconcilable clashes of principles. How could it find the will to take on its shaky shoulders the gigantic historic task of building a new International?

If the real content of the SAP's politics is ignored, the whole struggle against it can only be sterile and fruitless. But if we take the bull by the horns, then we will understand and make others understand that the question of the Fourth International symbolizes a whole outlook, a whole political system, which is in sharper and sharper opposition to the outlook and the political system of the SAP. For to anyone who has eyes it is no secret that the SAP has gone backward in the past months in a completely reactionary way.

A few days ago I wrote a fairly long article on the British ILP, and I hope you will soon receive the German translation.[5] The question of the Fourth International is analyzed in this article in relation to the British workers' movement, and perhaps this analysis can also be useful to the Dutch comrades.

Best regards,
L. Trotsky

Introduction to Fred Zeller's Pamphlet
November 7, 1935

This little pamphlet should meet with the warmest welcome. Along with large sections of the youth, Comrade Zeller—secretary of the Seine youth organization, an active member of the Socialist Party—has traveled, during the recent period, a most important road—from centrism to Marxism. This road need not be described in the preface; the reader should turn to the pamphlet itself. The reader would do best, perhaps, by first turning to Zeller's presentation, which provides valuable factual and political material, and then turning back to this introduction, the purpose of which is to draw the most pressing conclusions.

The expulsion of the leaders of the youth in Paris and of the leading members of the *Vérité* group (the Bolshevik-Leninists) from the Socialist Party is a fact of major importance. At the present moment a political regroupment is taking place in all the countries of Europe in the face of the maturing war danger. A differentiation along this line has begun in the ranks of the proletariat. Just as the extreme left leaders of the bourgeoisie discard democratic parliamentarianism once the defense of their property is at stake, so the opportunists trample party democracy underfoot whenever their social patriotism is threatened by

---

From the pamphlet *The Road for Revolutionary Socialists*, published in New York in 1936.

revolutionary internationalists. Herein is the crux of the question. That the party leaders have violated all the "statutes" and all the "norms" of democracy has been irrefutably proved by Marceau Pivert, who, as is well known, continues to believe in statutes just as certain naive "republicans" believe in the immutability of bourgeois democracy.

The traditional social patriots—Léon Blum, Lebas, Zyromsky, and others—found themselves in an extremely difficult position after the experience of the great war for "democracy." They feared the defeatist criticism of the Communists and the distrust of the masses. For this reason they sought to evade the question of national defense, to postpone a solution of it until the outbreak of the war, when the toilers would once again be caught off guard and it would be much easier under cover of military censorship to chain the party and the proletariat to the chariot of national defense. Suddenly—a stroke of luck! Soviet diplomacy arrived at the final conclusion that the reformist bureaucracy, hand in hand with the Radical bourgeoisie, is much more useful and reliable an ally than the revolutionary proletariat. A command is issued from Moscow to fall in line with the social patriots, and together with them to fall in line with the Radicals, the left party of French imperialism. What a pleasant surprise! Stalin, with both hands, hoisted Blum into the saddle of national defense. To be sure, in so doing he moved so energetically that Blum became frightened lest he tumble over the other side of the horse. Hence Blum's plaintive articles: "It cannot be done so crudely; one must act more cautiously; one must not scare the leftists. . . ." The Seventh Congress of the Comintern took heed of Blum's counsels and enveloped its social-patriotic resolutions in a maximum of obscurity. What more could be desired? The "united front" has slipped almost noiselessly into national unity.

But from the left there suddenly came sharp, even threatening voices of protest. Moreover, not only from the Bolshevik-Leninists (they are an "alien body"!) but also from the majority of the Paris Young Socialists. What is to be done? Debate with them? Unfortunately, easier said than done. Where are the arguments to be found in defense of the social-patriotic betrayal? What is there to counterpose to revolutionary internationalism? Zyromsky tried to raise as a cardinal argument the need of defending the USSR. It was Guesde himself, if you please, who taught the necessity of defending the Russian revolution. . . . Not only are the youth laughing but even the Pioneers are beginning to laugh at this argument, particularly from the lips of Zyromsky. We know how Guesde defended French democracy: by becoming the minister of the imperialist government during the war. The Zyromskys, too, have in mind these very same methods—in essence if not in form—when they speak of the defense of the USSR. To this the revolutionary youth and the Bolshevik-Leninists together reply: we will defend the USSR in the same way that we will defend ourselves, *by an irreconcilable revolutionary struggle against our own bourgeoisie.*

In view of these arguments of the left, the most extreme wing of the social patriots fails to have any effect—the youth are for Karl Liebknecht and not Zyromsky—what else was there left to do? Stifle, expel, crush! Casting aside the tinsel of phrases, *the expulsion of the revolutionary internationalists is equivalent to an action by the patriotic police with the aim of preparing national unity in the event of war.*

Naive people will object that there is some misunderstanding here. For Chochoy himself, the new national secretary of the youth, is "also an internationalist," he is "also" against national defense, and yet he was for the expulsion of Fred Zeller and his comrades. Obviously, the guilty one is . . . Zeller. As a matter of fact, "internationalists" of the Chochoy type exist in nature precisely in order to assist Léon Blum to befuddle credulous people. The "internationalist" who places his friendship with the social-patriotic bureaucracy above the duties of revolutionary action, is, in reality, only a left link in the imperialist chain. At certain times, in order to screen its intentions and calm the masses, finance capital requires a Daladier, a Henderson, even a Lansbury. Once the setting shifts, finance capital shoos Daladier away, replacing him by Doumergue or Laval. In the same way, the social-patriotic bureaucracy during certain periods has need of Chochoy for certain operations, in order, then, at the next stage, to remove and even expel him, should he attempt to open his mouth. Anyone who has failed to understand this cunning mechanism—even if his beard is grey—remains a blind kitten in politics.

The centrists of the so-called Revolutionary Left lecture us that they too are waging a struggle against the *ideas* of social patriotism, but they were not expelled. Their mistake lies in the fact that the Bolshevik-Leninists and Fred Zeller, together with his comrades, did not confine themselves to an ideological struggle, but resorted to personalities, permitting themselves attacks upon the "respected leaders" of the party. This is not a new argument, but it is well worth dwelling upon. At a time when the social patriots by their apparatus repressions prepare and facilitate the coming police repressions against the defeatists, the centrist rationalizers, whether they wish it or not, provide the bureaucracy with arguments to justify the expulsions. Let us bear this firmly in mind!

"It is necessary to wage a struggle against *ideas* and not *leaders!*" But this happens to be the classic argument of the "left" Mensheviks against Lenin during the war. There is a German proverb that covers this case: there is no washing the sheepskin without getting the wool wet. Ideas do not hang suspended in midair; they are borne by living people, people who unite in organizations and select their leaders. It is impossible to fight against bourgeois ideas without fighting against those leaders who defend these ideas within the proletariat and who are once again prepared to sacrifice the workers on the altar of patriotism. Those, unlike Chochoy and his kind, who do not desire to remain content by playing on the flute of internationalism in a closed room on Sundays in order to console their own souls, those who approach seriously and honestly the slogan of Marx and Engels, "Workers of the world unite," are duty-bound to say openly and courageously to the French workers: *Léon Blum, Marcel Cachin, Léon Jouhaux, Monmousseau, and Company are leading you down the road to disaster!* Let Marceau Pivert tell the youth whether—from the standpoint and principles of party democracy—a Socialist has the right to speak the truth to his party, i.e., that the "respected leaders" are preparing a new betrayal. To all appearances, he has that right. As for us, in our opinion, the duty of revolutionary internationalists stands above all obligations toward the party bureaucracy and its "discipline."

Léon Blum, Zyromsky, and others are not at all content to struggle against the *ideas* of Marx and Lenin; they open a rabid campaign against the young *leaders* who defend these ideas. Such is the inevitable logic of the struggle. But the centrists refuse to understand this. The left Mensheviks rose up against Lenin's "sectarian" methods only because they were internationalists in words while in action they felt their indissoluble bond with the social-patriotic leaders of the Second International. So, too, the rationalizers of the Revolutionary Left, observing the expulsion of the internationalists, scurry between the two wings, but invariably end up by disassociating themselves from—the expelled. Why? Because the expellers are closer to them politically. They lecture to us that with our "sectarian" methods (i.e., the methods of Marx and Lenin) organizational unity would never have been achieved. In the meantime "the masses are striving for unity," and we must not "tear ourselves away" from the masses.

Before us here is the entire argumentation of the ill-starred leaders of the SAP,* who, it may be pertinently remarked, never had any masses behind them, haven't any now, and never will have in the future. We say in answer that the *instinctive* urge to unity is quite often an urge peculiar to the masses; but a *conscious* striving for unity on a *revolutionary basis* is peculiar to the *vanguard* of the proletariat. Which of these tendencies should revolutionary Marxists support? For example, the organizational unity of the working class has long existed in England. But at the same time it implies the political unity of the working class with the imperialist bourgeoisie. The traitor MacDonald sits in the Conservative government of Baldwin; the patriot-pacifist Henderson represented the Conservative government in the League of Nations to his dying day; Major Attlee, the new leader of the Labour Party, stands for imperialist sanctions set by the League of Nations under the dictation of the London Stock Exchange.[6] Under such conditions "organizational unity" is a conspiracy of the workers' bureaucracy against the basic interests of the proletariat.

But are things any better in France? In the days of Brest and Toulon, four bureaucratic apparatuses (the SP, the CP, the CGT, and the CGTU) were absolutely "as one" in strangling and slandering the uprising for the sake of a friendly smile from the Radicals. From its outset the united front in France was converted into an instrument of collaboration with the bourgeoisie. The organizational merger of the two parties, if realized, would signify *under present conditions* only the preparation for national unity. Jouhaux and Monmousseau have already achieved trade union unity, with the interests of their apparatuses guaranteed but with factions prohibited, i.e., they took measures beforehand to strangle revolutionary socialism. When centrists, tailing the rights, begin to declaim too much about unity, the Marxist is duty-bound to be on guard. *Unity between whom? In the name of what? Against whom?* Unless there is a clear definition of aims and tasks the slogan of unity can become the worst possible trap. The Marxists are for the unity of genuine revolutionists, for the fusion of militant internationalists, who alone are capable of leading the proletariat on the road of the socialist revolution.

This is not sectarianism. Marxists are the ones best able to find

---

*The émigré groups of the Socialist Workers Party of Germany (SAP), of which there are rather a considerable number, today play the role of a brake in the workers' movement of different countries.

a road to the masses, and those who are as yet unable will learn on the morrow. The school of Lenin is a great school precisely in this sphere. Should the social patriots arrive at an organizational agreement among themselves (and this is not so simple!), then the revolutionists—inside as well as outside the united party, depending upon circumstances—will wage an irreconcilable struggle for the emancipation of the workers from the *ideas* and *leaders* of reformism, Stalinism, social patriotism, i.e., against the Second and Third Internationals which have become *the agency of the League of Nations*. The struggle for the independent policy of the proletariat, for the fusion of its vanguard upon a Marxist program, for the international unity of the workers against imperialism—this is the struggle for the Fourth International.

In the ebb and flow of our epoch, amid great defeats and disillusionments, in the growth of the conservative Soviet bureaucracy, the oldest generation of both Internationals has largely spent itself, become a hollow shell, and fallen prostrate. The building of the new International in its main weight falls upon the young generation. The obstacles are great, the tasks colossal. But it is precisely in the struggle against great obstacles that fighting cadres are formed and steeled. The Young Socialists of the Seine and after them the provinces as well should and can assume an honored place in this work. More faith in ourselves, in our forces, and in the future! Let the philistines howl about the tactlessness, rashness, and exaggerations of the youth! Cadres of a revolutionary party have never yet been educated either in ballet schools or in diplomatic chancelleries. The revolution is not only "tactless" but ruthless when need arises. That is why Messrs. Bourgeois hate Leninism (they get along quite nicely with Stalinism). The social patriots translate the fears of the bourgeoisie into the language of "sanctions," expelling young Bolsheviks from the party, while centrist philistines curse on this account . . . the Fourth International. This need not worry us. All these processes take place in the thin layer of the bureaucracy and the workers' aristocracy. We must look deeper into the masses that languish in the chains of the crisis, hate their slave owners, seek to struggle, are capable of struggle, and have already made their first assault in Toulon and Brest. These masses need no hollow preaching on unity, nor the false "tactfulness" of salons, but clear-cut slogans and courageous leadership. It is our hope that Zeller's pamphlet will perform a service in the cause of educating the young cadres of the new International!

On Organizational Problems
November 1935

Trotsky asked me my opinion of the principal Bolshevik-Leninists in Paris. I spoke of them cautiously. Then there was a silence.

"You know," he said, "there isn't much choice! You have to work with the material that you have on hand. That is not always convenient. When I arrived in Prinkipo, I received long strings of letters from enthusiastic militants who offered to come visit me. In France, I had to put my confidence in the militants who, on the whole, shared the perspectives of the Russian Opposition. I had to reject the skeptics and the dilettantes. The movement had to prove itself by marching boldly forward. We had to have a periodical, first to defend and spread our ideas and reply to the Stalinist slanders, and then, little by little, to regroup in one organization all those who agreed with us and wanted to struggle. So, despite the friendship that I felt for Monatte, Rosmer, or Louzon, our disagreements over the role of the party and the trade unions, among others, did not permit constructive work with the anarcho-syndicalist militants of *Révolution proletarienne.* As for Treint, with whom I had a long correspondence, it was difficult if not impossible to gather his small group around my friends because of their determined hostility. Moreover, it is curious how Treint succeeded in making so many enemies on all sides!

"I also received Maurice and Magdeleine Paz, but what can you do? Although I appreciated their talent and their desire to help me, I didn't feel the spark that would have helped me to decide upon them. Something very important was lacking: the desire to act, to struggle with one's face bare, to assert oneself and, if necessary, to sacrifice everything to the independence of one's ideas. I did not feel that in those two dilettantes of communism. So . . .

"When Raymond Molinier arrived, a young man of twenty-five,

Excerpts from *Trois points c'est tout,* by Fred Zeller. Translated by Naomi Allen. Parts of these notes about what Trotsky said to Zeller in Norway were first printed in *La Vérité,* September 19, 1947. Trotsky's remarks were undoubtedly conditioned by the fact that Zeller was not yet a member of the GBL.

full of plans, of faith, of enthusiasm, of drive, though he might be somewhat adventuristic, and after him Naville, Gérard Rosenthal, the young Van, and all the others, they were the ones I put my confidence in. But their difficult characters and the inevitable struggle of people among themselves did not always make collective work easy. I know it; I know it well. But what about it? Without doubt, the arrival in the French organization of new and young fighters will cause things to fall into shape. . . ."

Trotsky often stressed organizational problems [in our talks]. He properly attached great importance to these.

"If you do not train good, serious administrators at every level of the movement, you will not win even if you are right a thousand times over. What the Bolshevik-Leninists have always lacked—and particularly in France—are organizers, good treasurers, accurate accounting, and publications that are readable and well proofread."

The most serious difference that I had with him, if I dare say so, was over democratic centralism, whose implacably authoritarian conception seemed to me as dangerous as the Social Democratic method, which never permits ordinary branch members to influence the party leadership in a decisive fashion.

Trotsky, while strongly insisting that Lenin's Political Bureau had applied a "democratic" centralism while Stalin's applied a "bureaucratic" centralism, remembered having come up against this problem at the Second Congress [of the Russian Social Democratic Labor Party, 1903], which separated him from Lenin for several years.

"Nevertheless," he added, "Lenin was right again. Without a strongly centralized party, we could never have taken power. Centralism means focusing the maximum organizational effort toward the 'goal.' It is the only means of leading millions of people in combat against the possessing classes.

"If we agree with Lenin, that we are in the epoch of imperialism, the last stage of capitalism, it is necessary to have a revolutionary organization flexible enough to deal with the problems of an underground struggle as well as those of the seizure of power. Hence the necessity of a strongly centralized party, capable of orienting and leading the masses and of conducting the gigantic struggle from which they should emerge victorious. Hence also the need to collectively make a loyal self-criticism at every stage."

He added that the application of centralism should not be schematic but should develop out of the political situation. He cited as an example the Russian Communist Party in 1921, passing from a military and ultracentralized type of organization required by a civil war to an organization based on factory cells as a function of the needs of economic reconstruction:

"Between congresses, it was the Central Committee and its Political Bureau that led the party and supervised the rigorous execution at every level of the policy decided by the majority. It was not permissible to return constantly to questions of orientation and thus to violate the execution of the policy decided on by the party."

He also returned often to one of the greatest dangers facing the workers' vanguard: sectarianism, which exhausts, withers, demoralizes, and isolates:

"That is what threatens the French section. It was one of the principal reasons that led us to urge our comrades to enter the SFIO as a 'tendency.' The experience has been shown to be a good one, in that it enabled them to work deeply among the masses, to confirm the correctness of their policy, to extend their influence and to consolidate themselves organizationally.

"All his life Lenin fought against sectarian deviations that will and have cut revolutionaries off from mass movements and from a clear understanding of the situation. Several times he had to fight against the 'Old Bolsheviks,' who were capable of nothing more in his absence than trying to make reality conform to the 'sacred documents.'"

Trotsky recalled what had happened in 1905 when the Bolsheviks played only a small role because of the sectarian position they adopted, in Lenin's absence, toward the Petrograd Soviet:

"Theoretical routine, this absence of political and tactical creativity, is no substitute for perspicacity, an ability to size things up at a glance, the flair for 'feeling' a situation while sorting out the main threads and developing an over-all strategy. In a revolutionary and especially an insurrectional period these qualities become decisive." . . .

Trotsky frequently returned to the need to strengthen the fraternal bonds among the comrades in struggle:

"It is necessary to preserve, encourage, and watch over those bonds," he would repeat. "An experienced worker member represents an inestimable *capital* for the organization. It takes years to educate a leader. We therefore should do everything possible to save a member. Don't destroy him if he weakens, but help him to overcome his weakness, to get over his moment of doubt.

"Never forget those who 'fall' by the wayside. Help them to

return to the organization if you have nothing irremediable to reproach them for on the level of revolutionary morality."

When we walked along the mountainside in the evening, it occurred to him to discuss the physical well-being of the members, what today we call the "shape" they are in. He was very concerned about this. He thought about looking out for those who had become exhausted, about conserving the strengths of the weakest people:

"Lenin was always concerned with the health of his collaborators. 'It is necessary to go as far as possible in the combat and the road is long,' he would say."

The internal atmosphere of the organization worried him. In the small vanguard movements which fight against the stream, internal disputes are often the most severe and heated. After being expelled from the SFIO, the Bolshevik-Leninist Group was divided into many hostile factions:

"If the comrades were to look a little beyond themselves and direct their efforts to outside and practical work, the 'crisis' would resolve itself," Trotsky said. "But it is always necessary to see to it that the atmosphere remains healthy and the internal climate acceptable to everyone. Comrades should work with all their heart and with the maximum of confidence.

"Building the revolutionary party requires patience and hard work. At any price, the best should not be discouraged, and you should show yourselves capable of working with everyone. Each person is a lever to be fully utilized to strengthen the party. Lenin knew the art of doing that. After the liveliest, most polemical discussions, he knew how to find the words and the gestures that would soften unfortunate or offensive remarks."

For Trotsky the essential thing in the period ahead consisted of creating an organizational apparatus. Without an apparatus there is no possibility of applying a policy: everything is limited to empty boasts without real weight. The difficulty in great human constructions is the judicious choice of the personality suited to a given function. The art of the organizer consists in accustoming a number of individuals to work together so that each one becomes the complement of the others. An "apparatus" is like an orchestra in which each instrument expresses its own voice in order to blend unobtrusively into the harmony that is thus created.

"Avoid placing members of equal ability and similar temperament on the same work committees," said Trotsky. "They will nullify each other's work and the results counted on will not be obtained.

"Learn how to choose comrades suited for a given task; explain patiently what is expected of them; act with flexibility and tact—that is the way a true leadership is built.

"Leave maximum initiative to the responsible comrades in their own field. If errors are committed, correct them by explaining in a comradely fashion how they are harmful to the party as a whole. Do not take administrative measures except in unusually serious cases. As a general rule everyone should be allowed to advance, develop, and improve.

"Don't lose yourselves in secondary details which conceal the total situation. Do only what you are able to do with the forces at your disposal. Never more, except, of course, in decisive situations."

The Old Man added that the nerves of the comrades must not be strained indefinitely. After hard efforts, one needs to catch one's breath, get one's bearings, restore one's energies, and rest.

At the level of organizational work, one must be methodical and precise, leaving nothing to chance.

"Whatever you do, set yourself an objective, even if very modest, but strive to attain it. Proceed this way in every phase of the organization. Then you should elaborate a short- or long-term plan, and apply yourself to it without weakening, with an iron hand. That is the only way to move forward and make the whole organization progress."

One morning the courier brought leaflets and an internal bulletin of the French Bolshevik-Leninists. Reading them, Trotsky exhibited impatience and annoyance. Equipped with a red crayon, he crossed out and underlined without stopping, and then said brusquely:

"Your mimeographed bulletins are very bad. It is very annoying to read them. Like your other journals and publications. I ask myself how, with modern machines, you manage to get out documents that may be good politically but are unreadable. Consult experts in this field. I assure you that the worker will not make an effort to read a badly printed leaflet.

"I remember my first leaflets, issued by our circle in Odessa. I wrote them in purple ink, hand-printing the letters. They were then transferred to a gelatin sheet and published in many dozens of copies. We certainly used primitive means, but our leaflets were very readable . . . and they made their way!"

His strongest criticisms were about our periodicals:

"A revolutionary paper should address itself primarily and above all to the workers. But your way of conceiving and editing *La Vérité* (which was then the paper of the Bolshevik-Leninists) makes it more of a theoretical journal than a paper. It interests the intellectual but not the worker. On the other hand, you have put out some good issues of *Révolution.*

"But what is inadmissible and scandalous is to let the papers come out with so many typographical errors and transpositions of type, which give the impression of intolerable and criminal carelessness.

"The paper is the face of the party. In great measure the worker will judge the party on the basis of the paper. Those for whom it is intended are not strongly with you or even your sympathizers. You ought not to repulse anybody with language that is too highbrow. Your occasional reader should not be made to think: 'These people are way over my head,' because then he will no longer buy it.

"Your paper ought to be well laid out, simple, and clear, with slogans that are always understandable. The worker does not have time to read long theoretical articles. He needs brief reports in a polished style. Lenin said, 'You have to write with your heart in order to have a good paper.'

"Stop thinking that you are writing for yourselves or your members. For them there are theoretical magazines and internal bulletins. The workers' paper should be lively, also humorous. Workers like to have the powers-that-be ridiculed and exposed with factual proof.

"Also make the worker comrades in your organization write in the paper. Help them in a friendly way. You will see that very often the short and simple article of a worker, on a particular fact of capitalist exploitation, is very superior to an article that is academic and erudite. Take Lenin's articles in *Pravda* as a model. They are simple, lively, readable, appealing as much to the worker in the Putilov plant as to the student in the university."
. . .

As I had told him about our financial worries, the problems raised by the regular publication of *La Vérité* or *Révolution,* and everything that concerned factory newspapers, leaflets, and personnel shifts, the Old Man said to me:

"What is well thought out is clearly expressed . . . and . . . the means of saying it are easily found. To the degree that you have a clear theoretical vision of things, you will also have the political will to put it into effect. If you want strongly to succeed in what you understand clearly, then you will also be capable of finding the means."

Party and Soviets
November 1935

It is repeated that it is a race between fascism and us. But it is very necessary to analyze the content of this formulation from the point of view of the revolutionary party. Will we know how to give the masses a revolutionary framework before the fascists wipe them out? It would be absurd to believe that we will have enough time to create an omnipotent party that would be able to eliminate all the other organizations before the decisive conflicts with fascism or before the outbreak of the war; but it is quite possible in a short time—with the help of events—to win over great masses, not for our program, not for the Fourth International, but for these committees of action. But once created, these committees of action would become a magnificent springboard for a revolutionary party. . . .

Here it is not a matter of one question or another; it is *the* question of life or death.

From *L'Organe de masse.* Signed "Crux." An excerpt from a letter to Jean Rous.

Slogans of Revolutionary Action
November 1935

We must find a formulation for this slogan: Local committees elected by the masses of workers and peasants.

To the slogans of passivity and slackness we oppose our slogans of revolutionary action.

But when revolutionary action is set in motion by the masses themselves, it is necessary to know how to counterpose to the opportunist apparatus an apparatus of revolutionary action created "ad hoc" by the masses to fill the needs of their action, and elected by the masses in struggle. If at the moment of the explosion in Toulon there had been a group with a sufficiently

---

From *Bulletin Intérieur*, GBL, no. 9, December 1935. Signed "Crux." Translated by Naomi Allen.

correct orientation to launch the clear and simple call "Every hundred workers send one delegate to the Toulon Committee of Action," the masses would certainly have responded to this appeal. This committee of action would have had quite exceptional authority, not only in the eyes of the masses themselves, but also in the eyes of the local authorities and in the eyes of the rest of France and of the purged traditional organizations. Even if the movement had been halted without assuming national dimensions, a healthy precedent would have been set.

And it would have been possible to resume at a new stage more easily and with more experience.

I rejoice that *La Vérité* called for committees of action in its last issue. But one article alone is not enough. *We need to prepare a campaign,* as we did at one time for the *workers' militia.* We need to win over the comrades of *Révolution* to this slogan. They could perhaps put out a special issue devoted to the committees of action.

Committees of Action and the Masses
November 13, 1935

The actual relations [between committees and masses] are the opposite.[7] The committees of action are necessary precisely to lead the masses. You do not say that these committees must emanate from the masses in struggle and be elected by them (!) and that the delegates must be accountable and subject to recall. . . .

From *L'Organe de masse.* Signed "Crux."

A Serious Lesson for the Future
November 1935

The National Council in any case has the merit of having created a clear situation [by confirming the expulsions]. In the last few weeks too much time and energy have really been spent on illusory and sterile maneuvers. . . . It is a serious lesson for the future! In any case, now the way is clear. Political progress is possible only through a ferocious offensive and through openly denouncing not only Léon Blum but also Marceau Pivert, albeit in different tones.

From *L'Organe de masse*. Signed "Crux." This letter to Fred Zeller was written after the National Council of the SFIO, meeting on November 17, confirmed the expulsion of the Bolshevik-Leninist leaders.

Take to the Open Sea!
November 21, 1935

Politics may be defined as the art of taking advantage of favorable situations. In France, at present, you have an exceptional situation, full of opportunities. It is necessary to know how to take advantage of it. That means not to try to stay in this calm bay, but to take to the open sea.

It would be false to assert that we are carrying out the new turn under the "dictate" of the reformist bureaucracy. I refer you to my letter at the time of the Mulhouse congress, when there was as yet no question of your expulsion ["A New Turn Is Necessary," in *Writings 34-35*]. The Seine congress shows once more that the opportunities for us within the SFIO are used up. And in the provinces too? But you cannot tell Paris to "mark time" and wait for the provinces to catch up. Besides, you will not be able to "mark time." We will win whatever is to be won in the provincial Socialist movement by other ways and means, imposed on us by the situation as a whole.

From *Bulletin Intérieur*, GBL, no. 9, December 1935. Translated by Tom Bias. A letter to the Political Bureau of the GBL.

To make concessions of *principle* to the reformist bureaucracy or to the narrow-minded Pivertists would only mean undermining our own future. *Your statement for the National Council is a little too mild. You don't mention revolutionary defeatism, which is accepted with reservations by this riffraff Zyromsky,* who is neither revolutionary nor defeatist and who does not accept the Fourth International. Why do you avoid raising this slogan in your statement to the National Council and in your motion to the Seine congress? Therein lies an error which will not appease our enemies but which could set back our friends.

Are there comrades among you who wish at all costs to remain cooped up in the SFIO? Doesn't the example of the youth show that remaining tied to the SFIO constitutes more of an obstacle than a springboard? If someone among you says, "Outside the SFIO we will be isolated, we will sink into futility, etc. . . ," we should answer, "Dear friend, your nerves are shot; take a four-week vacation, and then we'll see!" And at the same time we must engrave on our memory the attitude of these comrades in this moment of crisis: we will know more formidable crises in the future, and the same faint-heartedness can recur on a much vaster scale. Let us not forget that the attitude of Zinoviev and Kamenev in October 1917 was not accidental, just as Lenin says in his testament.[8]

I have just now received a letter concerning the National Council. Blum has sent some conciliators into the commission in the same manner that the imperialists use pacifists to confuse the workers. I sincerely hope that this ruse of war will not succeed in tricking our comrades. To muzzle them now would be fatal from the national as well as the international point of view.

The *ASR* group in Belgium is preparing its members for expulsion; Walter Dauge is beginning to talk about the Fourth International. If the French comrades yield on this essential point they will be politically weakened and they will disorient the entire organization.

The last issue of *La Vérité* seemed colorless and mediocre. *La Vérité* is the principal tool of the GBL. In order to be able to reach the masses with our ideas, it is necessary to formulate them. One may accede to *La Vérité's* appearing only twice a month, if that is really necessary, but we must take all the more pains to see that it preserves its character as the central organ of the tendency. To sacrifice *La Vérité* would constitute a crime tantamount to treason. It would be better in such a case to join the Revolutionary Left!

It is possible and necessary to develop *Révolution* into a mass paper. But it would be fatal to believe that the masses could be satisfied with a second-rate diet. The ideas and slogans which are to be presented to them must be previously analyzed and discussed and well formulated (*Vérité!*).

On the other hand, you must tell the *whole* truth. You must denounce by name the treacherous leaders of the two parties and of the trade unions. The masses have to know whom they can trust to lead them. The very idea that after scuttling *La Vérité* you can furnish *Révolution* with general articles without directly offending the all-powerful apparatuses—this idea alone is a serious error!

Whatever you undertake with the bureaucracy must be subordinated to this last perspective. No equivocation for a moment on this decisive point! I persist in my belief that there are not—maybe *not yet*—differences of principle between us. So it would not be appropriate to open a general discussion of tactical questions. We have to try, by whatever means, to amend our policy, beginning with an effort within the Central Committee, initiated by the Political Bureau. No resignations! Resignation is nothing but desertion, even when one is right; do not sow panic, since the situation is excellent and our opportunities are innumerable.[9]

It is also necessary to arrive at a fusion with the Fred Zeller tendency as soon as possible; co-opt several new comrades, including Fred Zeller, onto the Central Committee, even if they are not very "mature" politically, but are active and firm: the Central Committee would be a higher education for them.

These are a few suggestions which I would like to submit to you at this time.

Turn to the Masses!
November 25, 1935

Dear Comrades:

I must admit that the waverings and maneuvers with the SFIO, and now with the Revolutionary Left, seem to me perfectly inexplicable as well as extremely dangerous.

1. Why has mass work been almost totally neglected? Because your attention remains fixed on the SFIO's statutes and on Pivert's changing moods, but not on mass action.

2. Nothing has been done on the propaganda level in favor of committees of action elected by the fighting masses. *Concerning the committees of action, Motion C contains quite an obscure formula.* Why? Because your attention is centered on our reintegration into the apparatus and not on our integration into the masses.

3. The organization is marking time in Paris while making sacrifices in terms of principles (see the unfortunate Motion C; see also the last number of *La Vérité*) and losing its influence. Why? Because a wrong orientation has been adopted. You cling to the SFIO at a time when, since Mulhouse, it represents a politically completed stage.

4. Your memorandum concerning the expulsion (your memorandums are never dated!) contains two lines on the demand for readmission! These lines are scratched out with a pen! However, there were voices in favor of a new attempt to be readmitted, even after the National Council meeting. Incredible! You could do excellent things with the forces you are now wasting on these sterile and demoralizing maneuvers.

5. Your attitude toward the Revolutionary Left to me seems incomprehensible and absolutely opposed to our principles and tradition. What is the Revolutionary Left? It is a French SAP. If you flirt with those people, you are going to push them to the right and lose ground to them. You must denounce them without mercy. *La Vérité* is silent about the Revolutionary Left. It is unbelievable! Permit me to use the right word: it is scandalous!

6. In one of your memorandums (again, no date or number),

From *Bulletin Intérieur,* GBL, no. 9, December 1935. Translated by Mary Gordon. A letter to the Political Bureau of the GBL.

you deal with the "united front" with the Revolutionary Left. Fundamentally, this is an abuse of terminology. The united front implies mass organizations and you are only propaganda societies. If your conceptions are identical, you must merge; if your independent existence is justified by principled differences— and that would be the only justification—how can you carry out joint propaganda?

7. There may exist, in practice, cases where you act together— against the expulsions, against the fascists, etc. But even then, you must spell out your point of view. Do not confuse principles, organizations, and banners. March separately, strike together (please, do both).

8. The Revolutionary Left says that it differs from us only "in terms of tone." But the SAP, too, began with this assertion. With our relentless attack we obliged them to admit that an abyss separates them from us. Our German section lost a great deal of time flirting too long with the SAP, and the whole movement for the Fourth International, as a result, was paralyzed for a time. Since directing our fire against the SAP, we have been successful everywhere. The IAG is disintegrating; the movement for the Fourth International is becoming a reality. Is this the right time to tolerate SAPist or pro-SAPist tendencies in our ranks?

Comrade Van tells me that in the nineteenth arrondissement [of Paris] there is a Bolshevik-Leninist–Revolutionary Left "Revolutionary Action Group." What is it? What program does it have? Is it a new party of the nineteenth arrondissement? How can the discipline of the Bolshevik-Leninists reconcile itself with that of a new group, and what about the Fourth International? Maybe I have misunderstood Van's letter. I would be happy to receive clarifications about it.

9. Again and again, there is talk about a "mass paper." Not *La Vérité*, not *Révolution*. No, something entirely new. I must admit once again: I understand nothing about it. While *La Vérité* has been retreating and fading lately, because of its one-sided, conservative, and sterile orientation toward the SFIO, the youth have been able to put out a paper that is developing very well because it is supported by the devotion of the youth. You must help them and not hinder them. If not bureaucratized, *Révolution* may become a mass paper for young workers, which is the first layer we want to win; the adults will come only later. That is the logic of all revolution.

And the third paper? What could it mean? On what basis? On the basis of the alliance with the Revolutionary Left? But that would mean breaking with our principles and our politics. We can draw to *Révolution* and *La Vérité* the best representatives of centrism. But the paper must be ours. It must be the organ of the section of the Fourth International in formation.

If a hermaphroditic paper is actually in the works, I wish to announce in advance that I am not responsible, and I certainly hope the International Secretariat will make the necessary declaration.

Comrades, if since July I have insisted on the necessity of devoting nine-tenths of our forces to mass work and only one-tenth to internal maneuvers, today I say ten-tenths for mass action and nothing for Léon Blum or even for Pivert. You must turn your back on him; you must denounce him relentlessly. He has become the "extreme left" of the People's Front. To cling to Pivert, who himself clings to Blum, only means to passively play the People's Front game. No, we cannot tolerate such impulses for one minute.

Some comrades might find this letter too rough, maybe even unfair. But I am writing from far away. The information I get is fragmentary. That is why often I can formulate an opinion only after some delay. Comrade Van's last letter, combined with Motion C, the last issue of *La Vérité,* and your memorandums, have produced the greatest anxiety in me. I hoped that with the help of the bureaucracy we could carry out the necessary turn, though with some delay, still, without crises or shocks. I still want to hope so, but we must speak frankly. Let all the comrades speak frankly!

For Committees of Action, Not the People's Front!
November 26, 1935

The "People's Front" represents the coalition of the proletariat with the imperialist bourgeoisie, in the shape of the Radical Party and smaller tripe of the same sort. The coalition extends both to the parliamentary and to the extraparliamentary spheres. In both spheres the Radical Party, preserving for itself complete freedom of action, savagely imposes restrictions upon the freedom of action of the proletariat.

From *New Militant,* December 14, 1935.

The Radical Party itself is undergoing decay. Each new election gives added proof of the passage of supporters away from it to the right and to the left. On the other hand, the Socialist and Communist parties—because of the absence of a genuinely revolutionary party—are growing stronger. The general trend of the toiling masses, including the petty bourgeoisie, is quite clearly to the left. The orientation of the leaders of the workers' parties is no less self-evident: *to the right*. At a time when the masses by their votes and their struggle seek to cast off the party of the Radicals, the leaders of the united front, on the contrary, seek to save it. After obtaining the confidence of the masses of workers on the basis of a "socialist" program, the leaders of the workers' parties then proceeded to voluntarily concede a lion's share of this confidence to the Radicals, in whom the masses of workers have absolutely no confidence.

The "People's Front" in its present guise shamelessly tramples not only upon workers' democracy but also upon formal, i.e., bourgeois, democracy. The majority of the Radical voters do not participate in the struggle of the toilers and consequently in the People's Front. Yet the Radical Party occupies in this front not only an equal but a privileged position; the workers' parties are compelled to restrict their activity to the program of the Radical Party. This idea is most outspokenly advanced by the cynics of *l'Humanité*.

The latest elections to the Senate have illuminated with special clarity the *privileged* position of the Radicals in the People's Front. The leaders of the Communist Party boasted openly of the fact that they renounced in favor of nonproletarian parties several mandates [to seats in the Senate] which justly belonged to the workers.[10] This merely means that the united front reestablished in part the property qualification in favor of the bourgeoisie.

The "front," as it is conceived, is an organization for direct and immediate struggle. When struggle is in question, every worker is worth ten bourgeois, even those adhering to the united front. From the standpoint of the revolutionary fighting strength of the front, the electoral privileges should have been given not to Radical bourgeois but to workers. But in essence, privileges are uncalled for here. Is the People's Front intended for the defense of "democracy"? Then let it begin by applying it to its own ranks. This means: *the leadership of the People's Front must be the direct and immediate reflection of the will of the struggling masses.*

How? Very simply: through elections. The proletariat does not deny anyone the right to struggle side by side with it against fascism, the Bonapartist regime of Laval,[11] the war plot of the imperialists, and all other forms of oppression and violence. The sole demand that class-conscious workers put to their actual or potential allies is that they struggle *in action*. Every group of the population really participating in the struggle at a given stage and ready to submit to common discipline must have the equal right to exert influence on the leadership of the People's Front.

Each two hundred, five hundred, or one thousand citizens adhering to the People's Front in a given city, district, factory, barrack, and village should in time of fighting actions elect their representative to the local committee of action. All the participants in the struggle are bound by its discipline.

The last congress of the Communist International, in its resolution on the Dimitrov report, expressed itself in favor of elected committees of action as the mass support for the People's Front. This is perhaps the only progressive idea in the entire resolution. But precisely for this reason the Stalinists do nothing to realize it. They dare not do anything for fear of breaking off collaboration with the bourgeoisie.

To be sure, in the election of committees not only workers will be able to participate but also civil service employees, functionaries, war veterans, artisans, small merchants, and small peasants. Thus the committees of action are in the closest harmony with the tasks of the proletariat's struggle for influence over the petty bourgeoisie. But they complicate to the extreme the collaboration between the workers' bureaucracy and the bourgeoisie. In the meantime the People's Front in its present form is nothing else than the organization of class collaboration between the political exploiters of the proletariat (the reformists and the Stalinists) and the political exploiters of the petty bourgeoisie (the Radicals). Real mass elections of committees of action would automatically eject the bourgeois middlemen (the Radicals) from the ranks of the People's Front and thus smash to smithereens the criminal policy dictated by Moscow.

However, it would be a mistake to think that it is possible at a set day and hour to call the proletarian and petty-bourgeois masses to elect committees of action on the basis of a given statute. Such an approach would be purely bureaucratic and consequently barren. The workers will be able to elect a committee of action only in those cases in which they themselves participate in some sort of *action* and feel the need for revolutionary leadership. In question here is not the *formal democratic* representation of *all* and *any* masses but the *revolutionary* representation of the *struggling* masses. The committee of action is an apparatus of struggle. There is no sense in guessing beforehand precisely what strata of the toilers will be attracted to the creation of committees of action: the lines of demarcation in the struggling masses will be established during the struggle itself.

The greatest danger in France is that the revolutionary energy of the masses will be dissipated in spurts, in isolated explosions like Toulon, Brest, and Limoges, and give way to apathy. Only conscious traitors or hopeless muddleheads are capable of thinking that in the present situation it is possible to keep the masses immobilized up to the moment when they will be blessed from above by the government of the People's Front. Strikes, protests, street clashes, direct uprisings, are absolutely inevitable in the present situation. The task of the proletarian party consists not in checking and paralyzing these movements but in unifying them and investing them with the greatest possible force.

The reformists and Stalinists fear above all to frighten the Radicals. The apparatus of the united front quite consciously plays the role of disorganizer in relation to sporadic movements of the masses. The "leftists" of the Marceau Pivert type serve to shield this apparatus from the indignation of the masses. The situation can be saved only by aiding the struggling masses to create a new apparatus in the process of the struggle itself, which meets the requirements of the moment. The committees of action are intended for this very purpose. During the struggle in Toulon and Brest the workers would have created without any hesitation a local fighting organization, had they been called upon to do so. On the very next day after the bloody assault in Limoges, the workers and a considerable section of the petty bourgeoisie would have indubitably revealed their readiness to create an elected committee to investigate the bloody events and to prevent them in the future. During the movement in the barracks in the summer of this year against Rabiot [the extension of the term of military service], the soldiers without much ado would have elected battalion, regimental, and garrison committees of action had such a course been suggested to them. Similar situations arise and will continue to arise at every step—in most cases on a local but often also on a national scale. The task is to avoid missing a single situation of this kind. The first condition for this is a clear understanding of the import of the committee of action as the *only means of breaking the antirevolutionary opposition of the party and trade union apparatuses.*

Does this mean to say that the committees of action are

substitutes for party and trade union organizations? It would be stupid to pose the question in this manner. The masses enter into the struggle with all their ideas, traditions, groupings, and organizations. The parties continue to exist and to struggle. During elections to the committees of action each party will naturally seek to elect its own adherents. The committees of action will arrive at decisions through a majority (given complete freedom of party and factional groupings). In relation to parties the committees of action may be called a *revolutionary parliament:* the parties are not excluded—on the contrary they are necessarily presupposed—at the same time they are tested in action, and the masses learn to free themselves from the influence of rotten parties.

Does this mean then that the committees of action are simply— *soviets?* Under certain conditions the committees of action can transform themselves into soviets. However, it would be incorrect to call the committees of action by this name. Today, in 1935, the popular masses have become accustomed to associate with the word soviets the concept of power already conquered; but France today is still considerably removed from this. The Russian soviets during their initial stages were not at all what they later became, and in those days they were often called by the modest name of workers' or strike committees. Committees of action at their present stage have as their task to unite the toiling masses of France in a defensive struggle and thus imbue these masses with the consciousness of their own power for the coming offensive. Whether matters will reach the point of genuine soviets depends on whether the present critical situation in France will unfold to the ultimate revolutionary conclusions. This of course depends not only upon the will of the revolutionary vanguard but also upon a number of objective conditions; in any case, the mass movement that has today run up against the barrier of the People's Front will be unable to move forward without the committees of action.

Such tasks as the creation of a *workers' militia,* the *arming of the workers,* the preparation of a *general strike,* will remain on paper if the struggling masses themselves through their authoritative organs do not occupy themselves with these tasks. Only committees of action born in the struggle can assure a real militia numbering fighters not by the thousands but by the tens of thousands. Only committees of action embracing the most important centers of the country will be able to choose the moment for the transition to more decisive methods of struggle, the leadership of which will be rightly theirs.

From the propositions sketched above flow a number of conclusions for the political activity of the proletarian revolutionists in France. The cardinal conclusion touches upon the so-called Revolutionary Left. This grouping is characterized by a complete lack of understanding of the laws that govern the movement of the revolutionary masses. No matter how much the centrists babble about the "masses," they always orient themselves to the reformist apparatus. Repeating this or that revolutionary slogan, Marceau Pivert subordinates it to the abstract principle of "organizational unity," which in action turns out to be unity with the patriots against the revolutionists. At the very moment when it is a life-and-death question for the masses to *smash* the opposition of the united social-patriotic apparatuses, the left centrists consider the "unity" of these apparatuses as an absolute "good" which stands above the interests of the revolutionary struggle.

Committees of action will be built only by those who thoroughly understand the necessity of *freeing the masses from the treacherous leadership of the social patriots.* Yet Pivert clutches at Zyromsky, who clutches at Blum, who in turn, together with Thorez, clutches at Herriot, who clutches at Laval. Pivert enters into the system of the People's Front (not for nothing did he vote for the shameful resolution of Blum at the last National Council meeting!) and the People's Front enters as a wing into the Bonapartist regime of Laval. The downfall of the Bonapartist regime is inevitable. Should the leadership of the People's Front (Herriot-Blum-Cachin-Thorez-Zyromsky-Pivert) succeed in remaining on its feet in the course of the entire approaching and decisive period, then the Bonapartist regime will inevitably give way to fascism. The condition for the victory of the proletariat is the *liquidation of the present leadership.* The slogan of "unity" becomes under these conditions not only a stupidity but a crime. *No unity with the agents of French imperialism and of the League of Nations.* To their perfidious leadership it is necessary to counterpose revolutionary committees of action. It is possible to build these committees only by mercilessly exposing the antirevolutionary policies of the so-called Revolutionary Left, with Marceau Pivert at the head. There is of course no room in our ranks for illusions and doubts on this score.

Preface to Part Two

Things came to a head soon after the SFIO National Council on November 17, 1935. Molinier was encouraged at having received Rous's support, and therefore a majority in the Central Committee, for his "loyalty statement" maneuver and may have thought that Rous could be counted on to go along with him on other questions. On November 20 he began, with his friends in and out of the GBL, to make all the practical preparations for the publication of a new paper, and at a meeting of the Central Committee on November 23 he announced to its startled members that a mass paper named *La Commune* was going to appear the following week. To show that he meant business he displayed printed copies of a *Commune* poster and handbill ("appeal") and a list of sponsors of the paper, and made a motion that the Central Committee support *La Commune* as "the mass paper for the creation of the GARs and communes," to be controlled by the GBL. The motion was defeated 10-8, with 1 abstention. Rous made a motion to put Molinier in charge of launching *Révolution* as a mass paper for revolutionary regroupment under the political control of the JS and the GBL, in accord with Molinier's own previous proposals. This was defeated 8-4, with the others abstaining. Naville then made a motion to transform *La Vérité* into a mass paper published by the GBL but seeking the collaboration of revolutionaries from other tendencies in and out of the SFIO, and to state publicly that the GBL had nothing to do with Molinier's personal activities around *La Commune*. This was defeated 9-5, with 5 abstentions. Rous then introduced a motion condemning Molinier's announcement about *La Commune* as a factional ultimatum incompatible with comradely collaboration and threatening the unity of the GBL. Naville called this motion "juridical hypocrisy" and abstained. It was defeated 8-5, with 6 abstentions. Thus, no motion was carried.

The Central Committee responded to this leadership default by appointing a conciliation commission to explore possible agreements: it consisted of Rous and two of his supporters plus Molinier and Frank. The commission met November 24 and finally did reach some compromises which both sides said were acceptable. On November 25 a general assembly (membership meeting) of the GBL's Paris region met and heard reports about some of the differences over the mass paper, which must have been difficult for them to sort out; the members also listened to a reading of Trotsky's November 21 letter to the Political Bureau, which clearly ran counter to the Molinier line. The Molinierists thought it necessary to answer in a letter by Frank which was dated November 28 but seems to have been written and mailed a day or two earlier.

On November 26 the Central Committee approved the conciliation commission's proposals to proceed with GBL-JS copublication of *Révolution* as a mass paper, the back page of which would be called "La Commune," and to appoint an editorial board with Frank as its secretary. The same day Trotsky, having just learned about the stalemated November 23 meeting of the Central Committee, sent Rous a telegram warning that any further concessions to Molinier would be fatal.

By this time Molinier already had most of the concessions he wanted about the new paper, except its name. Apparently he thought he could get that too by continuing aggressively to present the Central Committee with accomplished facts. A professional bill-posting company began to paste up his *Commune* posters around Paris, to which stickers had been added announcing that the paper would appear December 6, and Frank was seen meeting with "Friends of *La Commune*" to promote the circulation of the first issue. Between these provocations and Trotsky's pressure the Political Bureau was in a new mood when it met on November 29. Basing itself on the Central Committee's November 26 decisions, the Political Bureau characterized *La Commune* as a paper that would inevitably be used against the GBL, ordered that no paper with that name should be published, prohibited GBL participation in the Friends of *La Commune*, and removed Frank from the post of editorial secretary of *Révolution*. Molinier refused to accept the Political Bureau's right to take such actions, which he said were violations of the Central Committee's November 26 motions, and he demanded that the Central Committee be convened immediately, a demand which was not granted. Meanwhile Trotsky, writing on November 28, called on the International Secretariat to intervene in the French section, and asked that his repudiation of *La Commune* be made public. When Frank's answer to Trotsky's November 21 letter was received in Norway on November 29, Trotsky sent a telegram calling it an example of centrist demoralization and saying he considered a split preferable to concessions to the Molinier group.

The next day he began an uncompromising political offensive against the Molinierists (letter of November 30).

On December 1 Molinier took another step outside of the GBL when he went to the JS executive committee and asked it to become copublisher of *La Commune*. This offer, which was rejected by the JS, convinced the GBL leaders that collaboration with Molinier was no longer possible.

The GBL had selected Molinier to serve as its member of the ICL international plenum in January 1935. On December 3 Trotsky asked the IS to urge the GBL Central Committee to withdraw Molinier from that post. Trotsky's motivation was that politically Molinier had gone over to centrist positions and that organizationally he was flouting both GBL and ICL discipline. On December 4, before Trotsky's request was received, the IS gave Molinier twenty-four hours to say if he would submit to discipline and renounce publication of *La Commune*. Molinier answered that he was only carrying out a Central Committee decision. On December 6 the first number of *La Commune* went on sale. In due course Molinier was removed as the GBL's representative to the international plenum and suspended from the Central Committee. The GBL was split.

The question that most disturbed GBL members at this point was: What is driving Molinier and his group; what is driving or encouraging him, a founder of the French section and its most energetic leader, to violate its discipline in such a way that the section is being split and its very existence is being threatened? Trotsky undertook to answer this question on the same day that he called for Molinier's removal as the GBL's representative to the plenum (letter of December 3). Choosing his words carefully, because such charges are not made lightly by responsible people in the Marxist movement, Trotsky said that the course of the *Commune* group represented "a capitulation to the social-patriotic wave":

> The approach of the war has (temporarily) given the social patriots a powerful weapon against the internationalists. Hence the expulsion of the Leninists. Hence Pivert's cowardly capitulation. . . . Hence, finally, the fear of "isolation" felt by the unstable elements in our own ranks and their tendency to go with the centrists at any cost and to be differentiated from them as little as possible. There is no other political content in the attitude of Molinier and Frank. They are capitulating to the social-patriotic wave. All the rest is only phrases, worthless in the eyes of a serious Marxist.

The Commune group of course indignantly rejected this

explanation as slanderous; far from being capitulators to social-patriotic pressures, they depicted themselves as the real continuators of Bolshevik-Leninism (they called their opponents "neo-Bolshevik-Leninists") and the best fighters for a new revolutionary party, who alone had the audacity to take the initiative to save the GBL from sectarian mistakes that would doom it to isolation and impotence. But Trotsky's analysis was accepted by a majority of the GBL adults and youth and reduced the sizable percentage of members that followed Molinier in the split.

In December Molinier threw all of his energies, resources, and gifts of improvisation behind the new paper and the GARs that were supposed to become its organizational base. At the second session of a JS congress in Paris on December 8 he went so far as to line up with Pivertists and other anti-GBL elements behind an unsuccessful motion to prevent the JS from copublishing *Révolution* with the GBL. But the high hopes and inflated expectations of the Molinier group were soon punctured. The masses were not attracted to *La Commune*. The GBL, the JS, and the GR were all hostile and ordered their members not to collaborate with Molinier in the GARs. Even the small group that had originated in the petty-bourgeois Social Front ("Frontists") withdrew from *La Commune*. By early January *La Commune* and the GARs consisted of little more than the members of the Molinier tendency in the GBL and their sympathizers. This should have strengthened the authority of the GBL leaders. But it didn't, chiefly because of their inept handling of the crisis and Molinier's skillful exploitation of their mistakes.

Instead of conducting a political offensive against Molinier, which would have educated the GBL ranks (among whom were many people conciliatory to Molinier or uncertain about the issues), and which might have won over some of the Molinierists, the Central Committee relied chiefly on organizational measures and formal discipline. When the Central Committee met on December 11, its first meeting since November 26, the Rous-Naville forces refused to sit with the eight Molinierist members, who insisted that Molinier should be present too; this refusal was based on the formal ground that the IS had expelled Molinier from the ICL, but invoking that formality now only resulted in preventing a political discussion in the leadership. With the eight Molinierists excluded from the meeting, the Central Committee expelled Molinier and warned his followers to abide by discipline or they too would find themselves out of the GBL.

Molinier was quick to seize on the openings thus provided, and he got better results in this area than he had with *La Commune.* With a flood of leaflets, bulletins, and open letters he and his group went after the GBL membership intensively. They published numerous documents showing how inconsistent, indecisive, and often arbitrary Rous and Naville had been, presenting themselves as loyal builders of the French section whose differences concerned only *how* to build a new party and as innocent victims of incompetent bureaucrats who resorted to suspensions, expulsions, and threats in order to avoid discussing political differences before the membership. They also strengthened their position by asking for a meeting of the whole Central Committee or a convening of a national conference to resolve the crisis, and they promised to abide by the decision of either body. When Rous and Naville rejected both the full Central Committee meeting and a conference, the Molinierists took up the demand as a crusade and followed it up with an offer to merge *La Commune* and *Révolution* (see letter of December 23). Instead of political measures to solve the internal problems, the Central Committee continued throughout December to depend on disciplinary sanctions. On December 23 it gave the Molinierists three days to choose between the *Commune* group and the GBL, and on December 28 it expelled fifteen Molinierists, including the eight Central Committee members. The disarray in the committee was expressed in the vote, five to four, with Naville and others favoring suspension instead of expulsion. As a result of all this, the GBL remained in a state of crisis and confusion despite the collapse of the *Commune* adventure. Trotsky was so appalled that on December 27 he asked the IS for a month's leave of absence to free him from the "disgusting trivia" of the French squabbles so that he would be able to accomplish other work ("Request for a Leave of Absence," in *Writings 35-36*).

In January the GBL leadership began at last to deal politically with the crisis and to take political steps toward a new party. On January 5 the Bolshevik-Leninists and their allies in the Seine Young Socialists, which had been deserted by the Pivertist minority after the December 8 congress, reorganized themselves as the Revolutionary Socialist Youth (JSR) and began functioning as an independent national organization. The GBL and the JSR leaders decided to draft an open letter calling for a new party and containing their proposal for its program; Trotsky was able to suggest amendments for the open letter (letter of January 4) before it was published at the end of the month. And on January

12 the Central Committee adopted a long resolution drafted by Naville on the causes of the crisis and the next steps toward a new party. This resolution was notable for recognizing some of the leadership's own mistakes, which helped somewhat to restore its credibility with the members.

The GBL's decisive steps toward a new party, taken on the heels of the *Commune*-GAR fiasco, led to a sharp switch in the tactics of Molinier, who could not now foresee any future separate from that of the GBL. On January 17 *La Commune* announced the formation of a new group, the Committee for the Fourth International (CQI, Bolshevik-Leninists), which promised to publish a monthly theoretical magazine to be called *La Quatrième Internationale*. On January 21, the CQI announced that it had signed the Open Letter for the Fourth International and wanted to adhere to the secretariat in Amsterdam designated in the Open Letter. On January 31 *La Commune* announced that it was now being published by the CQI instead of by "different tendencies" and that the CQI's chief aim was the building of a new revolutionary party in France. And within a week or two the CQI published a long pamphlet giving the Molinierist version of the struggle in the GBL, together with many documents from that struggle, and its proposals for bringing about unification of the pro–Fourth International forces in France *(La Crise de la Section Française de la Ligue Communiste Internationaliste [1935-1936])*.

As Erwin Wolf noted, Molinier's moves on the International and new party tended to deprive the GBL of its main political advantages over the *Commune* group, creating a new situation to which the GBL should have responded by taking the initiative for unification and saying, "See, the turn of *La Commune* proves that we were right. The split was all the more unjustified. It must be ended immediately." Instead, the GBL leaders, at the same time that their press was calling for a new party based on the ideas of the Open Letter, decided to ignore Molinier's campaign or to dismiss it as another of his adventures. Trotsky tried repeatedly to persuade them that they were only playing into Molinier's hands (letters of January 31 and March 4), but in vain. He also complained that they had bungled another opportunity when twenty "conciliators" proposed that a GBL leader and Molinier visit Trotsky in Norway for discussion of the crisis (letters of January 7, 8, and 14); the GBL leaders would not "legitimize" Molinier's position by doing anything like that, but their formalistic rejection certainly strengthened his position. So the *Commune* group recovered lost ground and made headway as energetic advocates of Fourth Internationalist unity, while the GBL and the JSR vegetated and lost both members and supporters.

Molinier took his next step at the end of February. The GBL and the JSR had announced their intention of holding a national conference for the new party on April 12, but its preparation seemed to be proceeding slowly and with difficulty. So Molinier decided to steal a march on them and announced that the CQI, the GARs, and *La Commune* would hold a constitutional congress launching a new party on March 7. That weekend witnessed the emergence of Molinier's Internationalist Communist Party (PCI), which described itself as "the French section of the Fourth International." The GBL leaders could no longer denounce or ignore the Molinier group; negotiations began for a reunification.

PART TWO
SPLIT
(November 1935-March 1936)

A Call for Action by the IS
November 28, 1935

Dear Comrades:

I have just received the letter from Adolphe with the appeal of *La Commune*. The call is empty, stupid, and shrill. *La Commune* does not want to multiply the tendencies, but it multiplies the mess. It proclaims adherence not to a program, but only to a few names; furthermore, unfortunately, I am named. But I categorically disavow any responsibility on my part. I do not belong to the "various tendencies" (see the appeal), all of which remain anonymous; I belong to one tendency only, which has its name and its program. The enterprise can only be a failure. All of us have the greatest interest in disavowing all responsibility.

I insisted by telegraph on a decisive intervention by Théodor. I know nothing of the results of this proposal. I accept the possibility that despite Théodor's intervention the enterprise is continuing and that the first issue may have appeared. In this case, if we find ourselves faced with an accomplished fact, what should our attitude be? This is what I propose:

1. To pass a short motion saying that Théodor and his friends decline all responsibility for an "organ" of "various tendencies" which are anonymous and have neither program nor banner. This motion should be communicated exclusively to the leaderships of our sections.

2. As for the French Central Committee, it would be necessary for a short time to maintain a wait-and-see attitude. It is necessary to wait for the reaction of the rank and file to the first

By permission of Jean-Claude Orveillon. A fragment of a letter to Théodor, a code name for the International Secretariat. Translated by David Keil. The last part of this fragment had been damaged and was only partly legible. Missing words were supplied by the Harvard College Library.

two issues of the organ of these anonymous "various tendencies." There will still be time to intervene, when the inevitable collapse takes shape. The purpose of the intervention should be to safeguard the organization, *La Vérité,* and the future.

3. But what is most important and urgent is the youth. While the adults have been marking time since July and have been wasting their energy and their time in order to court a few miserable Pivertists, the youth were carrying on effective and promising work. *Révolution,* which came out of this movement, is, despite its weaknesses, a living being capable of remarkable development. We should base ourselves on the youth. It is necessary to support *Révolution,* and help it become as quickly as possible the organ of the youth for the Fourth International.

During Fred [Zeller]'s stay here, we were in agreement on the broad lines concerning the steps to prepare for the Seine Alliance joining the Fourth International and the Bolshevik-Leninists fusing with the JSR group on the basis of the program of the Bolshevik-Leninists. The very fact that the promoters of *La Commune* (the organ of "various tendencies" of an anonymous character) have not understood the importance of the thrust forward of the youth, but are in a struggle with them and are creating an organ against them, is a complete condemnation of the enterprise. (Opportunists are always in conflict with the youth.) It is necessary for Théodor to invite Fred and other young people individually or in groups, in order to have a friendly meeting of minds with them on their national and international work. It is necessary to immediately name an international secretary (Van in practice boycotted international youth work, and not by chance).

If the GBL Central Committee, which has renounced the Bolshevik-Leninist banner in favor of "various tendencies," tries to haggle with the youth on the question of discipline, it would be necessary to give the Central Committee firm advice, not to insist. They have no right to demand discipline, since they have broken with the international organization and renounced the most fundamental principles, which is much more important. In short, we must continue to unstintingly support the youth who remain with our national and international positions, whatever the attitude of the Central Committee.

4. If the organization itself takes the initiative for a discussion, please publish my key letters to the Central Committee, . . . written since the Mulhouse Congress.

If the discussion becomes public (not by our initiative, of course), please have a short statement given to the press. . . .

What Is a "Mass Paper"?
November 30, 1935

To the Members of the Bolshevik-Leninist Group:

I have just learned that my letter to the Political Bureau on the new "mass paper" ["Turn to the Masses!"] was read to the general meeting. I can only rejoice if it succeeded in clarifying the situation a little. I addressed myself first to the Political Bureau in the hope that the question could be solved without a new discussion on the foundations determined by the last national conference. But it developed that the initiators of *La Commune,* after having prepared their undertaking outside the organization, and in fact against both the national and international organizations, decided to provoke a discussion after the fait accompli. In these circumstances it would perhaps not be without value if I enlarged in a more precise manner upon the criticisms and suggestions contained in my letter to the Political Bureau.

1. What is a "mass paper"? The question is not new. It can be said that the whole history of the revolutionary movement has been filled with discussions on the "mass paper." It is the elementary duty of a revolutionary organization to make its political newspaper as accessible as possible to the masses. This task cannot be effectively solved except as a function of the growth of the organization and its cadres, who must pave the way to the masses for the newspaper—since it is not enough, of course, to call a publication a "mass paper" for the masses to really accept it. But quite often revolutionary impatience (which becomes transformed easily into opportunist impatience) leads to this conclusion: The masses do not come to us because our ideas are too complicated and our slogans too advanced. It is therefore necessary to simplify our program, water down our slogans—in short, to throw out some ballast. Basically, this means: Our slogans must correspond not to the objective situation, not to the relation of classes, analyzed by the Marxist method, but to subjective assessments (extremely superficial and inadequate ones) of what the "masses" can or cannot accept. But what masses? The mass is not homogeneous. It develops. It feels the

From *International Information Bulletin*, WPUS, no. 3, February 12, 1936.

pressure of events. It will accept tomorrow what it will not accept today. Our cadres will blaze the trail with increasing success for our ideas and slogans, which will be shown to be correct, because they are confirmed by the march of events and not by subjective and personal assessments.

2. A mass paper is distinguished from a theoretical review or from a journal for cadres not by the *slogans* but by the *manner in which they are presented.* The cadre journal unfolds for its readers all the steps of the Marxist analysis. The mass paper presents only its results, basing itself at the same time on the immediate experience of the masses themselves. *It is far more difficult to write in a Marxist manner for the masses than it is to write for cadres.*

3. Let us suppose for a moment that the GBL consented to "simplify" our program, to renounce the slogans for the new party and for the Fourth International, to renounce implacable criticism of the social patriots (naming them by name), to renounce systematic criticism of the Revolutionary Left and of Pivert personally. I do not know if this newspaper would become, with the help of a magic wand, a mass paper. I doubt it. But it would in any event become a *SAPist* or *Pivertist* paper. The essence of the Pivert tendency is just that: to accept "revolutionary" slogans, but not to draw from them the necessary conclusions, which are the break with Blum and Zyromsky, the creation of the new party and the new International. Without that, all the "revolutionary" slogans become null and void. At the present stage the Pivert agitation is a sort of opium for the revolutionary workers. Pivert wants to teach them that one can be for revolutionary struggle, for "revolutionary action" (to borrow a phrase now in vogue), and remain at the same time on good terms with chauvinist scum. Everything depends on your "tone," you see? It is the tone that makes the music. If the tiger cooed like a pigeon the whole world would be enchanted. But we, with our rude language, we must say that *the leaders of the Revolutionary Left are demoralizing and prostituting revolutionary consciousness.*

I ask you: If we renounced the slogans which are dictated by the objective situation, and which constitute the very essence of our program, in what shall we be distinguished from the Pivertists? In nothing. We would only be second-rate Pivertists. But if the "masses" should have to decide for the Pivertists, they would prefer the first-rate to the second.

4. I take up the little appeal printed for "*La Commune*—organ of revolutionary (?) action (?)." This document provides us with a

striking demonstration (unsought by its authors) of some of the ideas expressed above. "*La Commune* will speak the language of the factories and the fields. It will tell of the misery which reigns there; it will express its passions and rouse to revolt."

This is a very laudable intention, although the masses know perfectly well their own misery and their feelings of revolt (stifled by the patriotic apparatuses with the aid of the Pivertists). What the masses can demand of a newspaper is *a clear program and a correct orientation*. But precisely on this question the appeal is utterly silent. Why? Because it wants more to conceal its ideas than to express them. It accepts the SAPist (centrist) recipe: in seeking the line of least resistance *do not say what is*. The program of the Fourth International, that's for "us," for the big shots of the leadership. And the masses? What are the masses? They can rest content with a quarter, or even a tenth, of the program. This mentality we call elitism, of both an opportunist and, at the same time, an adventurist type. It is a very dangerous attitude, comrades. It is not the attitude of a Marxist.

We find in the appeal, after the sentence quoted, a number of historical reminiscences: "To the sons and grandsons of the fighters of the Croix-Rousse, of those who manned the barricades of June 1848,[12] of the Communards of 1871, *La Commune* says," etc. (followed by rhetoric à la Magdeleine Paz). I do not know, truly, if the rebelling masses need literary reminiscences and somewhat hollow rhetoric disguised as a program.

But here is where the most important part begins: "*La Commune* is not going to add itself to the multiplicity of tendencies in the workers' movement." What sovereign scorn for the "multiplicity" of existing tendencies! What does that mean? If all the tendencies are wrong or insufficient, a new one has to be created, the true one, the correct one. If there are true and false tendencies, then the workers must be taught to distinguish among them. The masses must be called on to join the correct tendency to fight the false ones. But no, the initiators of *La Commune*, somewhat like Romain Rolland, place themselves "above the battle." Such a procedure is absolutely unworthy of Marxists.

After this a number of names are proclaimed in order to particularize, however little, the utterly vague character of the new paper. I set aside my own name, which *La Commune* claims without the slightest justification. Being among the living, I can at least defend myself. But the others, our common teachers, the real leaders of revolutionary socialism? Unfortunately, they are defenseless. The appeal names Marx and Blanqui. What does that mean? Do they want to create a new "synthesis" of Marxism and Blanquism? How will the masses disentangle themselves from the combination of these two names? A little farther on we find Lenin. But the Stalinists claim him also. If you do not explain to the masses that you are against the Stalinist tendency, they will have to prefer *l'Humanité* to *La Commune*. This combination of names explains nothing. It only extends and deepens the ambiguity.

And here is the high point: "*La Commune* is launched by militants belonging to various tendencies to bring about the rise of a great army of communards." What does this mean, this unknown crew of anonymous, unknown "various tendencies"? *What* tendencies are involved? Why are they (still unknown) grouped outside and against the other tendencies? The purpose of creating a "great army of communards" is laudable. But it is necessary not to forget that this army, once created (1871), suffered a terrific catastrophe because that magnificent army lacked a program and a leadership.

The conclusion: The appeal could have been written by Marceau Pivert (in collaboration with Magdeleine Paz) except for one point—the name of the author of these lines. But as for me, I repeat, I am implacably opposed to this equivocal and anti-Marxist appeal.

5. The adherence of the GBL to the SFIO has proved absolutely correct. It was a step forward. The Mulhouse congress was the high point of the Bolshevik-Leninist influence in the SFIO. It was necessary to understand that the limit of the possibilities within the Socialist Party was being reached (at least for the adults). It was necessary to utilize the newly won and fresh authority to influence new and virgin elements outside the Socialist Party, whose social composition is miserable. It is this suggestion which I expressed in a letter since published in an internal bulletin of the GBL (no. 6, letter of June 10), and which I permit myself to recommend to the comrades for rereading in connection with the present letter. Passing through Paris [on the way to Norway] I met with several comrades, especially some of the future promoters of *La Commune*, who were in strong opposition to the idea of a new turn. These comrades had taken a liking to their activity in reformist and centrist circles and hoped to be able to progress further and further. It was a mistake. Time and strength were wasted fruitlessly instead of emulating the youth, whose orientation was more correct because it was directed toward the young workers outside the Socialist Party.

Then came the expulsions at Lille. I, for my part, regarded

them as an act of liberation, because they expressed the reality: *the impossibility of fruitful future activity in the ranks of the SFIO,* especially with the approach of war and fusion with the Stalinists. It seemed that the fact of the expulsion was so eloquent as to spare us the need for any discussion as to what road to take. It was necessary to open up a vigorous and implacable offensive against the expellers, not as "splitters" (that's the small talk of Pivert), but primarily as the valets of French imperialism. It was necessary at the same time to criticize Pivert openly, since he had taken the place of Zyromsky in covering the left wing of the People's Front. It was necessary to develop the program of *committees of action,* to oppose collaboration with the Radicals, and to proclaim openly the necessity for preparing a *new party* to save the proletariat and its younger generation. Instead of that, the *Commune* group sought above all to win the sympathies of the Revolutionary Left by personal maneuvering, by combinations in the lobbies, and above all by abdication of our slogans and of criticism of the centrists. Marceau Pivert declared two or three months ago that the struggle against "Trotskyism" is the sign of a reactionary tendency. But now he himself, led by the SAP people, represents this reactionary tendency. *The Revolutionary Left has become the most immediate and most noxious obstacle in the development of the revolutionary vanguard.* That is what has to be said openly and everywhere, i.e., especially in a mass newspaper. But the *Commune* group has gone so far in its romance with the Pivertists that one is forced to ask if these comrades are still with us or if they have passed over to centrist positions. That is where one gets when one throws principles overboard and adapts oneself longer than is necessary to the reformist apparatus and its centrist valets.

6. We may ask: and *Révolution?* It is also not the paper of our tendency. Nevertheless we participate in it. That is correct, but *Révolution* is the paper of an organization which everybody knows—the Young Socialists. The newspaper is led by *two tendencies* which are drawing close and which must inevitably fuse. The progressive character of the Revolutionary Socialist Youth is determined precisely by this fact: that they are turning toward the Bolshevik-Leninists and not toward the Revolutionary Left. (The episodic adherence of Comrade Zeller to the Revolutionary Left, after all that had happened, was a mistake the responsibility for which must be shared by the *Commune* group.)

Révolution is a living, moving paper which can become the paper of the proletarian youth. To accomplish this task, however,

Révolution must not fall into the shadows of *La Commune*'s confusion, but must concretize its position—i.e., definitively accept the slogans of the Bolshevik-Leninists.

7. *La Vérité* is an absolute necessity. But it must liberate itself from the centrist influences which resulted in the appeal of *La Commune*. *La Vérité must resume its fighting, intransigent character. The most important object of its criticism is Pivertism, which is opposed to Leninism and has thus become, by its own characterization, a reactionary tendency.*

8. I do not want to analyze in this letter the extraordinary methods employed by the *Commune* group vis-à-vis its own national and international tendency. It is a very important question but nevertheless secondary in comparison with the question of program and banner.

I believe, dear comrades, that you have the greatest opportunities before you. You are at last going to reap the fruits of your efforts up to now, but on one condition: that you do not permit a confusion of tendencies, of ideas and banners; that you practice Leninist intransigence more than ever and orient yourselves openly and vigorously toward the new party and the Fourth International.

L. Trotsky

A Capitulation to the Centrists
December 3, 1935

Dear Comrades:

1. The differences that separate us from the *Commune* group are, as Comrade Frank's letter demonstrates, completely irreconcilable. It is useless to answer Frank. He has given no new argument: everything he says has already been said for a long time by the SAPists and Pivertists. It is a capitulation to the social-patriotic wave. Whoever doesn't understand this is not a Marxist.

The approach of the war has (temporarily) given the social patriots a powerful weapon against the internationalists. Hence the expulsion of the Leninists. Hence Pivert's cowardly capitulation (his vote for the Blum resolution on questions of general

From *Bulletin Intérieur*, GBL, no. 10, December 13, 1935. Signed "L.T." A letter to the Central Committee of the GBL. Translated by David Keil.

policy, his silence during the National Council on the question of the expulsions, etc.). Hence, finally, the fear of "isolation" felt by the unstable elements in our own ranks and their tendency to go with the centrists at any cost and to be differentiated from them as little as possible. There is no other political content in the attitude of Molinier and Frank. They are capitulating to the social-patriotic wave. All the rest is only phrases, worthless in the eyes of a serious Marxist.

2. I think that the majority of the Central Committee of the French section has shown an impermissible indulgence toward the opportunist tendencies of Molinier and Frank. (I will not dwell on Molinier's criminal and adventurist behavior.) This indulgence can only be explained from a psychological point of view, by the desire to preserve unity, etc. In this regard, the center group of Comrade Rous played an entirely positive role, to the degree that what was involved was cliques and personal struggles. But this spirit of conciliation became a serious fault once the capitulationist and centrist tendencies were clearly manifested inside the Molinier group. An open and honest break would be a hundred times better than ambiguous concessions to those who capitulate to the patriotic wave.

3. On *La Commune's* shameful appeal, I have already said all that I have to say. From the newly received letters, it is difficult for me to discern whether *La Commune* will appear or whether *Révolution* will be transformed into a "mass paper." But this isn't the decisive question now. Even if the *Commune* operation is buried, the question remains: in whose hands will *Révolution* be, and on the basis of what program will it be published?

When the time comes, it will be necessary to merge with the opposition Stalinists and with all the other revolutionary groupings, but not on the basis of . . . equal representation on the editorial board—without principles, without a banner (the Molinier method); rather on the basis of a *particular program.* Such a minimum program is provided in the Open Letter. Before having the Stalinists, etc., join, it is necessary to win the Seine Alliance for the Fourth International. Whoever opposes or holds back this work capitulates or prepares to capitulate to the wave of social patriotism.

The touchstone of a revolutionary tendency today is the so-called Revolutionary Left. It probably includes in its ranks a large number of revolutionaries. But every tendency is character-ized by its program and its leadership. Marceau Pivert is the left cover for Léon Blum. A "revolutionary" policy, within the framework of Léon Blum's discipline, after the expulsion, today means charlatanism and fraud. Is it true that Marceau Pivert, who voted for Blum's political resolution [at the National Council], was invited to collaborate with *Révolution*? If this is true, it reveals a tendency to hide behind centrism, that is, to hide one's banner.

The hesitations, experiments, and groping around were inevitable for a whole period. But now, after the tendencies have been defined as a result of a fierce struggle around the fundamental questions of our epoch (the war and the Fourth International), to pull revolutionaries backward toward a bloc with Marceau Pivert means accomplishing a reactionary task, means joining the social-patriotic front.

Every critical epoch engenders many temporary currents and countercurrents in which opportunists and adventurers swim, become caught up, and drown. Tenacity! The serious revolutionary crystallization will only occur around a Marxist axis. The uproar around *La Commune* will probably be forgotten in a few weeks, or will play directly into the hands of the social patriots. And the systematic struggle for the banner of the Fourth International will go on. It is times like these that verify ideas and temper characters. It is necessary to step over the political corpse of an old comrade-in-arms if he capitulates to social patriotism, or to its lackeys, which is hardly better. If we, before, when we were weaker, stepped over Zinoviev, Kamenev, Rakovsky, and other eminent old revolutionaries, we will step all the more easily today over the clique of capitulators who shamefully renounce their own banner.

L. Trotsky

P.S.—I have just received the circular letter of November 24, unsigned, but with the exclamation, "Vive *La Commune!*" We know the real nature of this *Commune,* under whose banner gathers a group whose members do not judge it useful to sign their names. The whole document consists of gossip and organizational intrigues which are not even verifiable for anyone outside the Central Committee. But this verification, in the last analysis, is not necessary. By its character of unprincipled intrigues, the document speaks sufficiently for itself. By radically changing their positions, by renouncing the fundamental slogans of Leninism, by trampling on its methods, by allying, behind the backs of the organization and its leading bodies (national and international) with direct opponents of Leninism, the centrist capitulators cannot advance a single *principled* consideration in defense of their betrayal. "Let's go out into the arena," their statement concludes. Which arena? That of opportunism.

Every serious Marxist will reject this scheming document and will examine *the root* of the question, that is, the attitudes toward centrism on the one hand, and toward Leninism on the other.

Molinier's opportunistic tendencies do not date from yesterday and are no mystery to any of us. Molinier's participation in leadership work has been justified only to the degree that other comrades, more solidly grounded in Marxist principles, supervised and corrected him. From the moment Molinier escaped from national and international control and tried to transform his adventuristic impulses into a "tendency," he immediately fell into the swamp of opportunism. This swamp he pompously calls an "arena."

L.T.

A Letter to the International Secretariat
December 3, 1935

Comrade Raymond Molinier continues to be formally a member of the plenum [of the ICL]. I do not believe that his political attitude permits us to keep him even formally inside the leading body of our international organization.

Politically, Molinier has gone over to centrist positions.

Organizationally, he has made a bloc with the centrists against our tendency. He has not consulted the International Secretariat about his "turn." He allowed himself to present ultimatums to our organization, relying on semicapitalist methods of "surprise attacks." His activity becomes more and more demoralizing. I propose to invite the Central Committee of the French section, by decision of the IS, to recall Comrade Molinier. At the same time, I propose the convening of an international control commission, to investigate the activity of Comrade Molinier and possibly that of other comrades associated with him.

From *L'Organe de masse.* Signed "Crux." The IS was a small body responsible for administrative decisions; the plenum was a larger committee, meeting less frequently, and bearing the highest political responsibility of the ICL between international conferences.

An Abdication of Principles
December 4, 1935

Dear Comrades:

If one wishes to know what an abdication of principles is, one must read P. Frank's letter attentively. It is politically inconsistent, but it reflects very well the state of mind of a skeptical and disoriented *intellectual* (not to say a petty bourgeois).

What is the reply of an "advanced" French petty bourgeois to your arguments? He is "very far left," "very revolutionary" ("The fatherland? Who cares? . . . General strike, insurrection!"). He answers you immediately: "We don't want any of your organizational domination." . . . "A new party? A new International? No, we've had enough of that." That is the typical response.

And Frank, what does he do? He slavishly transmits this mentality. "No organizational ultimatism whatsoever." "No group currently in existence can pretend to organizational domination." It is humiliating, even for a Marxist, to reply to such arguments. Do we ever concern ourselves with "organizational domination"? For us the important thing is a *program* that corresponds to the objective situation. If another organization, more significant than ours, accepts this program—not in words but in deeds—we are ready to merge with it without the least pretention to organizational domination. Look at the United States and Holland.

But in P. Frank's letter, in all his thinking—as in the well-known appeal of *La Commune*—there is no mention whatsoever of program, and not without reason: program constitutes a serious obstacle to the general fraternization with the petty bourgeoisie, with intellectuals, pessimists, skeptics, and adventurists; we, for our part, believe that program determines everything.

"No organizational ultimatism." What a revolting distortion of the Leninist formulation! No ultimatism whatsoever in relation to the masses, the trade unions, the workers' movement; but the most intransigent ultimatism in relation to any group that claims to lead the masses. The ultimatism that we are talking about is called the *Marxist program*. How can we get the masses to accept it? That, naturally, is a very serious question. If one wants to

---

From *Bulletin Intérieur*, GBL, no. 10, December 13, 1935. Signed "Crux." A letter to the Political Bureau of the GBL, in reply to a letter from Pierre Frank. Translated by Susan Wald.

create a mass paper, the editors themselves must possess a program, and it must be a Marxist program. In place of such a program, however, we find an adventurist type of devil-may-care attitude. Nothing more.

"Workers' militia and revolutionary defeatism" does not constitute a program. Everyone accepts that now, with this or that reservation. The program now concerns the fight for the new party, against the two Internationals, and against Marceau Pivert (SAP, IAG), the servant of unity between the reformists and the Stalinists. To fill one's mouth at this time with "organic unity," and likewise with "revolutionary organic unity," is to mislead the masses along with Marceau Pivert and other servants of social patriotism. *Committees of action, the revolutionary party, and the Fourth International:* this is where an adequate program for the present moment must begin. To limit oneself to insufficient or outmoded formulations means to play a reactionary role. And it is difficult to imagine a more reactionary document than the appeal put out by *La Commune*, unless it is Frank's letter. The weightiest argument in the letter, namely, "Why have the Bolshevik-Leninists remained weak in Germany and in France?" is nothing but an echo of the centrist objections, "Why were you beaten by the Stalinist bureaucracy, by the reactionary coalition in China, etc. . . ?" For quite some time we have been explaining the reasons for these defeats, and we never promised any miracles. Our international work began only in 1929—and not on virgin territory, but on territory saturated with old and powerful organizations, and with new, confused, and often treacherous organizations that claimed adherence to our principles. We have fought constantly against the Pierre Franks in Germany and in Spain, against the skeptics, and against the adventurers who wanted to perform miracles (and broke their necks in the process). The very fact that Frank uses arguments as arbitrary and confused as he does demonstrates that he feels himself to be an outsider in our organization. But in spite of all the skeptics and all the adventurers, ours is the only organization that knows where it is going, is going forward, and embodies the future of the working class.

Only little children could believe that what is at issue between ourselves and the *Commune* group is the question of a "mass paper." The real issue is the question of program, of the historical orientation of the tendency. The issue is a new chapter in the struggle between Marxism and centrism—a struggle that characterizes our epoch.

Crux [Trotsky]

P.S.—I would like to draw your attention once again to the absolutely intolerable methods of the *Commune* group. Here is how Frank himself describes them: "Having made the decision to launch *La Commune*, having taken the first steps, we turned toward the existing organizations (the GBL, the Young Socialists, the Social Front minority, the Revolutionary Action Groups), telling them: 'Your discussions are going on dangerously long. We have gotten a newspaper under way *for you*; go ahead, take it.'" Now, it is the so-called Bolshevik-Leninists who launched *La Commune*, and who afterwards, from the heights of the position they had attained, addressed themselves to the mere mortals of "various tendencies and organizations" thus: "Go ahead!" What have these audacious innovators thus created? *La Commune*. And what is *La Commune*? A doctrine, a program, some slogans, a banner? Nothing of the kind. It's a headquarters, some posters, and . . . the cashbox. It's a question of a certain amount of money. That is the truth. And it is from the height of this purely material position that the initiators are trying to lead and even command the Bolshevik-Leninist Group. That is where one ends up when one loses one's compass! No, our organization cannot be led by such methods. In the centrist swamps they are much more amenable. Go try your methods on them. "Go ahead!"

Molinier's Latest Adventure
December 4, 1935

My Dear Friend:

If I haven't responded to your document concerning the USSR, it was not because of negligence, as you yourself well know. In your criticism you declare—naturally, with reason—that it is necessary not to be satisfied with ready-made formulations from Trotsky. Other French comrades have complained, more than once, that I "stifle" the discussion with my premature interventions. That is the only reason (but you will recognize that it is a good one) that I have adopted a wait-and-see attitude under the circumstances.

In a private capacity I can only repeat the basic argument: the USSR is now the only state in the world where the productive

From the archives of the late Isaac Deutscher, in a collection of Trotsky's letters held by Leon Sedov and provided by Jeanne Martin. By permission of Tamara Deutscher. Translated by Naomi Allen.

forces are developing with a rhythm that cannot be equaled. Thanks to what? Thanks to the nationalization of the means of production and despite the faults and crimes of the bureaucracy. You can label the bureaucracy an "exploiting class" if you want to (sociologically that would be wrong), but you cannot eliminate the fact that the enormous development of the productive forces nationalized by the state is the most progressive fact in contemporary history, since it paves the way for socialism. To place the USSR on the same plane as the capitalist states would be absurd and criminal. To defend Ethiopia despite the Negus and to refuse to defend the USSR because of Stalin would truly be the height of incoherence. Politically it would be the equivalent of suicide. "Conditional" defense is an empty formulation. We defend the USSR against imperialism unconditionally just as we defend the reformist trade unions against fascism unconditionally.

You are surely well informed about Raymond's latest adventure, which I consider to be irreparable (for him, of course, not for the movement). He wanted to perform a "miracle." He always wants to perform miracles, and on all subjects. When great events approach (war, revolution), great alterations begin in tendencies and in thinking. I have already observed this phenomenon many times. In the general swirl of events it is easy to lose one's head, and Raymond is the first candidate for this loss. He decided to embrace everyone and everything (except his own tendency), and to demonstrate to imbeciles who do not want to admire Raymond that he is capable of performing a real miracle. Unfortunately he will break his neck, and that is all.

I would be very happy to have a few lines from you about your health, your work, and the general situation. Natalia sends you her best regards. And I do too.

L. Trotsky

P.S. Our health is not very good. (Our machine has neither accents nor circumflexes.)

Committees of Action
Versus Elected Communes
December 6, 1935

Dear Comrades:

La Commune's second appeal contains nothing of interest except an attempt to confuse the slogan for committees of action with the slogan for "elected communes." But what was the [Paris] Commune? It was the *municipal government* elected *after the seizure of power.* How can you call for the election of communes (outside the framework of bourgeois legality) before seizing power? It is absolutely incomprehensible. *Committees of action* are formations for the conquest of power and not at all "elected communes." Naturally, we want to support the tradition of the Commune, but not by imitating its organizational forms, and especially not by imitating its confusion. (At the least, you should read Pierre Dominique's book on this subject.)

This juxtaposing of committees of action with "communes" was invented specifically to justify the name of the newspaper, while spreading confusion.

The only excellent point is the invitation to participate in the "Chameleon Contest." We could even call the new tendency "chameleonism" and put a picture of a chameleon on its banner.[13]

From *Bulletin Intérieur*, GBL, no. 10, December 13, 1935. Signed "L.T." Translated by Russell Block. A letter to the Central Committee of the GBL.

Critical Remarks on Révolution
December 9, 1935

Dear Comrades:

I congratulate you for the first issue of the weekly *Révolution.* You will allow me, however, to formulate my criticisms: it is the only Marxist way of serving the movement.

From *Bulletin Intérieur,* GBL, no. 10, December 13, 1935. A letter to the editors of *Révolution,* on the occasion of its first number as a joint GBL-JSR enterprise. Translated by Mary Gordon.

1. One of the most important slogans is for "committees of action." But this slogan is formulated differently in almost all of the articles and never in a precise manner. You speak of "committees of revolutionary action" (the formulation is from Molinier and M. Paz). Rigal merely speaks of "mass committees." Another demands the creation of "committees to prepare the general strike." Such methods will only confuse your readers. Leave to *La Commune* the stupid slogan for "communes." When we say "Long live the Commune!" we mean the heroic insurrection, not the institution of the "commune," that is, the democratic municipality. Even its election was a stupidity (see Marx) and even then, this stupidity was only possible *after* the conquest of power by the central committee of the National Guard, which was the "action committee," or the soviet, of the time.

2. Each article should raise a different question, but all the articles should lead to the same conclusions. Unfortunately, many articles deal with the same question, but use different formulations, which confuses the reader. The effect of the propaganda greatly suffers from that.

3. Corvin characterizes the Laval government as a "*pre*fascist government." This is the second time that this serious mistake is repeated. The reader will conclude from it that Laval will give way to fascism. Unfortunately, it is possible; but fortunately, it is not at all certain. Laval may hand over his place to Daladier and Daladier to the proletariat. Laval as well as Daladier, according to this hypothesis, would be intermediary Bonapartist governments. That is the only Marxist characterization (it is very well developed in the article on the special edicts.) At any rate, we must avoid spreading a pessimistic fatalism by characterizing the current government as *pre*fascist.

4. The Nazi army was dissolved, not by the Schleicher government, as is stated in the article on the "defense of the Republic," but by the Brüning-Groener government. The thing is well explained in Röhm's *Memoirs*, and it is repeated in a leaflet of *La Vérité*.[14] It is absolutely necessary to publicize this episode more widely in *Révolution*.

5. The greatest defect is political anonymity. You fight against ideas without naming their representatives (Cachin, Blum, Zyromsky, Pivert, etc.). This gives your fight an abstract and academic character. The article "Frauds," which names people, gains a lot in effectiveness. You must, however, avoid certain vulgarisms (the serious worker does not like them). The idea of the Revolutionary Left, according to which we must attack the *mistakes* and not the personalities, is absurd. The worker wants

to know whether or not he can trust Blum or Pivert. You must frankly answer no, since Blum is a confirmed lackey of French imperialism, and Pivert confesses to being Blum's lackey. The "blunt" truth is a revolutionary factor. The most "courteous" lie is a reactionary one. *La Commune* will perish because it bases itself on lies.

6. The declaration against war and the "sacred union" contains excellent formulations and is a credit to its authors. Unfortunately, its value is considerably lessened by an incomprehensible gap. The declaration blames the reformists and the Stalinists and refuses to resort to anarchist and pacifist methods. Very good. But after establishing the bankruptcy of the old parties, the declaration does not mention the need to prepare a *new party*. It is incomprehensible. It is not easy for a worker to admit the bankruptcy of the two parties and of the two Internationals. But from the moment he understands that, he needs a revolutionary perspective. Otherwise, you can spread only pessimism.

La Commune presents itself as a revolutionary "paper of regroupment and action." What regroupment? What action? This way of acting characterizes very aptly people who try, with hollow formulas, to deceive the workers with the confusion that reigns in their own ranks and in their own heads. The Marxist revolutionary must speak clearly of the need to work for the new party and the *new International*. Otherwise, despite all the revolutionary formulas, there is always the risk of becoming the agent of one of the old parties. *Each example of vagueness will serve the enemy class, whose pressure on the working class becomes tremendous as the war approaches.*

7. *Révolution* hardly mentions international questions. It is a serious gap. In Belgium Godefroid is preparing to betray the Young Socialist Guards in order to curry favor with the bureaucracy. *Révolution* should take a position on this question, as well as on many others in the international movement. This does not necessarily mean articles. Sometimes, five lines are enough to communicate a fact or to define one's attitude. The international column should be well done.

Dear comrades, these critical remarks do not prevent me at all from regarding *Révolution* as infinitely superior to *La Commune*. *Révolution* represents a progressive organization (the youth) and a historical tendency (the Bolshevik-Leninists). This gives it a serious basis. *La Commune* represents only a few dissident cliques, with neither principles nor order, which adapt themselves to everyone and spend themselves in shrill formulas in order to camouflage their total inconsistency. Such enterprises abound during all critical prerevolutionary periods, and they disappear without a trace at the first turn of events.

My best revolutionary regards,
L. Trotsky

A Turn to the Right
December 11, 1935

Dear Friend:

I have received your letter of the fifth of this month. Also the announcement of *Rote Front*. (Comrade Braun will take care of circulation, etc.) I hope that this attempt will not fail too.

I find your work on Austrian matters outstanding—without going into the details, which are not totally clear to me (the possible boycott seems doubtful to me). One cannot educate the youth without an implacable struggle against those who remain passive and speculate on aid from the class enemy.

You are certainly already informed about Molinier's betrayal. These fellows do not want to remain "isolated" and so they capitulate to the Pivert tendency, which has in turn capitulated to Blum. If you tell them that they are participating in the preparation for the sacred union they will naturally be indignant. But that is only the simple truth. That is what is going on now. This is the first wretched capitulation to the powerful chauvinist pressure that bourgeois public opinion is putting on the working class with the indispensable aid of the Stalinist bureaucracy. We must be prepared for other casualties.

Some idiots will connect this with the entry into the SFIO. For such folk the whole issue is reduced to the question of whether we should have carried out entry at this time or that, in this country or another, etc. That there are still *other* factors in the world which carry a thousand times more weight remains a mystery to them.

As for that muddlehead Molinier, the following is interesting: In June, he came to us in Isère [in France] with his great idea of creating a Socialist "left": We're running out of time. Tomorrow

From the archives of James P. Cannon. By permission of the Library of Social History in New York. Translated for this volume from the German by Russell Block. A letter to Werner Keller (Jan Frankel).

will bring inflation and to overcome the political consequences of inflation the bourgeoisie will allow fascism to come to power. I replied: First of all, I don't see why there must be inflation and why immediately. Secondly, if we have so little time, we should not use this time to spread confusion and demoralization. Molinier bit his lip and forgot his fantasies for the moment. Instead of inflation, we had the decree-laws, i.e., a "deflation." And in the six months since the Mulhouse congress, we have grown significantly, especially in the youth, and despite our "very bad"—i.e., Molinierist—line.

Now these people suddenly declare: Tomorrow will bring de la Rocque's coup d'état. We're running out of time. We have to do . . . "something." Now, as if to make a mockery of these prophets once again, instead of de la Rocque's coup d'état we have had "general disarmament."[15] Of course, in the final instance this "disarmament" is on the one hand a deception and on the other a betrayal of the workers. But only in the *final instance*. This means that for the next period, French capital needs not de la Rocque but Laval. In other words, the coup d'état, if it really was planned for the immediate future (which is possible) now has been *postponed*. It goes without saying that no coup d'état could justify political betrayal and malevolent undermining of the revolutionary wing. But the fact that events have again given Molinier's "prognoses" the lie is, so to speak, the first punishment administered by political developments. Future punishments will be far more severe.[16]

But it is a historical law: When the workers begin a march to the extreme left, the unsteady elements within the left wing respond by making a turn to the right, against the stream, and usually sink in the stream for good.

With warm greetings,
Your old man [Trotsky]

Against False Passports in Politics
December 16, 1935

A friend has written to me about that lamentable *Commune:* "But it is no longer anonymous tendencies that are involved. Everyone has signed up." Is that so? Then that only makes the situation worse. When I spoke of "anonymous tendencies" I meant that neither their past record nor their program were known to anyone. But what do we see now before us? *Defectors* from different tendencies—the Bolshevik-Leninists, the Revolutionary Left, the Social Front.

The Bolshevik-Leninist Group is not anonymous at all; the "Revolutionary Left" is not revolutionary at all, but all the same, everyone knows what it is. The "Social Front" is a somewhat ambiguous enterprise, but everyone can nevertheless form an opinion of that formation. But the defectors from these three groups, who have come together not on the basis of principles but on the basis of "parity"—What do they represent? What is their political character? What is their program? Bolshevik-Leninists who found it necessary to launch an actual conspiracy against their own national and international organization (now in such a critical situation) must have had decisive reasons for acting as they have acted. What then are these reasons? In other words, what is the *new* program of those former Bolshevik-Leninists who so brutally abandoned their own organization? No one knows anything about this. And if these defectors say "But we have renounced nothing," we are forced to choose between two hypotheses: they are either simple fools, who set fire to their own house, or cynics who take others for imbeciles. And I do not hesitate for a single moment to choose the second alternative.

Political anonymity is intolerable. But there is something worse: that is, when someone tries to pass under the name of a tendency he has betrayed. *False passports* in politics are a hundred times worse than anonymity. And Molinier and Frank are presenting false passports to the workers. It is a crime!

La Commune, such as it is, is nothing but imitation and falsification. A few examples: In its first issue my work on civil war was quoted with approval.[17] But I have never separated the

From an undated GBL circular letter to the members. A letter to the Political Bureau of the GBL. Translated by Jeff White.

problems of civil war from the Marxist program and the revolutionary party. But the methods of *La Commune* are diametrically opposite to all my conceptions of the organization of a revolutionary party. "No domination"—in other words, no program. "On the basis of parity" means parity in cynicism with regard to principles, a scarcely enviable kind of parity. A "mass paper" is in reality an imitation of *l'Oeuvre,* dressed up in slogans borrowed from the right and the left and aimed at radicalizing petty bourgeois who are not even able to understand that the preparation for civil war begins with the *elaboration of a program* and that a "mass paper" can be nothing other than one of the instruments of this program.

In the second issue, it is explained "how the Chinese revolution was betrayed." This time, they take hold of Treint, who, alas, has been somewhat slow to understand the Chinese revolution (even now!), as well as some other questions. *La Commune* says, not incorrectly (though our Comrade Held has pointed this out much more firmly), that the People's Front is repeating the experience of the Chinese Kuomintang. But the editors do not at all understand that the beginning of the catastrophe rested on the fact that the young Communist Party was deprived of absolute independence from the "revolutionary left" in the name of "revolutionary action." The Communists abandoned their banner and their principles in order to gain "parity"—indeed questionable—with the left wing of the Kuomintang. Now *La Commune* is repeating the same experience under even worse conditions. "Parity of the different tendencies" means a miniature French Kuomintang.

But what, in this case, was the meaning of our entering the SFIO, some sophists or naive persons will object? The temporary entry into the SFIO, or even into the Kuomintang, is not an evil in itself; however, it is necessary to know not only how to *enter,* but also how to *leave.* When you continue to hang onto an organization that can no longer tolerate proletarian revolutionaries in its midst, you become of necessity the wretched tool of reformism, patriotism, and capitalism. This was the case with the Chinese Communists after the "little" coup of Canton in March 1926.[18] This was the case with the Pivertists after the Lille congress, and especially after the last national convention. After having declared that the struggle against "Trotskyism" is the unmistakable sign of a reactionary tendency, Pivert, in latching onto Blum and Zyromsky, had to launch a "new tendency" whose essential purpose is to struggle against "Trotskyism." And the poor Molinier clique is already obliged to sabotage the youth organization and its paper, and to oppose our national and international tendency every step of the way. That is what it means to remake the Kuomintang on a small scale.

La Commune's cornerstone—of its castle-in-Spain—is "revolutionary action." But what does this mean, at bottom? Nobody has said. There is the "Revolutionary Action Group" of the nineteenth arrondissement; there is another one, even less revolutionary (if that is possible), in the ninth arrondissement, *with Paz* in the leadership. Just like Molinier, Paz too seizes upon the phraseological refuse of Leninism. Is it a new party? No. Paz is completely attached to "his party." And the members of the nineteenth arrondissement's "Revolutionary Action Group"? *They are silent on the matter.* "But it is only a united front," they will reply. But the united front is an alliance of the forces of the mass organizations with a view to concrete action. In the case of *La Commune,* there are *neither forces nor action.* It is a "united front" for the publication of a newspaper. Now that is the exact opposite of a united front as it is conceived and interpreted by Marxism. The fundamental rule of the united front, in the meaning of the Bolshevik-Leninists, was and remains: *March separately, strike together.* Now the so-called Revolutionary Action Group is a deliberately ambiguous institution for *marching together* with the centrists and for striking . . . the Bolshevik-Leninists. Such is the real character of "Revolutionary Action Groups," *Molinier's as well as Paz's.*

The "program" of Revolutionary Action Groups presented in the second issue of *La Commune* is far inferior to the program of the Revolutionary Left. It seems a little too confused and too ambiguous even for Pivert. And Pivert's ringing program does not prevent him—far from it—from fulfilling his essential function, namely, to support Blum, Lebas, and Lagorgette in their attempts to break up the youth and the Bolshevik-Leninists. And moreover, it is *the only kind of "revolutionary action"* that Molinier practices—and it, too, is in the form of "direct action." With what success remains to be seen.

La Commune is equivocation turned into a paper. Let us take the extremely significant question of Pivertism. What is termed Molinier's "influence" in the nineteenth arrondissement, in the TPPS, etc. . . . is, *at its root,* only adaptation to Pivertism. In reality the Molinier group has played the role of slave in the service of centrism. Molinier's whole policy, above all in the last five or six months, has remained oriented toward fusion with Pivertism. The result? This policy has made Pivert's betrayal easier, weakened the influence of the GBL, and masked the *empty politics* of all this activity in the nineteenth arrondissement and in the TPPS, and this weakness has driven him right into a fatal adventure. Now, caught between the Bolshevik-Leninists and the "Revolutionary Left," *La Commune* sees itself obliged to denounce (meekly enough) Pivert's attitude at the youth congress. It expresses ambiguous sympathies to the youth while trying to break them up. At the same time, *it continues to be tied to the Pivertists*—against the youth and the Bolshevik-Leninists. Under these conditions, lies become an inevitable tool of this desperate struggle, which can only end in a new bankruptcy, even more disastrous for the promoters of *La Commune.*

A sentimentalist writes: "But you don't know these comrades personally; they are full of good intentions," etc. . . . Good intentions, however indisputable, are not enough. They must be guided by correct principles and controlled by a cohesive organization. Otherwise . . . but I prefer to give an example. Pierre Frank wrote a small pamphlet about February 6, 1934, containing some altogether scandalous passages calling the arming of the proletariat a "romantic" slogan.[19] The other comrades had to bring the necessary pressure to bear. *La Vérité* took a correct position on the question of militias and armaments. And the regrettable page of Frank's pamphlet luckily passed unnoticed.

But let us imagine for a moment that Frank had left the organization in February 1934, had insisted on his point of view on arms, and had launched a so-called "mass paper." Would Frank's "good intentions" have sufficed to make up for the reactionary consequences of his wrong conception? Now, the recent letter of Frank's that substitutes for the program of *La Commune* (see the internal bulletin) is full of errors and contradictions. But this time Frank's "good intentions" are altogether unchecked, since he has placed himself outside of the organization that has many times in the past saved him from the consequences of his "good intentions." The split, provoked by a disloyal plot, forces and will force the deserters to develop ideas, tendencies, and inclinations which will become their weaknesses. Where will they end up after such a beginning? I have no idea. That is why, for my part, I *distrust them absolutely.*

At the same time as the case of Frank, I contemplate above all that of Raymond Molinier: he has indisputable qualities of energy, a capacity for improvisation, and élan. But along with that, he shows an often very dangerous theoretical confusion, an impatience that drives him to adventuristic actions, and an almost absolute inability to discipline himself. A comrade from a country where the dairy industry plays a big role in the economy told me once: "Our peasants liken such characters to the kind of cows that give a lot of milk but always kick over the pail." That's really the case with Molinier. Numerous comrades, serious and objective, have often asked themselves uneasily whether the balance sheet of Molinier's activity (these overturned pails) was not rather on the negative side. For my part, I have never wanted to give up hope: I would tell myself that a stronger and more cohesive organization could perhaps educate him. But now that Molinier is improvising a "mass paper" controlled only by his "good intentions," I cannot but say openly: This inclination will end up being fatal for the man.

The example of Doriot is still very fresh. He was a leader of the CP for years, and not just during its degeneration. Since leaving the CP, he has not wanted to choose a program, a tendency, a banner. . . . He looks for gimmicks, advances high-sounding slogans (workers' unity, the commune, etc., . . . what you will), and he too has his "mass paper" and even his own proletarian base. All that has not prevented his catastrophic degeneration. And nevertheless he too, in his time, must have had *"good intentions."*

Must we then consider that all the promoters of *La Commune* have been definitively lost for the movement? I have no idea, and, to tell the truth, that question is not uppermost in my mind at present. Let them suffer the consequences of their confused, adventurist, and disloyal attitude. As for the Bolshevik-Leninists, they must learn to draw some helpful lessons for the workers' vanguard from this painful experience. *Program first!* "Mass paper"? Revolutionary action? Regroupment? Communes everywhere? . . . Very well, very well. . . . But *program first!* Your political passports, please, gentlemen! And not false ones, if you please—*real ones!* If you don't have any, then pipe down!

Without the new revolutionary party, the French proletariat is doomed to catastrophe. The revolutionary party can rest only on the principles of Marx and Lenin. Aside from the Bolshevik-Leninists, no other tendency has even tried to draw from these principles a program that is equal to our epoch. The party of the proletariat can only be international. The Second and Third Internationals became the greatest obstacles to the revolution. It is necessary to create a new International—the Fourth. We must openly proclaim its necessity. They are petty-bourgeois centrists who falter at every step before the consequences of their own ideas. The revolutionary worker can be paralyzed by his traditional attachment to the Second or Third International, but when he has understood the truth, he will pass directly to the banner of the Fourth International. That is why we must present the masses with a complete program. By ambiguous formulas, we can only serve Molinier, who himself serves Pivert, who in turn covers for Léon Blum. And the latter puts all his forces behind de la Rocque . . . and the King of Prussia.

Under czarism, liberals and democrats treated us like fools, because of our propaganda in support of the slogan for a *republic.* Why frighten the people? they would object. There is enough in our propaganda to develop the content of a republic (various freedoms, universal suffrage, etc.) without actually saying that terrible word. We would reply: In order for the revolution to become possible, we must instill and maintain in the people an implacable hatred against the nobility, the bureaucracy, etc. . . . And every worker, every peasant, who learns to hate the czar will accept the slogan for a republic without difficulty.

The people of the SAP only repeat in connection with the Fourth International the reasoning of our old "democrats" in connection with the republic slogan. Such reasoning is character- istic of the mentality of a petty bourgeois—very "daring" in abstract critique, but always halting before the effort of revolutionary will. The working class mentality is quite different. We must teach the workers to hate Blum, Thorez, Jouhaux, etc., as the worst enemies in the ranks of the workers, and, *at the same time,* we must open up to them the perspective of the new party and the new International.

The class struggle is unforgiving, especially in a revolutionary epoch that counterposes the poor, faltering logic of the petty- bourgeois centrist to the powerful logic of great events.

If the youth of *Révolution* have well understood the lesson to be drawn from the affair of Molinier and Company, they will mature quickly and become much more sure of themselves in the accomplishment of the great tasks that history has placed before them.

A Clarification
December 20, 1935

To the editors of *La Commune:*

Please insert the following statement in your next issue:

In its first appeal your newspaper made use of my name, among others. In your first issue you reproduced an excerpt from something I had written. Some of your editors persist in calling themselves "Bolshevik-Leninists." Under these circumstances, in order to avoid all confusion, I consider myself obliged to declare that I do not support your publication in any way.

Leon Trotsky

From *La Vérité,* December 27, 1935. Translated by Russell Block.

The "Political Basis" of La Commune
December 23, 1935

To the members of the GBL

Dear Comrades:

I have just read *La Commune*'s proposal to *Révolution* for a fusion (a) on the political basis . . . of *La Commune,* and (b) on the basis of parity for all the formations entering this regroupment.

This proposal is not only wrong, it is also outrageous.

The "political basis" of *La Commune* is approximately that of the Revolutionary Left. This basis has been tested by experience. Its political result was the betrayal of the Bolshevik-Leninists and a servile attitude toward the social-patriotic apparatus. If a simple worker has not yet arisen above this "basis," we will enlighten him, we will lead him forward. But when we are offered

From *Bulletin Intérieur,* GBL, no. 11, January 6, 1936, where it was undated and signed "L.T." The date was supplied by Nicolle Braun, in *L'Organe de masse,* where this letter to the members of the GBL was partly quoted. Translated by Mary Gordon.

such a "basis" for a political organization claiming to lead the masses, we reject this "basis" with a kick.

But there is a second "basis." It is "parity for all the formations." The principle of proletarian organization is *democratic centralism.* In order to get the leadership of an organization you must convince the majority of its members. But no! This principle always seemed intolerable to the arrogant petty bourgeois. What? They have to work in the same way as the common herd? Oh, no! They are going, right away, to create a formation of their own. (For this, there is no need to have ideas. A few banknotes are enough.) After this heroic act, the deserters propose to their "friends," that is, those whom they have betrayed, a "fusion on the basis of parity." This would mean that an organization of hundreds or even thousands of workers should have the same rights as a group of petty bourgeois having only the material means to create their own "paper." To accept such a proposal as a "basis" would mean to accept demoralization and corruption.

The revolutionary paper is nothing other than the tool of the proletarian party. The point of departure for the building of this party is the Marxist program. In the course of eighteen years of merciless struggle all over the world, the Bolshevik-Leninists have formulated this program. It does not contain superfluous, artificial, incidental things. Each thesis is tested under the pressure of tremendous events. This program has no ballast that can be thrown overboard. On the basis of the program, which is a unified whole, the Bolshevik-Leninists have entered into fraternal collaboration with the Seine Alliance, which will develop its activity on the basis of democratic centralism. The GBL will seek to win to its program the majority of the youth, as well as the thousands and thousands of workers outside of it. It is the only "basis" worthy of a revolutionary organization.

P.S.—I want to make my opinion explicit. The idea of "parity of formations," that is, of tendencies, is inherently absurd and vicious. The tendencies are not equal in numbers; but what is most important is the different ideological and political value of the tendencies. There are right and wrong tendencies, progressive and reactionary ones. Adventurists, who hold nothing sacred, may well accommodate themselves with all the possible tendencies. But Marxists are obliged to mercilessly fight the unprincipled tendencies and not to make alliances with them on an equal basis. The parity of tendencies means the parity of Marxism, centrism, adventurism, etc. One could easily find in

Marx, Engels, Lenin a mountain of sarcastic quotations against analogous pretensions from petty-bourgeois formations of the time.

Another side of the same question: *Révolution* has established its reputation through the congress of the Seine Alliance, which, by the way, rejected Molinier's proposal. But the congress of the Seine Alliance does not exist for these manipulators. They expect *Révolution* to annul the decision of its own organization. Can one have the least confidence in people who with incredible levity betrayed their national and international organization (which is not at all "equal" to Bergery's Social Front or to the Revolutionary Action Group of the nineteenth arrondissement) and propose now to *Révolution* to betray the youth and the Bolshevik-Leninists? *The slightest concession to these methods would be fatal to the revolutionary education of the youth.*

Lessons of the SFIO Entry
December 30, 1935

Dear Comrades:

. . . It is useless to proceed with an analysis of the conditions in which the entry was accomplished. Not only because we need a closer look into the concrete circumstances of the working class movement in your country, but especially because the results of Bolshevik-Leninist work within reformist-centrist organizations do not really depend upon statutory clauses, but rather upon the spirit that animates our own friends, their resoluteness, their inner cohesion, their capacity to relentlessly oppose the demoralizing centrist influences.

It is precisely from this point of view that the French experience takes on the greatest importance. The most zealous defender of the entry into the SFIO was R. Molinier. Even at that time he was advocating the move with *opportunist* arguments ("Long live organic unity!" etc.). Nevertheless this move was not

---

From *Bulletin Intérieur*, ICL, December 1935–January 1936. Signed "Crux." Translated from the French for the first edition of *Writings of Leon Trotsky (1935-36)* by Candida McCollam. The recipients of this letter were not divulged in the ICL bulletin. But it is likely that it was written for the Polish Bolshevik-Leninists, who had entered the Polish Socialist Party (PPS) in November.

only necessary, but salutary. Before its entry the French section was in a state of complete stagnation. The opponents of the entry were precisely those elements who were satisfied with the group's vegetating passively, and who began more and more opportunistically to adapt to the united front [between the CP and the SFIO] from the outside. The split and its subsequent effects obviously damaged the political results of the entry. In spite of this, everyone, including yesterday's opponents, had to admit that the move that had been taken was correct. The first seven or eight months of the Bolshevik-Leninist activity within the SFIO was their best period. For the first time, they were able to present their analysis and their slogans before a larger audience, test their Marxist superiority over their opponents, and at the same time recognize their own tactical and organizational deficiencies and eliminate them by making changes in their practice. The culminating point was the Mulhouse congress (June 1935). For the youth, this period of "prosperity" lasted much longer and gave much greater results.

But here a turning point arose. The bureaucracy knew exactly how to assess our group's danger. Even at Mulhouse Léon Blum was pronouncing his readiness to achieve "organic unity" without the Bolshevik-Leninists. This warning frightened those (in R. Molinier's circle) who, exhilarated by the initial successes, were anticipating a long period of untroubled activity within the reformist party. And it was precisely these elements, leaning on new allies and semi-allies on the right, who began to exercise a very big influence on the political line of our group. All the warnings and exhortations (they really were not lacking) had no effect for some time.

Another factor of decisive importance was added to this: the threat of war. The social-patriotic wave, greatly reinforced by the treason of the Stalinists, enabled the SFIO apparatus to exert tenfold pressure on the left wing. Zyromsky, head of the traditional left wing, had succeeded in collaborating on social-patriotic theses on the war with the Menshevik leader Dan, and at the same time was a public defender of Stalinism within the SFIO.[20] Following several hesitations (for example, he declared: "Struggle against Trotskyism is the sign of a reactionary tendency"), the left centrist Marceau Pivert revealed himself to be a SAPist, that is, the most inveterate enemy of the Bolshevik-Leninists and the cover for the leading social-patriotic clique. By way of his Radical friends, the bourgeoisie made it known to Mr. Léon Blum that on issues concerning war and peace it did not tolerate jokes. Léon Blum himself made this known to the left. At the Lille congress (July 1935) the expulsions of the Bolshevik-Leninists began.

At that moment, if not earlier, our group should have understood that no feats of magic could save us from the combined attack of the bourgeois and social-patriotic apparatuses. The only slogan was: *Relentless revolutionary offensive against the apparatuses of treason, under the banner of the Fourth International.*

If this political line, the only correct one, had been applied six months ago without hesitation, consistently and courageously, the French section would be in an incomparably better position today than it now is. Unfortunately, this was not the case. It was precisely at this time that the opportunist group around R. Molinier gained a thoroughly pernicious influence: leaning on the psychological inertia of the first period already past, advocating and explaining adaptation and concessions, and sliding more and more toward the right, it finally openly betrayed. Only at this point did the majority of the group pull itself together.

Instinctively, the youth group had followed a more intransigent line after the Lille congress, and one that was consequently more correct. But they had been systematically sabotaged and somewhat demoralized by Molinier's group.

We are now at the end of this second period. It still is not possible to draw up an exact balance sheet. But one thing can be said with absolute certainty: In spite of the two splits, both at the time of the entry and the time of the exit, as well as big mistakes and hesitations, the group did conclude the SFIO chapter with a large and incontestable gain. The group has increased in size; it has a significant youth organization; it learned how to produce a mass weekly paper; and what is perhaps still more important, it has acquired precious practical experience.

Comrades can draw important lessons from the French experience:

1. Entry into a reformist centrist party in itself does not include a long perspective. It is only a stage which, under certain conditions, can be limited to an episode.

2. The crisis and the threat of war have a double effect. First, they create the conditions in which the entry itself becomes possible in a general way. But, on the other hand, they force the ruling apparatus, after many sharp fluctuations, to resort to expelling the revolutionary elements (just as the ruling class after long vacillations finds itself forced to resort to fascism).

3. Entry at the present moment, one year later than in France—and what a year!—could mean that the duration would

not be too long. But this by no means decreases the importance of the entry: in a short period an important step forward can also be made. But what is necessary, especially in light of the French experience, is to free ourselves of illusions in time; to recognize in time the bureaucracy's decisive attack against the left wing, and defend ourselves from it, not by making concessions, adapting, or playing hide-and-seek, but by a revolutionary offensive.

4. What has been said above does not at all exclude the task of "adapting" to workers who are in the reformist parties, by teaching them new ideas in the language they understand. On the contrary, this art must be learned as quickly as possible. But one must not, under the pretext of reaching the ranks, make principled concessions to the top centrists and left centrists (like the SAP, which, in the name of the "masses," prostrates itself before the reformists).

5. Devote the most attention to the youth.

6. The decisive condition of success during this new chapter is still firm ideological cohesion and perspicacity toward our entire international experience.

The Appeal "To Revolutionary Organizations and Groups"
January 4, 1936

To the Central Committee of the GBL

Dear Comrades:

Before I make some critical but secondary remarks on the draft of the appeal "To revolutionary organizations and groups" (December 30, 1935), I want to ask the question: What can be the meaning of this appeal to the *Commune* group, which is proposing (in its own way) fusion with *Révolution*?

Let us leave aside for the moment the fact that the leaders of *La Commune* are deserters from our own organization. The question

From the archives of James P. Cannon. By permission of the Library of Social History in New York. Translated by Naomi Allen. The final text of the appeal "For a Revolutionary Party of the Proletariat," published in the January 26, 1936, *La Vérité,* was described as "an open letter upon which the GBL and the JSR base their appeal for the constitution of a new party."

of desertion is separate. But *La Commune*, as a centrist, confused, and contradictory organization, exists independently from the measures that have been taken and that have yet to be taken toward the deserters. But I believe that your appeal to *La Commune* (not to the deserters) has the following meaning: "You propose that we merge our newspapers? Very well. We are quite ready to prepare for and facilitate this task of revolutionary regroupment. But the Marxist newspaper cannot be based on a few slogans that are deliberately vague or conjunctural and transitory. A mass newspaper is the instrument of the Marxist party in preparation. A newspaper must have a complete program. We are proposing the draft of that program. We consider a discussion of this draft, and especially of the slogans of the new party and the Fourth International, to be a preliminary condition not for collaboration on this or that point with this or that organization, but for the fusion of the mass newspapers, that is, for organic unity, these two things being equivalent."

Unity is an excellent thing. But demarcation on the question of the Marxist program must precede unity (fusion of the mass newspapers) in order for that unity to be honest and long lasting.

From the same point of view, *Révolution* could very well respond to the sugary and hypocritical proposition of *La Commune* in this sense: "The four paragraphs of *La Commune*'s platform—which moreover change every week—are absolutely insufficient to guide a mass newspaper, especially in our complex, catastrophic epoch, which is so rich in changes and turns. The Seine Alliance is now in a discussion preparing its program, which will at the same time be the program of our mass newspaper. We, *Révolution*, will be very pleased if you will adopt the same Marxist program, which is the only condition on our part for the fusion of the two papers."

This clear and sound attitude will necessarily destroy once and for all the machinations of Molinier and Company, which are directed not only against the GBL and the youth but also against the sincere and naive members of *La Commune* itself.

It is clear, on the other hand, that we cannot tolerate in our ranks elements that use the authority of the Central Committee of the GBL with the left centrists, and at the same time use the support of the left centrists, whom they have deceived, to extort "parity" with the GBL and with the youth, where they remain a hopeless minority.

The letters that R. Molinier writes me—I have received three since his betrayal—are only self-indictments. They demonstrate that he seeks only to add to the confusion in order to cover up his political and moral bankruptcy. If he had even a small vestige of revolutionary scruples, he would have to resign immediately from the workers' movement, retire to the background, reflect, study, and then seek to resume his place in the revolutionary ranks. But this personal question no longer concerns us. He has been expelled from the IS and from the plenum. I too voted for his expulsion. The matter is settled. Now you must settle the matter of those who follow Molinier instead of the ICL.

The formal separation of the deserters is the preliminary condition for a reasonable and independent policy toward the Revolutionary Action Groups. By their heterogeneous composition they are not at all suited to serve as the basis for a mass newspaper. Their slogans are in part confused, in part deliberate lies. (The lies come not from the rank and file but from the leaders; especially from the former Bolshevik-Leninists who are trying to hide their bankruptcy.) But after weeding out the deserters, in my opinion, our comrades could participate in these groups (if they are worth the effort) to raise our slogans and also to expose the adventurers within them, who could give these groups quite a dangerous orientation in the future.

Some conciliators are frightened by the split. But in revolutionary politics it is necessary to take facts as they are. The first great social-patriotic pressure has uncovered everything that was inconsistent, or even rotten, in our own ranks. It is necessary to take the facts as they are. To allow the Molinier group to perpetuate its confusion would mean gangrene.

Now to the text of the appeal itself. I have too little time to analyze it more closely. I restrict myself to several remarks that may be secondary but are important:

1. (page 1) *All* the signers of the Open Letter should be listed (as well as the different youth), not only the initiators. Comrade Adolphe [Rudolf Klement] must carefully establish the list of signers.

2. (page 2) "The powerful *antifascist* sentiment of the people . . ." Today, the word *antifascist* is useful only to muddle people's minds. It has no meaning. It covers up for the "People's Front." It must be ridiculed, and not used seriously, above all in programmatic documents.

3. (page 3) "The CP is . . . a dead sect." The CP has nothing in common with a sect, which is a scientific designation. It would be idiotic to call the leading party of the USSR a "sect." There are sects where the internal discussion is permanent (for example,

Mot-Dag). There are mass formations whose internal life is almost completely stifled (the CGT, for example), and which are not sects at all. This abuse of terminology must stop.

4. (page 4) "Thus the GBL, and then the Young Socialists . . ." etc. This formulation lacks precision. It is necessary to say that the Bolshevik-Leninists entered the SFIO without the slightest illusion about the possibility of regenerating this party, given its miserable social composition and the hereditary demoralization of its omnipotent apparatus. The experience helped the revolutionary socialist youth and adults to reach analogous conclusions.

5. (page 3) "The internal regime in the SP is rapidly being modeled after that in the CP." The formulation is not felicitous. In any case, it will seem exaggerated. The experience of the GBL and of the youth demonstrated the "real" (that is, the false) nature of democracy in the SFIO and its absolute limits: it ends where revolutionary action begins. After that irrefutable demonstration, the function of Pivertism clearly emerged in all its ignominy. It decks itself out in all the revolutionary slogans, but for each dose of "poison" it provides an immediate antidote: the general strike, arming [of the workers], defeatism, etc. . . . but all this with the authorization of Léon Blum. It is necessary in a few lines to expose more clearly the demoralizing function of Pivertism (SAPism).

6. (page 3) "To follow us on the road to the new party . . ." A more modest formulation would be preferable. For example: "Together with us . . ."

7. (pages 3-4) In the first paragraph of the summary of the platform, you speak of the dictatorship of the proletariat in general and of the committees of action that are necessary today. It is necessary to separate these two ideas and speak more of the committees of action later on, in a special paragraph, and in a clearer and more concrete way.

8. In the same paragraph, you say, in parentheses: "Paris Commune, soviets . . ." In a whole series of letters I have insisted on the fact that it is impermissible, when speaking of the organizational form of the government, to identify the Commune with soviets. The Commune was the democratic municipality. It is therefore necessary to choose between soviets and the Commune. The revolutionists of 1871 wanted to *combine* their "soviet" of yesteryear (the central committee of the National Guard) and the Commune (the democratic municipality). They only created more of a mess by this hodgepodge. In 1917 in Petrograd, after the conquest of power, we had the soviet and the

democratic municipality. Despite the fact that the Bolshevik Party absolutely dominated the commune, we dissolved it in favor of the soviet. It is *La Commune* that speaks of government based on local communes. This formulation of a democratic municipal federalism is most agreeable to the Bakuninists or to the Proudhonists. It has nothing in common with the dictatorship of the proletariat and soviets as its instruments. This is a fundamental question. Instead of combating *La Commune* on this level too, you have adopted part of its errors.

9. (page 4) "The absolute denial of all national defense *of capitalist regimes.*" It would be better to say: *for the imperialist countries.* Egypt and China are both capitalist and colonial. National defense of them is a revolutionary duty.

Firmness and Concessions
January 7, 1936

Why not accept this proposal? . . . The trip can be mutually informative. This *outward* concession to the conciliators will achieve the best results, because Molinier obviously will gain nothing from it, but on the contrary, when he returns his situation will be much more difficult. The Central Committee will thus definitively demonstrate its goodwill toward the conciliators. To round off an essentially firm policy by such "concessions" of form has always had its advantages.

From *L'Organe de masse.* Signed "Crux." A letter to "D." In the beginning of January a group of more than twenty conciliators from both *La Commune* and the GBL proposed to send Molinier and a representative of the GBL Central Committee to Norway for discussions with Trotsky. "D" was Leon Sedov, Trotsky's son and a member of the IS.

Reply to Conciliators
January 8, 1936

Comrades:

In your collective letter you totally abandon the question of the program, that is, you put yourselves on the same level as Molinier-Frank. Under those conditions, your so-called spirit of conciliation is nothing but a camouflage which must facilitate *La Commune*'s recruiting.

To be sure, you provide a refuge for your program, especially in *La Vérité*. But in the "mass paper," you replace the Marxist program with opportunist improvisation. The English bourgeoisie has always kept the House of Lords in order to maintain the "great traditions." But to act on the masses it relies upon the House of Commons. You practice the same double bookkeeping.

You state that I am not well informed: the youth are supposedly not that strong, etc. But people who seek numbers at any price must choose *Le Populaire* or *l'Humanité*, which are real "mass papers," that is, real papers of mass demoralization. People who seek the Marxist basis, for a paper also, must decide for the GBL and the youth linked to the GBL. As for *La Commune*, it is zero, in terms of numbers as well as of principles.

You propose that two comrades come here to meet with me. I have never refused to meet with comrades, not even with former comrades, when it is a matter of aiding the efforts of our national and international tendency. I am at your disposal in the present case as well. Naturally, it can only be a matter of personal explanations that could in no way alter the decisions made by the responsible bodies.

My best wishes for your Bolshevik-Leninist regeneration.

Leon Trotsky

From *Bulletin Intérieur,* GBL, no. 11, January 6, 1936. Translated by Mary Gordon.

Bureaucratic Pigheadedness
January 14, 1936

Your worst enemy appeals to a person who is entirely on your side. What should you reply? "Very well! Crux's opinion is important to you. It is important to us also. Let's go listen to him. . . ." What could be wrong—not from the point of view of bureaucratic pigheadedness but from the point of view of reason—with listening to the opinion and advice of an older comrade, before making a final decision? . . . But the . . . bureaucrat . . . replies: "We cannot accept any arbitration." What has this got to do with arbitration? . . . This formal side of the affair is not worth an eggshell. . . . This proposal by Raymond's supporters should have been seized with both hands and exploited thoroughly. . . .

If each one had been invited separately and dealt with in an official meeting with minutes, it would have been possible to get to know the different groupings and tendencies and to become thoroughly familiar with the differences among them. . . .

Molinier wanted to demonstrate his "goodwill." People will learn only through their own experience that behind that "goodwill" is hiding ill will. . . . The correct policy would have shown Molinier to be bankrupt a long time ago, but as it is his bankruptcy will not be demonstrated for months, because you are helping him with all your might.

From *L'Organe de masse.* Signed "Crux." A letter to "D" (Leon Sedov).

A New Situation Exists
January 31, 1936

You see only Molinier, whereas on the political plane what exists is a *new* organization for the Fourth International. This organization is the product of earlier political and organizational mistakes. But that doesn't matter. It exists.

A "statement" by the Amsterdam secretariat would be a

From *L'Organe de masse.* Signed "Crux." An excerpt from a letter to Jean Rous.

gesture of bureaucratic powerlessness.[21] What can they say? That Molinier is an adventurer? That *La Commune* should change its orientation? But everyone now will judge *La Commune* according to its *new* orientation, based on the Open Letter for the Fourth International. How is it possible not to see that there is a new situation (created by the old mistakes) that demands a somewhat more serious intervention and one that is more comprehensible to the outside world than a futile statement?

Politically, a new grouping for the Fourth International exists and demands a clear and flexible attitude on our part if we want to avoid accumulating more difficulties by bureaucratic obstinacy.

Molinier's New Ploy
March 1, 1936

Dear Comrade:

I must confess that I do not believe you are making good use of your time, sending me letters full of insults against our national and international organization, which you deliberately deserted. My mind is made up, and not even very strong language is going to change it. During these troubled times anyone can create an organization—without a program, without ideas, without perspectives, and without international ties—but such an organization is going to collapse like a house of cards at the first serious shock. We are an international organization. The workers who turn toward the Fourth International will find their way toward us.

When your group threw overboard its improvised "program" in favor of the Open Letter, I said to myself: maybe they have understood the crime they have committed. In that case they will address themselves to the Secretariat of the Fourth International in order to try to make at least partial amends. But it turns out that this is not the case. You create a "Committee for the Fourth International" while turning your back on the very same Fourth International. But allow me to tell you that our international organization has too high an opinion of its mission to tolerate

From *Bulletin Intérieur,* GBL, no. 12, March 18, 1936. Translated by Mary Gordon. This was a letter to a member of the Molinier group who had written to Trotsky after it abandoned its makeshift program and declared itself in favor of the Open Letter for the Fourth International.

such conduct. We may be a little slow (precisely because we wanted to allow the most reasonable elements, or rather the least unreasonable ones, to retrace their steps), but we will find effective means against these procedures, which have nothing in common with ours. Since you address yourself to me, I can only repeat that I do not have personal politics: my activity is indissolubly linked to the IS in Geneva and the bureau of the Fourth International in Amsterdam.

In short: you can expect no intervention on my part until you yourselves come to the understanding that you cannot keep to yourselves, and that you are obliged to look very humbly for the road toward the organization of the Fourth International.

The Most Inept Policy Imaginable
March 4, 1936

It is not a political program . . . to say "We don't want to have anything to do with Molinier." Because it is not a matter of Molinier but of an important group, *La Commune*. This group came into existence because of the errors of our section. It is possible to change an incorrect policy, but the material consequences of the past period do not disappear with this change; they continue to block the way. It is incontestable that Molinier in the past months has been more harmful to our movement than he could be useful in several years. . . . By your whole policy in the past period you have only helped him. . . . There is talk of a congress of the new party, but you proceed as though *La Commune* did not exist. If you want to wipe it out you must declare a holy war, in words and on paper. . . . But to simply remain silent about *La Commune* is certainly the most inept and dangerous policy imaginable.

From *L'Organe de masse*. Signed "Crux." Translated by Naomi Allen. This was a letter to Ruth Fischer.

Preface to Part Three

Spring 1936 was a time of hope, ferment, and political awakening for the workers of France. In neighboring Spain the year-old People's Front routed the right-wing parties in parliamentary elections and took over the government in February; if it could be done in Spain, why not in France? On the other side, Hitler marched his troops into the Rhineland in March, remilitarizing the region against the provisions of the Versailles treaty and strengthening the social-patriotic rationale for the People's Front in France. In the same month the two major French labor federations, the CGT and the CGTU, ended a fifteen-year split of the union movement by a merger based essentially on the People's Front program. At the end of April and the start of May, French parliamentary elections were held and were decisively won by the parties of the People's Front. The SFIO won 21 percent of the vote, increasing its seats in the Chamber of Deputies from 97 to 146. The CP got around 15 percent, increasing its delegation from 10 seats to 72. The Radical Socialists fell from 159 seats to 116. Out of 598 seats in the Chamber, the People's Front parties held 378. As the largest party, the SFIO demanded and received responsibility for the new cabinet, with Léon Blum as premier. But the workers did not wait for him to take office. In May and June they launched the biggest strike wave the country had ever known. Displaying a spirit of combativity that spread panic among the capitalists, they introduced new forms of struggle (sitdown strikes, factory committees), and they poured into the unions, whose membership jumped from around one million to five million in a few months. In Norway, Trotsky wrote an article entitled "The French Revolution Has Begun."

But the incipient revolution was arrested and diverted into safe channels by the SFIO and the Stalinists. The French section of the ICL was unprepared for the upsurge it had been predicting and proved unable to become a revolutionary pole in the strike wave by attracting support for a clear class-struggle line as against the class-collaborationist treachery of the traditional workers' parties. In part, its failure was due to governmental repression and the very unfavorable relationship of forces, but it was also due to the fact that the GBL and the PCI were still locked in factional combat when the working class began to move and their attention was only partially focused on the political openings around them.

The GBL leadership's response to the PCI congress at the start of March was predictable; but the IS, which understood that the split had been poorly executed and inadequately motivated, intervened to say that as a result of the *Commune* group's new orientation since January unification might now be possible and should be explored. Without pretending enthusiasm the GBL leaders concurred and indefinitely postponed the projected April 12 conference in order to conduct negotiations with the PCI. Both sides often acted more as if they were justifying a split than pursuing a reunification: they were belligerent, often over trivial details, and the negotiations were broken off or suspended more than once. During one of these intervals, both sides ran candidates in the April-May parliamentary elections; although they were on the road to a unification the GBL leaders refused to collaborate with the PCI in these campaigns, where neither side got more than a few hundred votes per candidate. Agreement was finally reached despite mutual suspicion and recriminations. On May 31 the GBL and the JSR met together and set up a short-lived organization, the Revolutionary Workers Party (POR), which then met jointly with the PCI the following day to merge as the Internationalist Workers Party (POI), the new French section of the ICL. The delegates were reported to be representing 615 members.

The unification was not much better led than the split had been. Most differences were left unresolved—even undiscussed— or postponed to a congress announced for August 15. The Central Committee was composed of seven members from the GBL, seven from the PCI, and three from the JSR, which put the PCI people in a minority there and in the Political Bureau. At the demand of the PCI it was agreed that "personal" cases, meaning the role of Molinier, would not be taken up at the congress; the ex-PCI people put him on the Central Committee but, at his request, not on the Political Bureau. The adoption of a party constitution was deferred to the August congress, which was an almost certain invitation to contention and chaos. The party's paper got a compromise name, neither *La Vérité* nor *La Commune* but *La Lutte ouvrière,* but the spirit of compromise was not much in evidence at the congress. Some PCI members, regarding a unification where they became a minority as a capitulation, refused to participate, while those who attended did so because after their five-month pro-unity campaign they saw no political alternative; apprehensive about the outcome, they resolved as they left the congress not to let themselves be pushed around as a minority.

The editors of this book have been unable to locate any letters by Trotsky about the crisis of the French section between March 4 (at the end of Part Two) and the article he wrote on June 7, a few days after the POI's founding congress. Molinier later complained that during this period Trotsky had not written anything supporting the proposed unification or done anything to overcome obstacles to it. In any case Trotsky did not withhold an opinion once the merger had taken place. His June 7 article was in the form of an introduction to a pamphlet by his secretary in Norway, Erwin Wolf, writing under the pseudonum Nicolle Braun, which was entirely about the French crisis and Trotsky's differences with the French leadership since the Mulhouse congress (printed as Appendix A in this book). Trotsky said he could "only be delighted" by the unification but he was not very optimistic about the future, especially since those who had lightmindedly split from the national and international organizations did not seem to have learned anything from their experience. Nor did he conceal his opinion that the non-Molinierist leaders had missed an opportunity for serious growth in a prerevolutionary situation. To prevent such harmful adventures and such weaknesses, he said, the leaders needed to be actively supervised by the ranks of the French section and by the international organization.

The unification was doomed from the start, given the attitudes on both sides. Political differences, small or large, were obscured or submerged by organizational gripes and suspicions. The Central Committee majority acted as if it did not expect the unification to last and was only going through the motions before the minority inevitably stepped out of line. With the first Central Committee meeting in June, the Molinierists began to complain that they were being discriminated against factionally in the assignment of responsible posts; they pledged they would still abide by Central Committee decisions but started making the point that the ex-GBL did not really represent a majority of the party. From the time that Trotsky's June 7 introduction was published, they accused him of leading a campaign behind the scenes to drive them out of the movement because they lacked the docility he allegedly demanded in the ICL.

The blow-up came over Molinier's personal business activities. After the merger the IS reminded the Central Committee that Molinier, whom the IS had expelled in December, was only provisionally a member of the French section. Soon after, it adopted a resolution ruling that if Molinier wanted to support the POI by his business activities, he should do so outside of the party, and if he wanted to be in the party he should discontinue his business affairs immediately, not just in words but in fact. The Central Committee adopted the IS position. Three Molinierists, including Frank, denounced the resolution for irresponsibly threatening the security of party members who had for years worked to strengthen the organization financially. Then they presented the Political Bureau with a plan to set up a financial commission to find badly needed material resources for the party aside from normal income through dues, pledges, literature sales, etc.; the party would take complete responsibility for this commission's decisions and actions under the Central Committee's control; since the commission's work would have a clandestine character, loose talk and rumors about it by members would have to be prohibited; and only the Political Bureau and the Control Commission would have the right to audit the financial commission's work.

In the eyes of the Molinierists this appeared to be an excellent party-building proposal. To the Central Committee majority it was a brazen repetition of Molinier's previous efforts to force the section through financial pressure to accept his policies. The IS called it an attempt to cover up Molinier's shady business affairs. The Central Committee promptly suspended the three Molinierists. Molinier himself submitted a written statement agreeing to cease his "business affairs." He also attended a meeting of the Central Committee where he discussed this and the proposed financial commission. When minutes of this discussion were sent out, the Molinierists charged that they had been falsified and, for this reason, refused to attend a meeting of the Central Committee called for July 12. The Central Committee majority replied just as heatedly that the charge of falsification of the minutes was a vile slander typical of the minority.

Trotsky's letters to France during this period dealt with both general political problems and the section's internal life. Most of his articles about the May-June strike wave and its aftermath will be found in *Leon Trotsky on France,* but Part Three also contains valuable advice about problems arising after the first wave of strikes had subsided, tactics toward police repression, and how to take into account the masses' initial confidence in the Blum government (letters of June 21, July 11, and July 19). After establishing formal arrangements about his literary collaboration with the new POI (June 12), he registered the complaint that the first issue of *Lutte ouvrière* looked too much like *La Commune* (June 18), urged the POI to open its own printshop and pay more attention to what was going on inside the CP, and angrily protested a decision, initiated by Molinier, to hold open meetings of the Central Committee (June 19). Although several of these letters contain severe criticisms of Molinier, it was not until July 11, after the Molinierists had annouced their boycott of the coming Central Committee meeting, that Trotsky expressed his judgment that Molinier did not belong in the POI and called for action to oust him (July 11).

While this letter was in the mail, the Molinier group decided to send a delegation to visit Trotsky: Molinier himself and Desnots, also called Le Ricard, who was supposed to express the views of the ex-PCI members who had never belonged to the old GBL. They met with Trotsky and took notes of the discussion, which they dated July 16 and later published. Their version of that discussion is included here, with the warning that this version was prepared at a time of intense factional heat and was never verified by Trotsky himself.

On July 14, while Molinier was in Norway and the Molinierists absented themselves, the Central Committee met and expelled him for having once again used financial blackmail against the French section. Its resolution noted that he had indicated that he would appeal to the ICL, and therefore his case would be settled by the ICL's coming international conference. The Central Committee also voted to postpone indefinitely the national congress that had been scheduled for August 15. Later in July the international conference, with only one negative vote, endorsed the expulsion, warned that any collaboration with Molinier was incompatible with membership in the POI, and urged the POI minority to conduct itself henceforth in a loyal manner. The Molinierists had no intention of remaining in the French section without their leader. They soon withdrew from the POI, reconstituted the PCI, and resumed publication of *La Commune*. The split continued for another seven years.

PART THREE
REUNIFICATION AND NEW SPLIT
(June-July 1936)

Introduction to
The Mass Paper
June 7, 1936

Comrade Braun's work on the latest major crisis of the French section seems to me to be of great interest and value to the French section itself, as well as to all the other sections. After the study had been completed, a unification took place between our section and *La Commune,* the group that had left it, and naturally we can only be delighted by this. But the unification does not by any means signify that the organization will be cured of its infirmities. The split did not happen by accident. The splitters got shipwrecked. But nothing proves that they have all drawn an important lesson from their shipwreck. Anyone who knows the main leaders cannot have any illusions about the future. France's development in the coming period will be very rich in crises, and each turning point within the crisis situation can bring about opportunist or adventurist reactions within the leading layer of the French section. If I feel it my duty to express this so bluntly, it is because my observations over the course of seven years do not allow me to entertain an excessive optimism on this score.

Comrade Braun analyzes carefully, and, in my opinion, in a completely objective manner, the heated correspondence between the leading French comrades and myself during the latest crisis. But that crisis was far from the first, and in the course of the many preceding crises the correspondence has been at least as heated and as plentiful. At present, after seven years of experience, I cannot say that my epistolary efforts have had positive results. I do not want to go into the reasons for that here. Perhaps I was unable to find the necessary arguments. In

---

From *L'Organe de masse.* Signed "Crux." Translated by Art Young.

any case, it is really time to abandon attempts at convincing certain comrades and inducing them through private letters to understand reality better. That is why I made my archives available to Comrade Braun, so that every member of the French section as well as of the other sections might learn the necessary lessons from the latest crisis and obtain an exact picture of the role of this or that comrade—something which, in the selection of a leadership, is of the utmost importance.

We have called the political stage which is now ending in France *prerevolutionary*. During that stage, our French section's task was to get up the necessary momentum. The situation was difficult, but not unfavorable. If, after the Mulhouse congress, the French section had unleashed the vigorous revolutionary internationalist offensive that all circumstances dictated, it would now have a very much larger membership and an infinitely greater authority and capacity for struggle. Here we now have in our own history an important example of an opening that was missed, or rather bungled; for—and I think Braun's work proves this—the leadership did everything possible to take as little advantage as it could of this opening.

How can we avoid repeating similar harmful adventures, on the one hand, and such weaknesses, on the other? Through active supervision by the ranks, that is, by the members of the French section, and through equally active supervision by our international organization. The aim of this document is precisely to furnish the necessary bases for such supervision.

Despite all these difficulties, the French section now has about five times as many members as it had at the time of the entry and is able to carry out much more work. But it would certainly be two or three times stronger today if the leadership had acted in a genuinely Bolshevik fashion. That proves how necessary it is not to make fetishes out of purely tactical or organizational turns. In the first place, certain persons didn't want to enter the SP under any conditions; and then later, some persons—usually it was the same ones—didn't want to leave it under any conditions. There they are, the two sides of the same conservative sectarian mentality.

Let us hope that in this respect the Belgian experience will be much more positive. In any case, the comrades who belong to reformist and centrist parties (England, Poland, America, etc.) must draw the necessary conclusions from the French experience: entry into other and even opponent organizations not only opens up considerable possibilities but also harbors dangers. Only obstinate and thoroughgoing conservatives can assert that entry is inadmissible, whatever the circumstances. But the attempt to make entry a cure-all leads inevitably to the brink of betrayal, as we can see and experience precisely by means of the French example.

First of all, we must all learn not to have too much confidence in those leading comrades, even if they return to us, who at the first opportunity express their discontent by quitting the national and international organization and considering themselves snipers for as long as they please. We must not entrust them with important posts except after a long and serious test. *That is what the self-preservation of any really revolutionary organization demands.*

To the French comrades and particularly to the youth, who have come to us so courageously from the reformist party, we should perhaps say again: although this study is devoted to the past, it must not serve to revive the differences of yesterday, but, on the contrary, to avoid their repetition tomorrow or the day after. Every member must, *from this point of view,* study carefully and without bias the documentation that has been submitted. In the last analysis, this can only be salutary for the French section.

Terms for Collaboration
with the French Section
June 12, 1936

Dear Comrade B:
I find in your letter no answer to my question, which is, nonetheless, quite simple. Given the extreme seriousness of the situation and the political responsibility that I bear before the French workers by my political collaboration with your paper, I want to be assured that neither my name nor my writings will be abused. I can accept collaboration only on the condition that the ideas and suggestions I consider decisive be published in your paper, under my personal responsibility, with all the reservations

From *Bulletin Intérieur*, POI, no. 2, June 14, 1936. Signed "L.T." Translated by Mary Gordon. Trotsky's letter was in reply to a question from J. Boitel, POI administrative secretary, about differences Trotsky had alluded to. The Central Committee accepted Trotsky's proposal in this letter.

and criticisms that, should the occasion arise, you would find necessary. Like other comrades, I happened to collaborate in emigration with the Russian press under the same conditions.

I do not at all want to oblige you to publish *all* my articles: you will choose what suits you; but when I have something to say to .the French workers, I must have the opportunity to do so in the next issue of the paper, even if the editor does not agree with me. That's all! (My last two articles, "The Decisive Stage" and "The French Revolution Has Begun," in my opinion, have this character of political urgency and I demand their unabridged publication.[22])

As for the differences I had with you, they are revealed in a study by Comrade Braun with my introduction: it is mostly a matter of your systematic concessions to the pernicious politics of the Molinier group. I have nothing to add on that subject for the moment. On current questions, I want to completely give up personal correspondence, which has taken too much of my time and which, as experience shows, has minimal results. From now on I want to replace this correspondence with a few leadership comrades by articles intended for all the readers of your paper. That is why I beg you to cable me a "yes" or "no" answer so that I can make consequent arrangements.

My best greetings,
L.T.

The First Number of Lutte ouvrière
June 18, 1936

To the Central Committee, POI

Dear Comrades:

I have finally received the first number of your paper, *Lutte ouvrière*. What is striking at first glance is that it represents an imitation of *La Commune*. What is the purpose of this? Do you want to indicate that you carry on the tradition of this ill-fated

From *Bulletin Intérieur*, POI, no. 2, June 14, 1936. Signed "L.T." Translated by Mary Gordon. A majority of the POI Central Committee shared Trotsky's complaints about the format and other features of the new paper.

paper? It puzzles me. At any rate, I believe that after the zigzags, the twistings, and the tricks of *La Commune*, which tremendously damaged the idea of the Fourth International in France, many readers—and I count myself among them—are disgusted to see on the masthead of the paper this histrionic fellow rushing—one never knows where—with his banner—one never knows which. If this assimilation with *La Commune* is being accomplished with your agreement, please insert this letter in your next issue of *Lutte ouvrière* so that I might at least fulfill my responsibility. If it is only a matter of bad faith from the group which, after its fiasco, wants to impose itself through inexcusable conduct, please insert this letter in the internal bulletin, with necessary explanations on your part.

My best greetings,
L.T.

A Matter of Life and Death
June 19, 1936

To the Central Committee, POI

Dear Comrades:

1. We received the first number of *Lutte ouvrière* after a long delay. That proves that the mailing is still badly done. This was always the misfortune of *La Vérité*. I believe that the names of the comrades responsible for the editorial work, printing, and mailing should be published in the paper. The organization must be able to control its leaders.

2. You announced in *Révolution* my pamphlet on the new Soviet constitution. As far as I understand, it was just another plan that was not realized. This is not the first time such methods have been seen in our French section. You announce publicly the forthcoming appearance of *Lutte de classes*, of *Vérité*, of a pamphlet, of *Quatrième Internationale*, and then no more is heard of it. You simply deceive the reader for one or two weeks. The serious worker will say: If these people are so uncertain of their own affairs, how can I have confidence in their political

From the archives of James P. Cannon, in a translation from *Bulletin Intérieur*, POI, no. 2, June 14, 1936. By permission of the Library of Social History in New York.

statements? I find such methods purely criminal because they sap the future of the organization.

3. For several years I have insisted upon the necessity of the French section's having its own printshop, which could be of inestimable value for the revolutionary period. Unfortunately, in this question, as in all others, I was unable to convince the leadership. Why? Because even the meaning of a revolutionary organization is not understood. Naville unfortunately has not the slightest interest in these things. Molinier considers the revolutionary organization from the point of view of a "promoter": colored posters, kiosks, phony publicity—in short, bluff, which costs a great deal but produces nothing. The revolutionary organization must base itself not on quasicapitalist methods but on the devotion of its members, on untiring work, intensive and at the same time systematic; on its own printshop, with two printers entirely devoted to the organization; on a fast and efficient mailing system; on energetic and tireless salespeople; on perfect bookkeeping. There is no other way for a revolutionary organization.

La Vérité devoured enormous sums, enough for two printshops. The American comrades, with more modest means, have created a printshop which does magnificent work. Besides the weekly and monthly, it issues 400-page books. And the Americans were neither richer nor more numerous than the French.

You are now suffering repression, which should win you sympathy. Couldn't you start a special collection for the printshop? Better late than never!

4. I found in the internal bulletin your decision to open the doors of the Central Committee to every member of the organization. I confess, I cannot understand this at all. The Central Committee is the revolutionary general staff. How can it sit publicly? You must have in the organization a serious percentage of police agents, Stalinists, GPU agents, etc. These will be the first visitors to the Central Committee. At every session of the Central Committee there are secret or confidential questions. There is the need to discipline different comrades, etc. To have a little "gallery" for the sessions means to *hinder* the normal work of the leading body. I am not at all astonished to find the name of Molinier as the initiator of this disastrous proposal. Is it for purposes of democracy? No! It is for purposes of demagogy and personal intrigues. To provide timely information for the organization; never to take it by surprise; and above all not to dictate its will by financial pressure—these are the most elementary rules of democracy!

I find this question very serious. It is impossible even to correspond with a Central Committee that sits publicly. I propose to settle this question again by a roll-call vote and to publish the result in the internal bulletin. The organization must have the opportunity to control its leaders and their methods. It is the only way to prepare a good selection of comrades for the leadership.

5. I read in the bulletin the statements of Comrades Molinier and Frank concerning your policy. I find them totally false. From the opportunist and capitulatory stage these comrades have passed directly into their "third period."[23] The first counterblow, which is inevitable, will throw them back into the baldest opportunism. In the opportunist period, as at present (the "third period"), Molinier remains faithful to his adventurist conception of revolutionary activity. Since the objective situation requires a mass paper and the organization is not yet capable of creating one, Molinier wants to "promote" one over the head of the organization.

Since the objective situation imposes on the proletariat the struggle for power, Molinier wants to solve this task over the heads of the unions, the existing organizations, and the working class itself. Instead of revolutionary work, he wants to perform some new "miracle." He can only perform a new *fiasco*, which this time can become *disastrous for the organization, if it does not take rigorous measures to force the miracle-makers to submit or get out.*

I use this language because it is a matter of life and death for your organization, which is, in addition, the only lever of the proletarian revolution. This is no time for pleasantries or for adventures. The least indulgence in this respect would be a crime.

The objective situation demands the conquest of power; but this demand is addressed to the proletariat and not to you. You cannot take power in the name of the proletariat—it has not yet given you its mandate. Your task is to win for the revolutionary solution the vanguard of the workers, which is now grouped principally around the Communist Party. Since the Mulhouse congress all your attention and activity should have been bent in this direction. It is necessary to find a language comprehensible to the Communist workers. The moment is extremely propitious. While the leaders turn more and more away from the workers, seeking to win the confidence of the "progressive" bourgeoisie, to persuade it, to convince it, we must try to win the confidence of the Communist ranks. It is necessary to adapt all of your activity, and especially the tone and content of your paper, to this objective. That is also why I proposed your paper be named *Le*

Soviet. After the great strike this name would resound in the
streets of Paris and elsewhere much better than the dull name
Lutte ouvrière. A name corresponding to the situation and to the
consciousness of the Communist workers would be a hundred
times more important than posters, kiosk sales, dubious photomontage, and all the claptrap of petty-bourgeois journalism. The
question of the name is naturally not decisive, but it is very
symptomatic.

6. We must orient ourselves toward the factories, as well as
toward the unions. But it is absurd to think that we will find
virgin territory there. The influence of the Communists must
now be quite great in the unions and in the factories, and it has
yet to pass its high point. It is to this twist in the evolution of the
revolutionary consciousness of the masses that we must adapt
ourselves in advance. *Without losing its character for a single
instant,* the newspaper must accelerate the evolution of the
masses and not thwart it by extravagances.

7. The most important task is to *make thorough preparations*
for the forthcoming party conference. In these preparations full
democracy must have play. To contribute to the preparations for
it, I ask you to publish this letter in the internal bulletin.

Crux [Trotsky]

P.S.—This letter was written before I received the news of the
repressions directed against you by Blum-Salengro. It is not
necessary to state my full solidarity with the comrades under the
threat of repression (which is only beginning) and my certainty
that our comrades shall not lack courage. Nevertheless, I feel
obliged to send this letter as it is. The ills of which I speak are not
and cannot be eliminated by the Socialist-bourgeois repression,
but only by the criticism and action of the organization itself.

Still another question. You sometimes use the formula: "De la
Rocque is at liberty," or *"l'Action française* has not been seized,"
etc. Leave that to *l'Humanité.* Salengro might very well seize
l'Action française or even have de la Rocque arrested. That
doesn't amount to much. We must pose the question quite
differently: "You have promised to dethrone the 200 families?[24]
What is their paper, which systematically prepares for resistance
and which takes care of *l'Action française* like a barking dog in a
chicken coop? It is *le Temps.* To attack the 200 families you must
begin by seizing *le Temps.* Arrest de la Rocque? That's not much.
You must arrest the big magnates of finance capital." You have, I
remember, formulated this slogan, and with good reason.

The fact that *le Petit Journal* gives you free publicity is a very important symptom of the state of mind of the petty bourgeoisie. You should make systematic and clever use of this by sending a press release at every favorable occasion (not too often) and to this end even establish friendly relations (with reporters, etc.). In short, you must make use of the petty-bourgeois press just as Colonel de la Rocque uses *le Temps, le Matin,* etc.

New Stage in the French Revolution
June 21, 1936

To the Central Committee, POI

Dear Comrades:

I hope to outline my assessment of the present situation in France more fully in my next article.[25] But I will be unable to do it for the next several days. I hasten, therefore, to communicate a number of preliminary considerations.

The first wave seems to be calming down. The masses are digesting the experience and determining their gains. The 200 families and their numerous aides are preparing the great revenge, which will not be delayed. We can expect to see lockouts, for which the responsibility will be placed by capital on the government. If, to speak conventionally in "Russian," we call the first wave "the February revolution," then *it is the July events which are being prepared now.* And between February and July there was the not unimportant accident of *April.*[26] Please reread the respective chapters in my *History of the Russian Revolution,* especially what I say about the quasi-inevitability of a partial defeat of the proletariat between its first, rather imaginary, victory and its final, definitive, victory. Without keeping this whole perspective in view, there is the risk of getting lost in details.

You popularized the general strike. The first experiment with it is accomplished. To repeat the slogan now, without definition or concretization, would be a mistake. It is necessary for us to

From the archives of James P. Cannon, in a translation from *Bulletin Intérieur,* POI, no. 2, June 14, 1936. By permission of the Library of Social History in New York.

understand that the next strike will be directed in all likelihood not against the Blum government, *but against its enemies*: the 200 families, the Radicals, the Senate, the upper bureaucracy, the general staff, etc. The strategic art consists in orienting the vanguard toward the inescapability of this new, intense struggle against the enemies of the proletariat outside the People's Front, but also inside the ranks of the People's Front. In short, it is a question of preparing for a new strike just to assure the partial first conquests, not to speak of more ample ones. We do not put Léon Blum in the same bag with the de Wendels and their de la Rocques. We accuse Blum of not understanding or foreseeing the formidable resistance of the de Wendels. We must repeat that despite all of our irreconcilable opposition to the Blum government, the workers will find us in the front lines in the fight against its imperialist enemies. This is a very important distinction, even a decisive one, for the coming period. It is in this sense that systematic propaganda has to be carried on for the second general strike, not to overthrow the government but to break the obstacles before it.

But that is not enough. The first strike took the enemy (and, alas, the friends) unawares. The second strike will meet a formidable retort. A process of selection is taking place now in all domains of social life. The second strike cannot occur spontaneously and without a general staff. It will need an adequate organization. Our agitation must have as its purpose not *accelerating* the outbreak of the second strike, but seriously *preparing* for it. It is quite possible, even likely, that the anarchists and the inexperienced youth are now going to play with the slogan of the general strike. We must not let ourselves be dragged in that direction. On the contrary! We must emphasize the enormous tasks and difficulties of the undertaking. The precondition for the success of a new general strike is factory committees and soviets.

Capitalist provocation can, however, bring the new strike wave sooner than might be desirable from the strategic point of view. We are not pedants. We participate in every revolutionary explosion, even when its chances of success are minimal. But under these circumstances, we do not push the masses to the end—i.e., to the abyss—but on the contrary, we try to withdraw from under fire with our forces more or less intact. At the same time we use the experience of "July" to convince the workers of the necessity of preparing for "October."

The French calendar will be quite different from the Russian

calendar, I am sure, just as its rhythm of events is, but I believe
all the same that the dialectic of revolution—in the most general
sense of the term—will remain the same. That is why I hasten to
communicate to you immediately these hasty considerations.

Crux [Trotsky]

More Difficulties in
the French Section
July 11, 1936

To the Political Bureau

Comrades:

1. The objections of some comrades that in my last letter I
attempted to "dissociate myself" can only make me rejoice [see
"Terms for Collaboration with the French Section"]. They prove
that the rank and file is at last beginning to occupy itself with
surveillance of the leadership. This is a necessary condition for
the cohesiveness of the organization.

However, have I earned these reproaches? Honestly, I am not
sure. The international plenum with my participation announced
the expulsion of R.M. from our organization. The commission
created by the IS under my chairmanship publicly declared that
La Commune and its organization had placed themselves outside
of the Fourth International. After the fusion with the PCI, the IS
declared that it would reaffirm its decision regarding R.M. before
the international conference. Under these conditions R.M., after
failing in his indescribable, unbelievable attempt to foist upon
our organization the name and the paper of his "party,"
nevertheless does leave his stamp upon your paper; that is, he
proves once more that he is making a joke of the formal decisions
of, the obligations undertaken by, and the public opinion of our
international organization, as well as of the national section.

I collaborate on your paper. But I am also a member of the
international plenum. I believe that under these very specific
circumstances it is not only my right, but my duty as well, to

From the archives of James P. Cannon, in a translation from *Bulletin
Intérieur*, POI, no. 2, June 14, 1936. By permission of the Library of Social
History in New York.

"dissociate myself." International discipline prevails in every case over national discipline. If I have carried it out in a form that might, perhaps, offend the democratic sentiments of the organization, I am the first to sincerely regret it, but I hope that this explanation will straighten out the misunderstanding. If you find it of use to yourselves, you are at liberty to publish this explanation in your internal bulletin.

2. I do not believe that Molinier's "business affairs" should be on the agenda of your organization. Whether he discontinues or continues his business is not, to my mind, of great importance. He has made so many worthless promises and assumed so many worthless obligations that one more or less cannot weigh very heavily in the balance. What is necessary is to proclaim the entire incompatibility between his conceptions (the real ones), his methods of acting, his attitude toward the organization as a whole as well as toward individual comrades; *it is all of that* which makes him a destructive factor in the organization.

In the plenum I was the final one to defend, not his methods, which are indefensible, but the necessity for a final attempt at collaboration. Now, the experience of *La Commune* and R.M.'s attitude after the most lamentable fiasco of this treacherous adventure prove in their very essence that there is nothing in common between R.M., on the one hand, and our principles, policy, methods, and rules of revolutionary morality on the other hand—I repeat, nothing in common. The very fact that the whole organization is obliged at every instant to occupy itself with R.M. and not with questions that are infinitely more important shows the incompatibility of R.M. with the revolutionary organization.

No, it is not a matter of his "business affairs" in themselves. It is a question, above all, of the policy of *financial pressure* in his own organization. That fact has been established beyond all dispute. The control commission has formally confirmed it. If the International Secretariat, including the undersigned, consented to the subordination of the R.M. question to the interests of the fusion, it was precisely for the purpose of giving the rank and file, especially the youth, an opportunity to go through experience *of their own* with R.M. It seems to me that this experience has been fully consummated. It is necessary to draw up a *definitive balance sheet*. That is my opinion.

3. As to the political resolution, it will be, to say the least, deficient if it permits a group of comrades to vote for it who only the day before expressed themselves in a contrary sense with particular vehemence, not to say ferocity. This is new proof that

principles mean nothing for R.M. and his group when they are concerned with personal difficulties. They vote for everything, make soft-soaping speeches, and prepare some new plot. A fictitious unanimity achieves nothing in such cases and even prevents the organization from educating itself. It is something like a repetition of the mistakes in the experience before the *La Commune* plot.

4. When I read *l'Humanité* and *Le Populaire* I repeat to myself: it is impossible for our French section not to have striking successes. The report about your discussions on the Lille case made by Fr. shows quite a high level.[27] Under the pressure of great events one learns quickly. What is needed now is a *firm nucleus* in the leadership capable of making decisions, giving directives, and placing the "freelancers," adventurers, and factionalists in a position where they can do no harm.

5. T. has sent you his third article ["Before the Second Stage"]. It is written in a very "objective" tone and is very much restrained in its form. This tone corresponds, it seems to me, to the present transitory period between two different stages. It is necessary to *explain*. Everybody around you must begin to reflect. By the seriousness of our analysis we will win over the best people.

6. I have heard on the radio about Salengro's "buildup" of preparatory measures against the "sit-down" strikers (conference of the prefects, etc.). Conflicts are inevitable. It is the duty of the revolutionists to orient these conflicts toward a *political,* not a *physical,* resolution, that is, toward one as little physical as possible. To be able to find every time the line between spinelessness and anarchic adventurism is not an easy task. Moreover, your influence over the masses is still quite limited. But the worst incidents provoked by the authorities can serve the development of the revolution on the condition that the vanguard knows how, *with the aid of the workers involved,* to throw the responsibility for them onto the shoulders of the class enemy, and at the same time to explain the political lessons that flow from them. The confectionery workers of Lille could, for example, address a manifesto to the workers of France, explaining that it is entirely possible for the workers to run the factories themselves provided that the banks and key industries are in the hands of the people. Some corresponding quotations from the Socialist and Communist programs could then be given and a conclusion drawn up pointing in the direction of a workers' and peasants' government. If the bourgeois Radicals oppose it, then it is

necessary to base oneself on the support of the real people, the four or five million trade unionists, etc. The manifesto need not necessarily criticize the government. It should make some positive proposals to the government in the name of one factory going through a great experience. Such a manifesto could have tremendous repercussions. It will be quoted, criticized, etc., in the entire labor and bourgeois press. If they give in to physical force at the last moment, that is, if the workers allow themselves to be evacuated one by one without entering, naturally, into a battle with the authorities, the manifesto of the factory still would retain all its importance for the future.

I also believe that in such a case the factory (or group of factories) engaged in a struggle, which is for the moment without any way out, could send delegates to plead its cause before the unions and the workers' parties, and naturally also before your own.

7. The TPPS disappeared in its time almost without a trace because *its leadership was a technical and not a political leadership.* They believed that by "action" alone they would win over the workers. But workers, like everyone else, want to understand what they are acting for. The political factor dominates and determines the physical struggle. This is not at all a matter of preaching spinelessness or of seeking to cover up personal cowardice with some learned exegesis. But it is necessary to understand the laws that determine the evolution of the masses. It is necessary to accelerate this evolution with political arguments, not to counteract it with inappropriate feats of courage. (At the same time it must not for one moment be forgotten that in this period there will indeed also be a great need for courage.)

8. It seems to me that you do not engage in special and systematic action in your penetration of the Communist circles. Yesterday I read again, after a considerable lapse of time, *Que faire?* (July 1936). They state that great discontent persists inside the CP. *Que faire?* is absolutely incapable of utilizing it, of orienting it, because this purely academic enterprise has no firm orientation of its own. *A special department* is necessary for the penetration of the Communist ranks. An explosion is inevitable, but if you are not prepared for it in advance, you will be unable— any more than at St-Denis—to profit from it. Isn't it possible to create a special bulletin for information and rumors concerning the life of the Communist Party?

9. To explain, to educate, to prepare public opinion, to furnish

the correct slogans: a paper even of a small format can suffice for this need, if one learns to say what is strictly necessary. Imagine yourselves in a situation in which you have already been driven out of the legal arena. Your illegal paper would of necessity have to be of very small format. But it could at the same time play a very big role, provided it assured the coherence of the organization by means of slogans corresponding to the situation.

10. It is also necessary to avoid another danger, that is, the attempt to impose our own calendar upon events. Toulon and Brest as well as the June strike are improvisations of the working class against all the official organizations, without the knowledge even of your own. What will this magnificent proletariat, so resourceful, so imaginative, so full of verve and of traditions, improvise next? It is necessary to have confidence in it. That is why it is necessary to pursue with the closest attention every move, every symptom, even every false rumor that passes through the working class. It is necessary to organize an information service: newspaper clippings, letters, reports, personal reports, etc. It is necessary for someone to make it his business to tirelessly classify documents, to study them, to trace the curve of the movement, etc. This is the only way to keep our fingers on the pulse of the working class. It is also the only means of building up the different departments of the "general headquarters."

You will perhaps say to me that it is much easier to give general advice than to orient oneself in practice from day to day. To be sure, dear comrades, I will be the last to deny that. Mistakes are inevitable; not to lose one's head or one's courage even in the midst of the worst misfortunes—that is the last bit of advice that I can give you in this letter, which has already overrun its proper length.

Crux [Trotsky]

P.S.—This letter, with the exception of the first point, is not necessarily meant for publication. But you can make whatever use of it that you wish.

Notes from an Interview
by Molinier and Desnots
July 1936

Trotsky: What do you want (*pointing to the July 12 letter*) with all of this? I understand and I do not agree, no matter how much you may twist my arm. In my view the political questions, which are long-standing questions, have stood the test of experience. (*Addressing Le Ricard [Desnots]*) As for the other questions, the personal ones, I have been acquainted with them longer than you have. If you are the majority, you will have the opportunity to fight it out within the organization.

Le Ricard (reproachfully): The party will be destroyed by these internal quarrels.

Trotsky: Rhetoric. Quarrels are human. You sound like Magdeleine Paz. Do you have a remedy for quarrels in your briefcase? I don't!

Le Ricard: It is not just rhetoric. Personal quarrels we can take care of by ourselves. But the nature of these quarrels is different, they are political questions.

Trotsky: You make vague, pathetic statements about the unity of the revolutionary party. . . . I support those who expelled M[olinier]. I am absolutely adamant about this. M. has done the worst disservices to the Bolshevik-Leninist movement in France. The M. clique has changed its position ten times over. I refer to this as a "personal clique" in the Marxist sense of the term, a grouping which surrounds an individual and covers for all his misdeeds despite numerous changes in political position. I have arrived at this position after seven years of experience with the French section. M.'s participation in our movement has been disastrous and destructive. And since M. cites my words, I will take the liberty of enumerating the facts.

From *La Crise des Bolcheviks-Léninistes* (1939), where Trotsky was identified throughout as "Crux." This transcript was signed by Molinier and Desnots (Le Ricard) and dated July 16, 1936. Translated by Russell Block.

In France, in Spain, in the IS, we have had dozens of instances of the "M. case." If all the others are injurious, it is necessary to draw the proper conclusions. But there are the facts. A biographical fact about M. which bears a heavy weight: his flight from the barracks, where every worker, every peasant is. Because of personal cowardice? He claims revolutionary work. . . . Why? The court has declared him insane. He has a certificate issued by the state according to which he is insane. . . . The doctors were called in, something which I will never understand. After that, I said to him: "You will not be able to hold any position that puts you in the limelight, because at any moment the police can throw up this fact—you are a deserter and you've been declared insane!" If M.'s nerves are so delicate that he can't stand the barracks, then he won't be able to stand prison; hence, he is not a revolutionary.

(Ray says he will reply shortly.)

Trotsky: I can't discuss political questions with someone who has been expelled.

Then there was the "affair" of business matters. When I arrived in France, I saw that business activities were a disorganizing factor and that M. was introducing a "commercial spirit." . . . M. has certain qualities that I appreciate in a revolutionary. Thus I tried to get the IS to pass a resolution for M. to cease his business activities. M. consented, the decision was approved unanimously, then the affair brought about rebellions within the organization. This was in July 1933. M. afterward deceived the international organization and me personally by resuming his business activities. There was another affair, less important but characteristic: the Lille affair.

On my arrival in France, I proposed to the Central Committee that it leave Paris, where an unhealthy atmosphere prevailed, to go to Lille and remove yourselves from this poisonous atmosphere. The Central Committee refused. M. went to Lille. I said: Very good! This was on his own initiative. He wanted to attribute it to me. He left for Lille to accomplish miracles. Always miracles! Financial, political, military! He did not accomplish any miracles in Lille, but he used his presence there to lambast the Central Committee and to declare that everyone was "rotten," including Frank. It was M. who was going to be the educator! He returned. Lille was a fiasco . . . in miniature, a preparation for the *La Commune* fiasco.

The *Commune* affair was an act of treason. This has been

amply demonstrated in Braun's pamphlet. Since M. believed that he could counterpose cash to the international organization you will not find a single Bolshevik-Leninist, either in Europe or in America, who can possibly believe that we can work with him. Not one person voted for him in the plenum. The vote was unanimous.

The launching of *La Commune* was a plot hatched by M. I understand how people plot in a reformist organization, but this is the Fourth International, and I assert that if it wasn't for his financial resources, this idea never would have occurred to M. It was only because he had the cash that he conceived the idea of forming his own party on the basis of three or four points. Then it declared itself a section of the Fourth International, which was a shocking act of usurpation. The Control Commission formed by the IS demonstrated his disloyalty, and I am prepared to write publicly that M. has introduced the commercial spirit into the organization and that his methods are incompatible with a proletarian organization. If I make such serious accusations, it is because I am convinced after seven years and the episode of *La Commune*, which I consider to be a lamentable fiasco.

When the question of unity was posed, I said: We were right in expelling M., but we shouldn't let the M. case stand in the way of the fusion. We will wait and see.

The attitude of M. and F[rank] since the fusion—absolutely incredible. After the fiasco they want to give lessons in politics and morality. That is a bit too much! There is no one in the international organization who will tolerate the presence of M. in our ranks. I say that the commercial spirit and the habit of regarding the organization as a business, all of this is becoming too much for him. Since the fusion there have been three episodes:

1. The financial opposition of Poly, Le Ricard, and Frank. As for you, Le Ricard, you are unaware of precedents or previous instances. He, F., knows about the tragic commercial episode, the Control Commission, and nevertheless he has dared to propose starting this commercial episode all over again, calling the decisions of the IS "chatter."

We throw out people who call the decisions of the IS "chatter." Frank has no character. When M. was in Lille, P.F. was with him. At that time, F., according to M., was "rotten."

Like Mèche, who is malevolent when directed by M., they change their colors, their organization, but not their leader.

Henri M., whom I esteem, for his part put pressure on his brother to lead a proletarian life.

2. Then there is this episode of the minutes. . . . I don't wish to take it up. M. is always ambiguous so that one can interpret his proposals from the right or from the left. When he wants to deceive, to equivocate, he finds evasive formulations. He can be brutal or ingratiating. He's a repeated offender. I've lost all confidence in what M. says and what he writes. I can imagine that he expressed himself in an ambiguous fashion. The comrades who edited the minutes are comrades of the highest integrity. The three Bardins are among the best elements.

3. The episode with *l'Intransigeant*.[28] In a bourgeois newspaper, an article directed against us, a vicious article where they try to use M. to compromise the organization. . . . What does this article prove? Our decision on M.'s business affairs was correct. Don't talk to me about rumors: the bourgeoisie has its own sources of information.

The only condition for a revolutionary attached to the organization is to understand at what point it was criminal to give these bourgeois scoundrels the opportunity to compromise the organization. Now, what does M. do? He turns the accusation against the leadership. That is the act of a madman!

How can one fail to see that this article is aimed at the organization far more than at M? M. is a destructive element. The expulsion of M. was correct, and its correctness has been demonstrated once again for the new elements.

I will repeat this before any audience whatsoever.

Le Ricard: We worked with M. in the PCI. There was no pressure, no impropriety. There was one single case that was settled with an expulsion and we did not come to Honefoss for that. I myself was subjected to slanders and lies by these "comrades of the highest integrity." The most important consideration, more important than the M. case, more important than anything, is the PCI's numerical contribution to the POI; above all, we must look to the well-being of the POI and the interests of its development.

Trotsky: You are pathetic! Development is a daily, ongoing process. We have to settle the question of M. and the Fourth International. Either you accept the decision of the IS, or you don't. If you don't accept it, then you make an appeal on the national or international level.

Le Ricard: I don't know the international organization! I've never seen it! All the terms are set by those people, the very ones who have deceived us.

(A reiteration of the conditions for unification. The GBL had avoided making common preparations and had decided not to propose individual expulsions.) Now expulsions are being proposed again. This procedure is bureaucratic. It is better to explain things than to assert them.

Trotsky: We don't want miracle workers in our organization! I have a thousand letters. I'm working on my diary. We will never tolerate adventurists.

Le Ricard: I can say that no one was ever put under any sort of pressure in our PCI.

Trotsky: Go back to your party!

Le Ricard: We do not have a shopkeeper's mentality. We want a strong party. . . .

Trotsky: You can stay in the POI without Molinier.

Le Ricard: The PCI was one entity, the POI is another. They deceived us with this unity.

Trotsky: I've lost all confidence in the old Bolshevik-Leninists of the PCI. They have learned nothing from experience. As Lenin said about Zinoviev: It's no accident. These old Bolshevik-Leninists betrayed our political principles. They burned their fingers. They come back wanting to apply their principles and go astray even on the trade union question. I wrote to M.'s older brother in good time. I said that the only issue was that of resigning from the revolutionary movement for the time being, for M. had betrayed our principles and had held the party up to ridicule. At that time I said: Resign and demonstrate that you are loyal to those principles and we will open the door to you. But now he must be expelled.

Le Ricard: What holds the party up to ridicule is the formulations in *La Lutte ouvrière.*

Trotsky: Lutte ouvrière will have its ups and downs, but it is our movement. What Rous wrote about the Blum government, the

Commune crew ought to study and appreciate.[29] Rous is one of the young people in our ranks. He's learned very slowly, but he's learned a lot.

Le Ricard: The source of the ridicule is the method of publishing public accusations in the bulletins of the organizations. . . . What compromises is the public distribution of these "internal" bulletins by the Bolshevik-Leninists!

Trotsky: If mentioning someone's business ventures can embarrass the organization, then he has to be expelled.

R.M.: The fact that I deserted did not prevent Crux from giving me posts and sending me on assignments, and the courts never declared me insane.

I had given up business up to the time I was with Crux in Lille. On my return I could not find any other work except in this firm and the chief officer of this company was himself cynically named treasurer of the organization, since there was a meshing of interests. The IS demanded that I give up business. This being done, the question is now one of "spirit."

Desertion in 1929, worked in the organization during period of desertion. This situation resolved in accord with the organization and Crux. The question of desertion being resolved, Raymond worked in the organization without anyone's raising an objection. Then political disagreements arose with Rosmer, who looked for arguments, using the desertion, etc. . . . Crux opposed this! Raymond carried out national and international responsibilities for Crux.

Lille. His stay was limited by the necessity of accompanying Crux, who was expelled. All ties to the north were established at that time. Back in Paris at the time of the entry, Raymond again found work in the business firm in question. There were never any objections, and things continued as they were.

Trotsky: In the case of M., above all, the time for resignation has passed. Expulsion is necessary.

Le Ricard: Posing the question in this way will disgust the organization. The party will be weakened!

Trotsky: Those who quit the organization out of disgust are not serious. We've already had losses, but we are entering into a very promising period. The party will grow. We have to expel him; the question cannot be put off.

(The discussion continues around the same questions. The upshot is that Crux says that Molinier can be readmitted if he is capable of bearing the consequences for acts prejudicial to the Fourth International on the outside and maintains his loyalty to the organization while outside of it.)

(. . . . All Le Ricard's proposals not to allow the difficulties of unification to revolve around the M. case, which should not have been done, were in vain. A meeting was set for the following morning on the French question. It is worth mentioning that in the course of the final minutes of the discussion, Le Ricard made the observation that the methods of the leadership were bureaucratic, and that Crux retorted: "With bureaucrats, you know where they are going, and it's possible to stop them; with adventurists, it's impossible to stop them." By designating as adventurists militants who have not acquired bureaucratic docility, this sentence sums up for us the lesson of the "affair.")

A Hasty Formulation on the People's Front
July 19, 1936

To the Political Bureau, POI

Dear Comrades:

The latest issue of *Révolution*, which, in general, makes a very favorable impression, has a surprising opening: "Under the vigilant protection of the French workers, the People's Front government will be able to carry out the program . . ." This formulation is doubly untrue: (1) Even under their "protection," the government could not carry out that program, for it is *unattainable*, since it assumes prosperity under the capitalist regime; (2) Our task is not at all to "protect" the coalition government between the proletariat and the bourgeoisie.

From *Bulletin Intérieur,* POI, no. 4, September 1936. Translated by Mary Gordon.

I am sure it is only a matter of a hasty formulation and not of a deep difference. But in order to avoid any future misunderstanding, I want to explain myself on that question again.

We and the People's Front have common enemies. That is why we are ready to fight them alongside the regular groups of the People's Front government, without taking the least responsibility for this government or posing as the "protectors" of Léon Blum. We consider this government as a lesser evil, compared to de la Rocque. But while fighting the greater evil we do not have to "protect" the lesser evil!

We must not conceal from the masses that the program is unattainable in the framework of capitalism or that the attainable parts of the program would always be sabotaged by the Radicals. When we say, "The moment has not yet come for a frontal attack on the Blum government," we do not mean by that that we have to protect it, but only that we must attack it from the side—its right side, the Radicals. We must distinguish and personalize our criticisms of the government by striking the heaviest blows at the Radical ministers and by explaining to the Socialist and Communist workers that it is Daladier, Delbos, Rucard, etc., who sabotage and cannot but sabotage everything that is progressive in the government program. The two-year draft remains. The reactionary officers will keep their posts. Léon Blum's paper, *Le Populaire*, is still forbidden in the barracks. Who is responsible for this? Daladier, the old agent of French imperialism. The Radicals are the line of least resistance for the revolutionary critique. By concentrating your fire against the Radical ministers, with really concrete examples, you will easily get the ear of the Communist and Socialist workers. You may rightly add: "Unfortunately, the Communist leaders support the Radicals against the Socialist leaders." At any rate, our slogan cannot be "Down with the Blum government!", but "Drive the bourgeois Radicals out of the Blum government!" That is where the slight difference of meaning lies. It is extremely important for this period, but it does not at all mean that we "protect" the Blum government.

We must maintain an explanatory terminology, rather than an agitational one. But it must remain, nevertheless, firm and uncompromising.

In the July 16 issue of *Le Populaire* there is an article by Collinet trying to reconcile our criticisms of the People's Front with the "protection" (or the recognition, if you prefer) of the Blum government as "our" government. Naturally, we cannot solidarize with Collinet, despite all his plagiarizing of our criticisms. We must oppose him precisely because of that, because he tries to reconcile revolutionary criticisms with the coalition between the proletariat and the Radical bourgeoisie. That is the crucial point of the overall political situation in France.

Your leaflet as well as your July 14 tract contain the slogan for a "workers' guard." Why have you given up the slogan for a "workers' militia"? Such changes are very prejudicial to your propaganda. You must carefully choose your slogans and formulations. But after you choose them, you must keep them until the objective situation has changed.

Crux [Trotsky]

Epilogue:
Trotsky and the French Section
After July 1936

The delegates at the ICL's First International Conference for the Fourth International in July 1936 decided, against Trotsky's advice, that the time was not yet ripe for the establishment of the Fourth International; instead, they set up the Movement for the Fourth International (MFI). Before it could even publish the conference resolutions, the MFI was thrown onto the defensive and into a struggle for its very survival in August when Stalin staged the first big Moscow trial, with Zinoviev and Kamenev as the chief defendants in the dock and with Trotsky and his movement accused of a terrorist plot aimed at restoring capitalism in the Soviet Union. For most of the next year Trotsky's time was almost exclusively devoted to exposing and explaining the Moscow trials, and he had very little to say about the French section.

The Molinierists remained in the POI until its first congress in October 1936. Each faction accused the other of trying to rig the congress with paper delegates. Even so, the report of the credentials committee disclosed a 23 percent drop in membership since the June 1 unification, that is, during the four-month period that had witnessed the most massive labor upsurge in French history. At one point before the Molinierists marched out crying fraud, several of the delegates threw punches at one another. The implications of this exchange were not lost on the police, whose informer supplied a most detailed report of the congress. In June the police had warned the government that the POI had the potential to become a formidable force, but this estimate was revised in September, even before the spectacle of the October congress: "Because of its internal struggles and the sectarianism of its militants . . . it can be affirmed today that this group for the moment is incapable of provoking and leading any kind of social movement."

After the congress the POI leaders tried to pull themselves together and get the party going. For a time there was progress:

both the POI and the JSR grew as some effective work was done
in the unions and in a propaganda campaign against the Moscow
purges. But the objective situation became unfavorable. The
People's Front moved to the right, the capitalists unleashed an
offensive to take back gains the workers had won in 1936, the
first Blum government fell in June 1937, and demoralization set
in among the French workers. The Moscow trials produced a
wave of pessimism and anti-Leninist sentiment among radicals,
which was reinforced by the Stalinist murder of revolutionists
during the Spanish civil war.

Under these conditions the ability of the POI leaders to work as
a team did not last long. Meanwhile the PCI came back into
business, still declaring its adherence to the Fourth International.
It did not reach the POI's size, but it too made gains and it
remained a thorn in the POI's side. "I fully understand the
immense difficulties created by the existence of two organizations
which make use of the same banner but at the same time fight
each other bitterly," Trotsky said in a letter to a French
correspondent on May 27, 1937 (see *Writings 36-37*). But the only
solution Trotsky saw at this time was for the PCI to recognize its
errors and rejoin the French section, with Molinier retiring from
the French scene for the time being. Since that last point was the
one thing on which the PCI would not compromise and on which
the POI would not budge, the split continued.

To Trotsky's statement that the two organizations bore the
same banner should be added the fact that they also presented
virtually the same program. In fact, the political differences
began to diminish as soon as the *Commune* group endorsed the
Open Letter for the Fourth International in January 1936. While
Trotsky never retracted his charge that the Molinierists had
capitulated to centrism and the social-patriotic wave in 1935, he
also did not continue to make such a charge after they changed
their course. From time to time both sides alluded to basic
political differences to justify their separate existence, but their
political differences rapidly became the kind that could normally
coexist in a revolutionary party. When Molinier was expelled the
second time in 1936, it was not because of his political positions
but because of his methods, and when his group left the French
section it was not because of the POI's or the MFI's political
positions but because of their methods. Most of this was
incomprehensible to people outside of the two groups and little of
it was attractive to anyone but perennial factionalists and
sectarian screwballs.

Trying to break out of the international isolation that their exit from the MFI created, the PCI leaders fished around for blocs with other dissidents inside and outside the MFI who had their own grievances against Trotsky's and the IS's "bureaucratic" practices and policies. Since most of these groups soon quit the MFI or turned against the Fourth International, the chief result of these efforts was to further discredit the PCI in the eyes of the MFI and the POI.

At the second congress of the POI in the fall of 1937, a debate over the class character of the Soviet Union took place, with at least a third of the delegates supporting the position of Yvan Craipeau that it was no longer a workers' state. Viewing this as an unhealthy symptom, Trotsky wrote an answer to Craipeau, "Once Again: The USSR and Its Defense" (*Writings 37-38*) and began following its development more closely. What he observed disquieted him even more. In the POI press and in its reports early in 1938 he thought he saw signs of political degeneration and organizational disintegration. As plans got under way in the spring for the founding conference of the Fourth International that was held in September, Trotsky thought the French section was in a "miserable state." "They do not communicate any statistics to us, which is a bad sign in itself. The newspaper does not appear regularly. The same is true of the so-called monthly. They have not a single man with organizational capacities." By contrast, *La Commune* was bigger and was published regularly and more frequently, along with leaflets, pamphlets, and theoretical material: "The competition is causing general confusion and is extremely prejudicial to our section. We can't simply ignore the *Commune* organization. We must help our section vanquish the *Commune* organization." In letters to Socialist Workers Party leaders James P. Cannon and Max Shachtman, who were going to attend the founding conference, he urged international intervention to shake up the French section and get it going in the right direction and suggested tactics to be followed toward the Molinier group, which he was sure would appeal to the conference for reinstatement. He also advised firmness toward the POI leaders, who would reject maneuvers toward the Molinier group as "capitulation" ("Thoughts on the French Section," April 19, 1938, in *Writings 37-38*).

A British delegate to the founding conference, C.L.R. James, noted that in the commission meetings preceding the conference the delegates devoted six sessions to the French section. The ten-page resolution adopted by the conference is probably the most severe criticism of a section ever approved by the Fourth International (see *Documents of the Fourth International: The Formative Years [1933-40]*). The resolution found the section to be stagnant and in a state of disorganization. It had lost 15 percent of its members and it lacked a serious party administration, a normally functioning treasury, a stable editorial staff, and even the most modest apparatus of fulltime functionaries. The leadership was held to be inadequate at mobilizing the party members, coordinating their work, and creating political, ideological, and moral cohesion and team spirit. This could not be attributed to objective conditions alone: the leadership had not assimilated what a revolutionary organization really is and had failed to apply the essential organizational principles that Bolshevism had developed throughout the years. "Revolutionary" amateurism, a do-your-own-thing spirit, work that was done anarchically, without organizational objective, order, or system— these faults of a leadership that did not know how to lead itself were responsible for confusion and demoralization among the rank and file. All these defects had been noted at a June 1938 POI conference, the resolution added, but corrective action was needed immediately. To this end it presented a series of suggested changes and offered the help of the International and financial aid from other sections to help implement them.

As expected, the PCI took the occasion of the founding conference to seek admission to the Fourth International and fusion with the French section. Negotiations were held between PCI delegates and a special IS commission but were broken off when the PCI delegates refused to give a categorical answer to a seven-point IS resolution, in particular the point that Molinier could not be a member of the unified section. An IS statement on the negotiations ("On the Molinier Group" in *Documents of the Fourth International*), declaring that Molinier had been expelled in 1936 "for attempting to use money obtained by dubious means to impose his personal control over the organization," concluded by saying, "Now, as before, the door of the Fourth International remains open, with full assurance of normal democratic rights, to the rank and file members of the PCI who are ready to accept the resolutions and decisions of its international conference and accept discipline. The door is closed to R. Molinier." Then, as before, the PCI rejected that condition for going through the door.

The POI's crisis of stagnation at the time of the founding conference was followed not by reorganization and recovery but by a new dispute that tore the organization apart. When the POI and the PCI were being organized in 1936, their leaders had lost interest in the Revolutionary Left, but the Pivertists continued to play an important role in French working class politics. Pivert himself had taken a post in Blum's first government, resigning in 1937 but still proclaiming the need to remain in the SFIO. A few months later the SFIO bureaucracy ordered the GR dissolved, but the Pivertists remained in the party as a left wing until June 1938, when they were expelled. They promptly set up a new organization, the Workers and Peasants Socialist Party (PSOP), whose first congress voted not to affiliate to the People's Front. Of the 30,000 supporters they had had in the SFIO before the expulsion, only around 6,000 or 7,000 joined the new centrist party, but it represented a significant pole of attraction for leftward-moving elements and therefore was both an obstacle and an opportunity for the Fourth Internationalists.

The PCI members entered the PSOP at the end of 1938, although they had to do it without Frank, who thought little could be accomplished in the PSOP, and without Molinier, who was excluded by the PSOP leaders. Inside the POI, a proposal for fusion with the PSOP, made by Rous and Craipeau, led to a new crisis that destroyed the POI. Pivert did not want a fusion although he was willing to have POI members join individually. A majority of the POI leaders (Boitel and Naville) also voted against a fusion in February 1939. Whereupon the Rous-Craipeau minority decided to go ahead and join the PSOP on their own. Trotsky at first was uncertain about the entry but he became convinced that it was better than continued stagnation and he tried to help the entry work by writing several articles about the PSOP (reprinted in *Leon Trotsky on France*). The Rous-Craipeau group, supported by the IS, made headway inside the PSOP, winning over the leadership of the PSOP youth group and becoming part of a left wing that got over one-fourth of the votes at the PSOP's second congress in June 1939. The IS called on the POI leaders to reconsider and join the PSOP. When they refused and persisted in their hostility to the Rous-Craipeau group, the IS withdrew its recognition of the POI as the French section of the Fourth International in July 1939, a few weeks before the start of World War II.

Prior to this, in April 1939, C.L.R. James had had a discussion with Trotsky in Mexico about the difficulties facing the Fourth International ("Fighting Against the Stream," in *Writings 38-39*) and much of the talk centered on the reasons for the poor state of the French section. James said that at the founding conference in 1938 Cannon and Shachtman thought it was mainly a question of leadership and organization, while he thought the problems were due to the social composition of the section. Trotsky agreed that the section suffered from the "traditional" French malady ("this incapacity to organize and at the same time lack of conditions for improvisation") and from a composition, historically determined ("the social composition of every revolutionary movement in the beginning is not of workers"), that was separated from the mass of the workers and found it difficult to work among them. Against both of these weaknesses, he said, it was necessary and possible to fight, but he strongly disagreed that either of these factors provided the main explanation for the difficulties in France. That could be found only in the general nature of the period: the uninterrupted series of international defeats, the spread of fascism, the degeneration of Stalinism, the demoralization created by the People's Fronts all combined to create extremely difficult objective conditions for a small revolutionary movement. "We are in a small boat in a tremendous current," he said. "There are five or ten boats and one goes down and we say it was due to bad helmsmanship. But that was not the reason—it was because the current was too strong. It is the most general explanation and we should never forget this explanation in order not to become pessimistic. . . ."

When World War II began in September 1939, the POI, the PCI, and the PSOP all fell apart and disappeared. Former members of the POI, led by Craipeau and those like Marcel Hic who had not joined the PSOP, slowly and painfully put together a new underground Fourth Internationalist group. Members of the PCI also constituted an underground organization. Rous and Gérard Rosenthal quit, later joining the SFIO. Naville quit, later becoming a founder of the centrist United Socialist Party (PSU). Molinier and Frank, faced with heavy prison sentences for their antiwar activities, left the country. Pivert escaped to America, where he became a supporter of de Gaulle; after the war he rejoined the SFIO. The Fourth International was shaken by a deep crisis in which a large petty-bourgeois opposition, led by Shachtman and James Burnham, sought unsuccessfully to revise the International's basic program and theories. In the course of that conflict, Shachtman charged Trotsky with making the same mistake when he defended the Cannon faction in the Socialist Workers Party that he had made in defending the Molinier group before the 1935 split. In January 1940, Trotsky replied:

> Molinier was accused not of retreating from our program but of being undisciplined, arbitrary and of venturing into all sorts of financial adventures to support the party and his faction. Since

Molinier is a very energetic man and has unquestionable practical capacities I found it necessary—not only in the interests of Molinier but above all in the interests of the organization itself—to exhaust all the possibilities of convincing and reeducating him in the spirit of proletarian discipline. Since many of his adversaries possessed all of his failings and none of his virtues I did everything to convince them not to hasten a split but to test Molinier over and over again. It was this that constituted my "defense" of Molinier in the adolescent period of the existence of our French section. . . .

In any case I did not make the slightest principled concession to Molinier. When he decided to found a paper on the basis of "four slogans" instead of our program, and set out independently to execute this plan, I was among those who insisted upon his immediate expulsion. But I will not hide the fact that at the Founding Congress of the Fourth International I was in favor of once again testing Molinier and his group within the framework of the International to see if they had become convinced of the erroneousness of their policy. This time, too, the attempt led to nothing. But I do not renounce repeating it under suitable conditions once again. . . .

A number of comrades upon acquainting themselves with my archives have reproached me in a friendly way with having wasted and still continuing to waste so much time on convincing "hopeless people." I replied that many times I have had the occasion to observe how people change with circumstances and that I am therefore not ready to pronounce people as "hopeless" on the basis of a few even though serious mistakes. . . .

It is an extremely difficult task to form an international proletarian vanguard under present conditions. To chase after individuals at the expense of principles would of course be a crime. But to do everything possible to bring back outstanding yet mistaken comrades to our program I have considered and still consider my duty [*In Defense of Marxism,* pp. 147-48].

In May 1940 Trotsky survived a Stalinist machine-gun attack on his home. Molinier and Frank, then in England, sent Trotsky letters expressing their solidarity and their desire to heal the split in France. On July 1 Trotsky answered that he did not understand the practical purpose of their message, which he found to be vague (on both sides, the correspondence was worded to get through war censorship), but if they really were ready to accept discipline loyally, reunification would be possible and he would cooperate to bring it about ("Avuncular Advice" in *Writings 39-40*). Molinier and Frank responded on August 5 that "we accept the rights and duties as defined in your letter of July 1, without any reservations and without equivocation." By the time this letter reached Mexico Trotsky was already dead, the victim of a Stalinist assassin. The International Secretariat decided to postpone merger proceedings in France for one year. Frank was interned by the British government for the remainder of the war. Molinier succeeded in getting away to Latin America. In 1944 the two groups that had descended from the POI and the PCI united with a third to form a new French section, named the PCI. Frank returned to France after the war, served as a delegate of the French section to the Fourth International's first postwar conference in 1946, and since then has been a member of the International Secretariat and its successor, the United Secretariat. Molinier never rejoined the French section.

Next to the 1939-40 fight with the American petty-bourgeois opposition, the French crisis unquestionably had the most serious consequences of all the internal struggles of the Fourth Internationalist movement in Trotsky's time. Pierre Frank did not deal with this French crisis in his short 1969 work *La Quatrième internationale,* but later he did write some brief comments about it in a note for a comrade preparing lectures on the history of French Trotskyism, a copy of which he supplied for use in this book (Appendix B). Frank's note does not seek to draw explicit "lessons," although one can be derived from his present opinion that the gains Molinier and he made by their tactic in the SFIO were meager when weighed against the drastic consequences of the split.

When Trotsky stopped in Paris on his way to Norway in June 1935, he had a discussion with émigré leaders of the German section about their underground work in Nazi Germany since Hitler took power in 1933. When Trotsky was asked about the feeling of some German members that the work of the last two years had been wasted, he replied that "no work actually performed is in vain, however negative it may seem," because "it is through work that we educate and develop ourselves." Mistakes are inevitable: "What good master tailor has not thoroughly ruined a dozen suits in his apprentice and journeyman's years?" Mistakes have a positive aspect if we can use them to overcome our weaknesses and shortcomings; "in general, people learn only from their mistakes—especially in the proletarian movement." Experience with all kinds of activity, negative as well as positive, is necessary for the formation of Marxist cadres. ("Zur Organisationsfrage," *Informations Dienst,* no. 7/8, August 1935)

The same thing probably could be said about the French crises discussed in this book. The current theory and practice of some sections of the Fourth International suggest that not all of their leaders have absorbed the lessons Trotsky tried to teach in 1935-36 about "broad" newspapers, the revolutionary attitude to centrist groups, etc. But the French section did learn eventually to exercise some restraints on dead-end factionalism. Other sections were able to avoid some of the costly mistakes committed by the French section in its long-protracted adolescence, not only when they made their own departure from the Social Democratic parties but in other ways. It came to be more widely understood that revolutionaries should think a thousand times before splitting a revolutionary party or even jeopardizing its unity, and that even then they should think some more when the differences are over tactics and not principles. Other sections were also given an opportunity to weigh the practical results that flow from a conception of the revolutionary party as a federation of factions rather than as a combat organization striving for political homogeneity and a collective leadership. Positive lessons for building the latter kind of party were drawn in Trotsky's *In Defense of Marxism* and Cannon's *Struggle for a Proletarian Party* during the 1939-40 fight against the American petty-bourgeois opposition.

It should also be remembered that the Fourth International did not spring forth in full maturity in the second half of the 1930s; it was then only being born, in travail and turmoil. The French experiences of 1935-39, when digested, undoubtedly helped the Fourth International to develop a wiser and healthier relationship with its sections than existed before the war and contributed to the further evolution of the Fourth International away from organizational concepts, practices, and abuses mechanically borrowed from the Comintern.

2 fr. français

NICOLLE   BRAUN

"L'Organe de masse"

Contribution sur la crise de la section française
de la Ligue des Communistes-Internationalistes
(Bolchéviks-Léninistes)

Edité par le
Secrétariat International
de la L. C. I. (B.-L.)

Juin 1936

The front cover of the mimeographed edition of *L'Organe de masse* (The
Mass Paper).

Appendix A:
The Mass Paper
By Nicolle Braun [Erwin Wolf]
June 6, 1936

I. Background of the Crisis

The Mulhouse Congress

The French League overcame with extraordinary speed the enormous weakening it underwent with the departure of sectarian and conservative-literary elements when it entered the SFIO in the fall of 1934:

> Before its entry the French section was in a state of complete stagnation. . . . The split and its subsequent effects obviously damaged the political results of the entry. . . . The first seven or eight months of the Bolshevik-Leninists' activity within the SFIO was their best period. For the first time, they were able to bring their analysis and their slogans before a larger audience, to test their Marxist superiority over their opponents, and at the same time recognize their own tactical and organizational deficiencies and to eliminate them by making changes in their practice. The culminating point was the Mulhouse congress (June 1935). (Crux, letter of December 30, 1935)

This congress was held shortly after the conclusion of the Franco-Soviet pact and the publication of the famous declaration of Stalin understanding and completely approving France's

Published by the International Secretariat of the ICL, June 1936. Subtitled "A contribution on the crisis of the French section of the International Communist League." Translated by David Keil. Trotsky's introduction begins on page 141.

Parenthetical additions or comments in the quoted passages, when set off by parentheses ( ), either were part of the quoted text or were added by Erwin Wolf. The editors have used square brackets [ ] to add an occasional clarification.

175

national defense policy. Sympathy for the Bolshevik-Leninists increased, as was reflected in the voting results for the congress. In his report of July 1936 in the international bulletin, Rous said:

> The GBL had drafted a Bolshevik-Leninist motion, and this motion had rallied 105 mandates nationally; this corresponds to more than 2,000 votes. It is worth noting that in the Central Federation (the Seine Federation, i.e., Paris) the GBL obtained 1,087 federal mandates out of about 4,000. . . . But more significant than these numerical results is the political role played by the Bolshevik-Leninists. It can be said that the membership was polarized around, for or against, the essential slogans advanced by the Bolshevik-Leninists.

The entire French bourgeois press had to note our presence; for example, *Le Temps:*

> The Bolshevik-Leninists expressed themselves more violently, through the voice of Mr. Naville who . . . addressed . . . various ministers with insults such as "scoundrels." . . . He . . . went so far as to assert, over the protests of everyone or almost everyone, that Mr. Léon Blum had said that the Communists, the Socialists, and all French people would unite behind the tricolor to march, if necessary, against the Hitlerites. In brief, he went after all elements of the party. (!)

Likewise the Stalinists could not maintain a total silence about us. *L'Humanité* wrote:

> The putschist conceptions of the Trotskyists were rejected by the congress, which counterposed to them propaganda to tear the masses away from fascist demagogy.

The SFIO leaders felt the pressure; Rous wrote in his July report:

> The power of the Bolshevik-Leninist policy is such that it was in relation to our slogans that the leaders Blum and Faure had to explain themselves.

The centrists were pushed to the left; here is what the report says:

> To break the tendency of militants toward accepting our slogans, the left (*Bataille Socialiste*) was forced to imitate them in its motion.

The SFIO youth felt the influence of the Bolshevik-Leninists even more strongly. Having in the past been more or less an association for recreation and education, the Young Socialists became an activist force inside the party. The endeavors of the secretaries of the Communist Youth International, who came from Moscow to win over Fred Zeller and with him the largest faction, failed miserably.

*   *   *

What was the secret of success? Was the mass sympathy gained by clever diplomacy? Were the name "Bolshevik-Leninists" and the slogan of the Fourth International hidden so as not to repel the "backward" masses, as Schwab-Pivert and later Frank put it? Did the comrades limit themselves to four or five points instead of a principled platform? Not at all! The June 8 *La Vérité* addressed itself to the working class public *saying what is*, without reticence, following the Bolshevik principle.

Similarly the following issue of *La Vérité* was bold and provocative. The headlines alone indicate the self-confidence which the whole organization had: "The Bolshevik-Leninists in the Vanguard of the Assemblage"; "Our Intervention for the Fourth International."

The report on the congress accused the reformists and centrists. In summary, it said (*La Vérité*, June 21, 1935):

> "The Trotskyists left isolated from the congress and from the working class," says Thorez. . . . You take your wishes for reality, Messrs. Bureaucrats, in this domain as in many others. But the bourgeoisie, through its most serious paper, *Le Temps*, sees things more clearly and says euphemistically, "The Bolshevik-Leninists did not leave the congress crushed." —No, we are far from being shaken.

In actuality a new decisive turning-point had been reached. Crux pointed this out the day of the congress (June 10) in a letter to the International Secretariat. We reproduce the letter almost without omission, because involved here are not *isolated* arguments, lessons, or similar things, but a *homogeneous* strategic battle plan for the next period, a plan which should be understood and appreciated as a whole. The letter has been reproduced, distributed, and read. Not a voice has been raised against it, but—as we will see—each of its points has been acted against:

Dear Comrades:

We are obviously entering a new period. Two events determine it: the development of our section in France and the definitive turn of the Comintern.

1. The correctness of our entry into the SFIO is now proved by objective facts. Our section, thanks to the entry, has changed from a propaganda group into a revolutionary factor of the first order. No one will dare to assert that our group, in adapting itself to the new environment, has become softer, more moderate, more opportunist. Quite the contrary. We can correctly say that the Bolshevik-Leninist Group in France at the present moment surpasses all our other sections by the revolutionary precision of its slogans and by the offensive character of its entire political activity. . . .

2. The definitive betrayal of Stalin and of his Comintern crew opens to us great possibilities not only within the Comintern but also within all the working class organizations, especially in the trade unions. . . .

3. The same circumstances demonstrate the necessity for the implacable struggle against the SAP that we have undertaken. . . . The more flexible, many-sided and, above all, daring our policy of penetration into the mass organizations, all the more intransigent must our general policy be, all the more aggressive must it be against all hardened and crystallized centrist ideologies. The banner of the Fourth International must be relentlessly opposed to all other banners.

4. The preparation for the Mulhouse congress (which has opened today, at the moment these lines are being written) was a remarkable schooling not only for our French section but also for our entire international organization.

The struggle centered around three motions: the right, the centrist, and ours. In all the districts in which our comrades, numerically weak as they are, have unswervingly counterposed our resolution to the others, they have gained votes and sympathizers; and, at the same time, they have compelled the centrists to draw away a little further from the right, in order not to lose their entire influence. And, on the other hand, in the few cases in which our comrades committed the grave error of entering into a combination with the centrists, they gained nothing for our tendency and, at the same time, pushed the centrists to the right. (!)

These experiences provide us with the key for our entire policy in this period: to enter into combinations with the leaders of the SAP, of the IAG [London-Amsterdam Bureau], and so forth would imply losing our own identity, compromising the banner of the Fourth International, and arresting the development of the diverse centrist currents on the road of the revolution. As regards our French section itself, the Mulhouse congress implies, or should imply, the beginning of a new period. Not only is the SFIO not a revolutionary party but it is not even a proletarian party. It is petty bourgeois, not only in its policies but also in its social composition. This party opened certain possibilities to us, and it was correct to have recognized and utilized them. But these possibilities are limited. The Mulhouse congress, together with the repercussions that will follow it, should more or less materially limit these possibilities. The prestige gained by the Bolshevik-Leninist Group must be transformed into radiance in the eyes of the workers. But the workers are primarily outside of the SP: in the CP, in the trade union organizations, and among the unorganized. The Bolshevik-Leninist Group *must know how to effect a new turn,* which is the logical development of the previous stage. Without, of course, making the slightest concessions, it is necessary to concentrate nine-tenths of our efforts upon denunciation of the Stalinist betrayal.

5. The struggle of the different tendencies against us coincides today almost entirely with the ideological indoctrination . . . for the new imperialist war. Opposition to the war must coincide to an ever-increasing degree with sympathy for the Fourth International. The condition for success is a ruthless struggle against the slightest concession to the theory of national defense. The inevitable regroupment in the different working class organizations (Communist Party, trade unions, etc.) must open for us an outlet to the working class masses. It is necessary to orient ourselves in this direction with all the required independence. This regroupment can result in *the creation of a revolutionary party* within a fairly short period of time.

6. It is absolutely essential to speed up the preparatory work for the Fourth International. The revolutionary elements that will separate themselves during the general regroupment inside the working class must have the possibility of directly joining an international organization that bases itself on the entire experience of the revolutionary struggles. (Letter to the International Secretariat, June 10, 1935)

The Lille Youth Congress

After the Mulhouse congress a process of rapid differentiation took place in the Young Socialists which was in fact a differentiation between reformism and the Fourth International. The intermediate centrist groups such as the SAPists-Spartacists crumbled.

July 14, the day of the People's Front of Stalin-Blum-Daladier, showed that the youth with its Bolshevik-Leninist slogans had found an echo in the *masses.*

The next two weeks were spent in preparation for the Lille congress. The relationship of forces in terms of votes at the youth congress in the decisive regional district, Paris, was as follows: Bolshevik-Leninists plus Zeller faction—370 mandates; right-wingers—130; Spartacists—90. In the "red belt" of Paris, this proportion was even more favorable for the Bolshevik-Leninists. Numerous precious links had been made with the provinces.

The bureaucracy of the SFIO, however, was already utilizing the Lille congress to rid itself of the radical wing of the youth organization, a wing which was becoming dangerous for it. Thirteen leading comrades (Bolshevik-Leninists, Zeller faction, Spartacus, etc.) were expelled by 3,678 votes to 1,534. This result was only obtained by careful bureaucratic manipulation. At Lille they could no longer enjoy the "luxury" of democracy. There, it was not ideas that decided but apparatuses. The youth were not prepared for this crude expulsion. Even the Bolshevik-Leninist faction was partly taken by surprise. Mireille Osmin, who belongs to the right wing, made "conciliatory proposals," but in practice these would have meant the complete gagging of the left. *La Vérité* of August 2 reports:

> Zeller cries that the Left accepts the conditions. Biau (maker of the expulsion motion): "I do not accept the conditions of Mireille Osmin."

There was neither conciliation, nor statutes, nor freedom to speak. Nothing of the sort.

The expulsions took place July 30. The same day Crux telegraphed: "New step forward. Vigorous offensive necessary to prepare for independence. Letter follows."

Hardly six days after the Lille events, the proletariat of the ports of Brest and Toulon began to raise its rude voice. The thousands who opposed the Garde Mobile seemed to say: You Bolsheviks! The ones who will make the revolution are not the lawyers and café owners of the SFIO, but us. Finish your business with the knights of statutes. We are ready to fight. But we need a leadership.

Two days after the events in the ports Crux warned:

> The rebellion of the sailors is a sign of the accelerated rhythm of the revolutionary movement. It is on this basis that we must now direct our campaign against the reformists and the Stalinists and also against the hesitations of our centrist allies (!) and semi-allies. All considerations of form, internal discipline, etc., must give way before considerations of direct action among and at the head of the masses. . . . None among us has ever considered that our opportunities inside the SFIO were unlimited and that we would remain linked

to this party indefinitely. . . . All statutory maneuvers must now, after the first flashes of the revolution, be subordinated to an implacable offensive on the basis of revolutionary strategy. . . . We must say to ourselves: The transitory period of adaptation to the regime of the SFIO is drawing to its natural end. We must orient ourselves in practice toward the *revolutionary party* with the shortest possible delay, opening up the period of independent activity among the masses.

The words fell into a void. . . .

II. Serious Indications of a Crisis

Timidity

Among the leading comrades of the GBL, not all were entirely convinced "that the SFIO chapter was more or less closed," as Crux had stressed incessantly in June 1935 in his conversations with the French comrades in Paris. The successes had dazzled quite a number of comrades. Frank, the future "theoretician" of *La Commune*, was already made their spokesman: In his "Perspectives and Tasks" (June bulletin of the GBL), he took a position directly contrary to that of Crux, without having the courage to *openly* polemicize against him. He wrote:

> In the present situation, it seems to me that three points in particular are holding back our activity.
>
> The Seine Federation. To join its leadership, by making a bloc with other revolutionary tendencies, is an objective of exceptional importance, nationally and internationally. . . .*
>
> It would in my opinion be criminal to think (!) of leaving the SP; the Mulhouse congress was a striking proof of this; it was by our presence in the SP and by a quite appropriate activity that we are able to be precisely in the best position to serve as a pole of crystallization for all whom we can regroup. . . . The reformists, open or disguised, know that we would be much less dangerous outside the SP, where they will want to put us by expulsion. . . . We will not allow ourselves to be isolated.

This was not an accidental opinion. To the "tasks and perspectives" written even before the bureaucratic expulsions from the youth at Lille, but published only afterward, Frank added the following remark:

> Since that time (i.e., after the Mulhouse congress) there was Lille and its provocation aimed at running us out of the SP. On the whole, that

---

*Frank had only repeated what his factional colleague Raymond Molinier had demanded, two months before, in his article analogously named "Present Tasks and Past Tasks" (April 12, 1935). There he said, "Our aim is the political (?) conquest of the branches and federations, orienting them toward a relative (?) autonomy of propaganda (!)."

changes nothing (!) in the perspective and tasks presented in this article. (Internal Bulletin, June 1935)

The same Frank, who in August 1934 had declared, "Decide what you wish, but as for me, I will not enter the SFIO," exclaimed hardly a year later, with the same pathos, "Decide what you wish, but as for me, I will not leave the SFIO." Such "theoreticians," especially if they view themselves as "Old Bolsheviks," in opposition to the "neo-Bolsheviks," must be watched closely.

The Frank tendency quickly consolidated itself. In vain Crux pressed the offensive against the bureaucracy, as for example in his letter to Rous, July 30, 1935.

> The expulsion makes the inevitable turn in course easier for us and gives us a convenient argument: that they are getting rid of us to be better able to sell out the new generation to French imperialism. The point of departure is excellent. There is only one condition: a vigorous and coherent offensive on our part.

It is true that they wanted to carry out an offensive, but instead of independence, they sought reinstatement. . . . Frédéric noted this danger in time, as his letter to Crux, August 4, 1935, shows:

> Our people (especially Rousset—no one contradicts this) believe that reinstatement is quite possible, provided that a vigorous offensive is waged in this (!) direction, invoking the statutory illegality and bureaucratic character of the expulsion. . . . Craipeau . . . demands the dissolution of the Bolshevik-Leninist youth fraction; Rousset, at the first major meeting of the Young Socialists after the split, did not at all speak as a Bolshevik-Leninist . . . and demanded in the general assembly of the GBL that the publication of the Open Letter for the Fourth International be postponed as inopportune at this time. . . . All that, in order to prevent the bloc from prematurely breaking up. Linked with illusions about reinstatement, this can have quite harmful consequences.

In reality the *political* offensive had already been replaced with a defense on the ground of *statutes* and *formal discipline*, where the bureaucracy would undoubtedly be the stronger. Externally they seemed to take an intransigent attitude. Rous wrote in *La Vérité*, August 23, on the subject of the mutinies in the ports:

> To prepare for victory by forging the combat tool, the revolutionary

party, is the only way to avenge the heroic workers who fell at Toulon and Brest. . . .

Unfortunately he limited himself to a rather confused statement on the new party. To carry out the operation, he lacked the strength, boldness, and experience.

The publication of the Open Letter for the Fourth International also met resistance from adults at that time. Crux sought information from Rous August 10:

> I am a little disturbed that *La Vérité* has not published the Open Letter. It seems some comrades think that this document doesn't interest "the masses"; they thus accept the SAP's arguments. . . .

The response showed that many Bolshevik-Leninists were already using a typically SAPist argumentation. Rous wrote to Crux, August 17, 1935:

> Regarding the publication of the letter on the Fourth International, I was quite disappointed to see that certain comrades opposed this for reasons of the moment. . . . I should tell you quite frankly that . . . the reactionary argument prevailed in the majority of the Central Committee: "We must not cut ourselves off from important elements!—It is not enough to shout everywhere, 'Fourth International.' It must be built. The lines must be drawn around concrete (?!) questions. . . ." On the occasion of the national conference against the sacred union I supported the idea that it should be *in essence* an occasion for us to propagandize for the Fourth International. The reaction was, "no ultimatism," "let's be concrete"; *both on the Molinier side and on the Naville side.* (!)

The discussion on the publication of the Open Letter ended with a compromise: it was published on the last page, and the appendix concerning the questions of organization was omitted. Obviously, the SFIO bureaucracy was not appeased. Later it used the publication of the Open Letter, even in this form, as a pretext for the expulsions. Nor had allies been won on the right. But on the other hand, truly revolutionary elements had been left aside:

> Finally (says a letter from Van to Crux on August 25) it must be noted that reflections like the following are heard among a minority, quite weak it is true, but composed of young workers (!): "Now it is high time to have a Fourth International"—"After all, we need to have an organization of our own," etc.

Despite that, the vacillators were soon to have the upper hand;

hesitation transforms itself in a short time into a *retreat all along the line*. The symptoms of crisis became clear. Naville wrote to Crux, August 27, 1935:

> The question of orientation is far from clear in the group. There is a tendency not to accept the expulsions . . . unless we can make a determined bloc with the left. So concessions are foreseen which will weaken our position instead of strengthening it, among other things the abandonment of *La Vérité* and the publication of *Révolution* (or another paper) as the sole paper of the new united tendency, on a "broad" basis. . . . I cannot help noticing that this question of the mass paper can, under acute circumstances, bring about a dispute. It must be resolved. In that case, we can achieve real successes.

In these equivocal words, there is no evidence of a desire to resolutely oppose opportunist tendencies, but rather there is the indecision which we will observe later in Naville as well, when political or organizational questions arise. Didn't he himself object to the publication of the Open Letter?

The Bureaucracy Strikes

"The question of orientation" was completely clear to Blum and Company. One day after Naville's letter, the CAP (the party leadership) made its decision, definite though cautiously formulated,

> that the newspaper *La Vérité* can no longer be considered an organ of the Socialist Party; . . . to inform the members that by distributing this newspaper, they solidarize themselves with an activity aimed at discrediting and defaming fine party comrades; (hence still no prohibition! and finally) to ask the next National Council of the party to take . . . all sanctions—however serious—which the interests of the party may require.

Immediately after the decision of the CAP was made public, Naville drafted a resolution, two and a half pages long, which began with these words:

> The August 28 decision of the CAP is not at all unexpected. It is the continuation of the plan announced by Blum at Mulhouse. . . . It is absurd to think that any trick or detour can avert this episode. . . . Therefore it is necessary to: at the same time *resist* and *prepare for independence*. . . . The dominant question is that of organizing the new party. . . .

Rous (who afterward became ill for several weeks) also stated: "We will wage an offensive in all the party branches" (letter to Crux, September 3, 1935).

But this did not prevent the "offensive" from remaining a pious vow. Neither the best intentions nor the best resolutions suffice. There must also be a *real will* to carry out the decisions, to take a series of organizational measures, to assemble and put in action all the forces of the party. In reality, Naville's draft resolution remained *on paper*. Instead of the alarm being sounded to all revolutionaries, with a special issue of *La Vérité,* no paper came out for an entire four weeks—so as not to "provoke" the enemies. *La Vérité* appeared only at the end of September, *Révolution* at the beginning of October. Instead of going on the offensive, they retreated. Rous's letter to Crux, September 11, 1935, shows this:

> We are in the midst of a discussion of what line to follow. Everyone says that independence is what is on the agenda. Fine. Then, parenthetically, they confess that it is necessary to "retreat" because it is not certain that the whole Pivertist left will follow. . . . Yesterday the Central Committee discussed the question: since the CAP has banned *La Vérité,* the following maneuver is necessary: We say to the CAP, if you want to retract your measure and your proposals for expulsion, we are willing to give up (!) *La Vérité* and to consider in what forms we can express our tendency viewpoint. . . . It is obvious that this is only a maneuver so as to be able to publicize throughout the party, "See how far we have gone and still they refuse. . . ."

But even while some wanted to "maneuver," to more easily win over the vacillators to independence, the Molinier-Frank group was ready to sacrifice independence in favor of maneuvering. Rous reported, September 11, 1935, to Crux:

> Today in the Central Committee, Raymond proposed to stop publishing *La Vérité* (which is entirely different from the above maneuver). The motive: *La Vérité* is banned and prohibited in the party branches: whoever sells it, whoever writes for it, will be expelled. . . . Finally the following proposal was agreed upon: to maintain *La Vérité,* but to say that, in respect of the prohibition (!), it will no longer be an organ of the [Socialist] Party. . . .

Molinier's demand to suppress the newspaper was at the same time that of the ultra-centrist Pivert. (Between the two there was at that time an active exchange of ideas through correspondence.) Crux intervened in the discussion with a letter addressed to Van, September 13:

Marceau Pivert calls for the discontinuation of *La Vérité,* as if that measure could appease the gods. And *Lutte de classes* as well? And *Révolution?* And the leaflets? Those wretches of Spartacus show more consistency by abandoning *Révolution.* But by doing so they will succeed only in whetting the appetite of Blum and Zyromsky. . . . Before they throttle you, they seek to deprive you of your means of defense. To consent to that is to commit political suicide.

At the same time that the heated debate was going on in the Central Committee on the question of the "line," the bureaucracy, seeing no resistance on the part of the Bolshevik-Leninists, prepared its second blow, stronger this time: to Molinier's appeal against suspension from the delegation for *one* year, the bureaucracy replied: "Arras, September 13, 1935. The National Disputes Commission inflicts on Citizen Molinier a suspension from all delegations for *three* years."

The same day, thirteen comrades and two youth comrades received a letter from the general secretary of the party advising them of the motion of expulsion against them for being responsible for:

slanderous attacks by the newspaper *La Vérité* against members invested with the confidence of the party and the campaign waged by this paper in favor of constituting a Fourth International.

On September 19, the expulsion motion was confirmed by the National Disputes Commission, but at the same time they pretended, with the skill of true bureaucrats, to leave open the possibility of conciliation. The letter of the secretary of the commission says:

Please tell me how you plan to remedy a situation which creates difficulties inside the party, which all of us have a duty of avoiding, in the interests of socialism itself.

And the reply? . . . It was yet another two weeks before *La Vérité* appeared. It was devoted to . . . the agrarian question. Only on the last page was there published, in almost three columns, in the form of an official judiciary journal, a chronological enumeration of the decisions of the different bureaucratic commissions. The slogans (even on the last page!) were filled with vain illusions: "The revolutionary voice will not be silenced in the party." "Against a split." (!) "For revolutionary unity." (!!)

To Maneuver

As for our experienced comrades, they obviously had no illusions in the SFIO. They had only participated in this policy, actively or passively, because of the maneuvers, but they had not taken the following into consideration:

> But the policy of maneuvering has its own rules, which must be strictly observed:
> (a) The maneuver must be well understood in all its ramifications by the leadership (from the outset);
> (b) The maneuver cannot be used for tricky purposes, which are apt to disorient your friends without fooling your enemies;
> (c) You must define the limits of the maneuver to avoid becoming its first victim;
> (d) At each stage of the maneuver your own organization must be kept informed and no important step must be undertaken in a personal capacity. (Crux to a Belgian comrade, March 16, 1936)

After the Lille expulsions, the youth had carried out its politics under the slogan "The [Seine] Alliance Continues." That lent itself to ambiguity. Craipeau tried to explain the maneuver to the Central Committee of the GBL. According to Frédéric's report to Crux, August 4, he said:

> All splits take place under the slogan of unity. Therefore it is necessary to prepare for our independence by demanding reinstatement into the Young Socialists.

It goes without saying that Crux also thought of maneuvering. In his letter of July 30, 1935, he gave Rous his opinion:

> We can condense the discussion. Clearly, it involves a new party. . . . By that I do not mean to say that the adults must *leave* the party. Oh no! We must not make their job easier for them (the bureaucrats). But we are naturally all in agreement that the struggle against the expulsions, eventually for the reinstatement of the youth, must have an extremely aggressive character: *We accuse!*

But to maneuver does not, in the first place, mean to demand reintegration, but:

> The secret of success now consists in not allowing yourselves to be

taken by surprise. On the contrary, without the knowledge of the enemy a vehement offensive must be carefully prepared that will take the adversary by surprise. (Letter of Crux, August 10, 1935)

The moment to abandon the maneuver of returning to the SFIO had come shortly afterward. On August 23, 1935, Fred Zeller, at that time leader of the strongest faction in the Young Socialists in Paris, wrote his "Open Letter" against the Spartaco-SAPists who were ready to capitulate, solidarizing himself with the Bolshevik-Leninists. On the most important question, that of the International, he declared:

> The slogan of the *new International* therefore has for us a positive content and will realize its full revolutionary meaning in the ardent battle which we will wage along with you in the coming weeks. . . .

The tone and the open language of the Bolshevik-Leninists, so much criticized by our own comrades, he defended in these words: "We are not diplomats or embassy attachés, we are revolutionaries."

And on the question of reinstatement he wrote, "I can state that the thirteen expelled militants fought all the way for reinstatement. . . ."

But while the centrists of yesterday came over to our positions, the "Old Bolsheviks" Molinier-Frank revived the anti-Bolshevik SAPist slogan, "It must be done without saying it" (quoted according to the letter of Rous to Crux, September 3, 1935). On September 14, 1935, Frédéric reported to Crux:

> The general line, whose most consistent spokesman is still Frank . . . is conceived as follows: "not to give the bureaucracy pretexts by noisy speeches on independence . . . but to achieve independence without speaking of it. (!!)

Crux intervened in the discussion, with the inevitable delay. Here is a passage from his letter to Rous, September 13, 1935:

> Is it or is it not necessary to speak openly about the perspective of an independent party? How can it be avoided? You would certainly like to remain in the SFIO to the limit of its possibilities. . . . We say openly to our friends: Defend your place in the SFIO zealously, but be prepared for independent struggle if it is forced on us—and it looks as though that will be the case. *How can we avoid saying that openly?*

September 16—three days before Crux went to the hospital

where he spent six weeks— he once again summarized his viewpoint:

> I have spoken many times in the past weeks about the situation in France. If my suggestions sometimes lack the necessary precision, that is because I cannot observe developments close up, and important elements of the whole picture fail to appear. But I will try to summarize my point of view in a few lines once again.
>
> There is the question of our *political line*. It must be directed toward *independence*, which is dictated by the whole situation, above all by the conscious will of our enemies (the imperialists, the reformists, the Stalinists, the centrists, the SAPists, etc.). But there is the *tactical* and *pedagogical* question. This has its own rights and obligations which—in the final analysis, of course—are subordinate to our political line. We can and should use every means that is likely to persuade the hesitant, the poorly informed, the inexperienced, of the ill will of our enemies. But these measures and these procedures must not fetter our will to action and our fundamental intransigence. We ourselves must understand fully the secondary character of the statutory struggle, of the formal concessions, etc., despite all their conjunctural importance. If there is a serious division over some important concessions, it is better to give them up, because in such cases there is always the risk of losing more than you gain. Nine-tenths of our forces, at the very least, for the political offensive, for mass work, etc. . . . One-tenth, at the very most, for the statutory struggle and the purely pedagogical measures.

The letter came too late. In a report by Frédéric to Crux, September 17, 1935, on the subject of a general assembly to prepare for the National Conference, we read:

> At the General Assembly there was an initial discussion of the perspective. . . . The opposition (against the line of independence) was from among the ranks and especially comrades who had been for a year under the exclusive influence of Molinier. This opposition amounted to taking the line of the SAP in the purest sense: discontentment, ostrich tactics in face of the bureaucratic offensive, no concrete proposal, but arguments like these: our mission in the party has not yet been completed: instead of 300 we should leave— later—with 3,000; to leave the party now would mean exhuming the old cadaver of the League, but an even sparser one; we should not separate ourselves from the left wing, etc. . . .

Molinier-Frank had already carried out good faction work, if not against the SFIO or against the Pivertists, certainly against the GBL, *without meeting real resistance from the Rous-Naville factions*.

III. Centrism as a Touchstone

Relations with Pivert

In his June 10 letter, Crux had indicated that the correct attitude toward the centrists is the *key to the situation*: to let oneself be led into combinations with the leaders of the SAP, the IAG, etc., would mean compromising the banner of the Fourth International and "arresting the development of diverse centrist currents on the road of the revolution." One might say that the whole policy of the GBL from July to December 1935 was an uninterrupted attack on the maxim recommended by Crux.

In such situations, the centrists are the most dangerous enemies, because without breaking from reformism, they temporarily appropriate some of the most radical slogans. A typical example is Marceau Pivert. The left pressure from his own ranks (especially the youth) provided, even for this Freemason, a few momentary breaks in the clouds. The high point of his profession of faith in and, at the same time, the supreme tribute to a revolutionary organization, are certainly these words: "The struggle against Trotskyism, at present, is the sign of a reactionary state of mind inside the workers' movement" (see *La Vérité*, August 2, 1935).

But an adroit centrist never forgets an escape route. His infallible trademark is his equivocation. An example: Pivert solidarizes equally well with revolutionaries ("revolutionary unity without comrades like Fred Zeller or Makarowski . . . is a lie"—*La Vérité,* August 23, 1935) as with the reformists ("it is impossible to imagine a youth movement that would try to isolate itself from the party and let itself be led into a muted struggle against the party"—*La Vérité*, August 23, 1935).

He made no distinction between revolutionaries and reactionaries:

> There is room for all! and liberty for all! To want to throw out someone who does not think as you do is moreover a sign of ideological weakness; it means "I could not take care of these troublemakers by loyal discussion, a confrontation of methods, so I will throw them out." If the party consented to that, it would simply commit suicide. (*La Vérité*, August 2, 1935)

That he himself would commit this suicide could be predicted by two facts. First of all, all Marxist criteria were foreign to him:

> Tomorrow as yesterday (he wrote), we will defend, for the reconstruction of organic unity, this fundamental conception of socialism: the party open to all, internal democracy, respect for the rights of minorities. (*La Vérité*, August 2, 1935)

Furthermore his closest political friends were anti-Trotskyists par excellence, i.e., according to Pivert's own words, reactionaries. It was the "Spartacus" grouplet, led by the SAP people, which "protested" in a leaflet against the expulsion of the thirteen youth comrades as follows:

> They (the Spartacists) consider themselves all the more qualified inasmuch as from the beginning of their activity they declared themselves against factional struggle as practiced in the Seine Alliance, a democratic and revolutionary body, and inasmuch as they also declared themselves against the Bolshevik-Leninist slogan of the Fourth International. This slogan, which is abstract and empty of practical (!) sense, has always been considered by the Spartacus comrades as likely to give a handle to accusations of a splitting policy. . . . They regret that the Bolshevik-Leninist comrades felt it their duty to publish in *La Vérité* the formula "on the orders of Laval-Stalin" and to speak of "the sacred union team of Blum-Thorez-Zyromsky-Stalin."

In reality, the Spartacists only used their "protest" against the bureaucracy to win the favors of the bureaucracy by attacks against the "Trotskyists." With them it was not a problem of "clumsiness of language," which is what the Bolshevik-Leninists were reproached with, but of the language of treason.

Two militants represented the left wing of the SFIO at that time: Zeller, the youth; Pivert, the adults. The first reacted against the SAPist action with an "Open Letter to the Spartacus Comrades," in which he unmasked their sordid haste to capitulate. The second assembled all the ridiculous arguments of the Spartacists.

Just as the attitude toward Spartacus was a touchstone for Pivert, the attitude toward Pivert was a touchstone for the Bolshevik-Leninists. The proof that they were not completely blind, however, in relation to the nature of the "ally" is given in this excerpt from the letter written after one of the visits organized by Molinier to Pivert, who was then in an isolated place in southern France:

Here are several notes on the visit to Pivert, according to Rous's account: . . . On the question of the new revolutionary party, Pivert is "of course" in agreement. But it must not be talked about publicly, nor even among ourselves! . . . The political meaning of the expulsion escapes Pivert. It is the work of "swine." His perspective is to proceed as quickly as possible to total unity; only in the united party is there salvation at this time. Split at this time is something incomprehensible and somehow "ill-timed." (Letter from Van to Crux, August 6, 1935)

It is obvious that, despite this, it was necessary not to reject all blocs *for definite objectives*, since the problem was separating the wheat from the chaff among the centrists. Comrade Crux averted in due time the dangers of such a bloc. On August 10 he wrote:

You are in the process of preparing for a bloc with Marceau Pivert. I am far from being opposed to it. . . . But this bloc demands an absolutely intransigent attitude on your part on the question of the Fourth International. The slightest concession on this point would be fatal to the further development of our section.

To give an example of a very critical attitude, at the same time loyal, Comrade Trotsky intervened publicly in the discussion against Pivert (among the Parisian comrades *not one* was found who wanted to attack Pivert openly; at that time, Naville and others objected to the publication of the Open Letter so as not to "provoke" anyone "unnecessarily"). In his article " 'Labels' and 'Numbers' " (published in *La Vérité*, August 23, 1935), Trotsky bared the Achilles heel of all the centrists:

The misfortune of Pivert is that until now he has not cut the umbilical cord that binds him to the small world of the Blums and the Zyromskys. On every new occasion he looks at his "friends" and feels their pulse with anxiety.

Toward the end he wrote:

The Bolshevik-Leninists consider themselves a faction of the International which is being built. They are completely ready to work hand in hand with other truly revolutionary factions. But they categorically refuse to adapt their politics to the psychology of opportunist cliques and to renounce their own banner.

These words were probably aimed not only at Pivert, but also at our own comrades, seized by doubt. Nevertheless, Trotsky was mistaken here. For the next six months his article was the last open attack of the Bolshevik-Leninists against Pivert.

The Molinier-Frank Plot

The Molinier faction was peculiarly well informed about Pivert's plans. On August 26, 1935, Marceau Pivert wrote personally to Molinier:

> . . . A "cold" operation of the same order as the creation (?) of the Fourth International is vitiated (!) from the outset. Even now I still persist in thinking that the creation of the Fourth International was an error and that it was necessary to liquidate the reformists in the heat of battle. . . .

On September 3, 1935, Pivert expressed himself quite clearly in a letter to R. Molinier:

> At any price, it is therefore necessary to *remain in the party* (emphasis by M.P.), abandon this impossible attitude of being affiliated (?) to two Internationals at the same time. . . . But I believe that *the sacrifice of La Vérité is required.*

On September 11, Rous informed Crux: "Raymond has proposed discontinuing *La Vérité.*"

What it meant to want to remain in the SFIO at all costs was explained by Crux in his letter of September 13, 1935, concerning the same proposal made by "Spartacus":

> The Spartacists' notion that it is necessary to remain inside the SFIO *at any cost* is treachery. The reformists say, we will do everything within the framework of bourgeois legality. But bourgeois legality allows "everything" except the most important things. Blum's legality is nothing but an adjunct to and a reflection of bourgeois legality. It allows you to do, or rather to say, "everything" except those things that would effectively oppose imperialist patriotism.

This very important argument could not remain unknown to Raymond Molinier and his group. Just as Pivert wanted to remain in the SFIO at all costs, Molinier wanted to achieve a political bloc with Pivert at all costs. That explains his capitulationist and liquidationist line for the GBL. Frédéric, in his letter to Crux of September 14, wrote concerning Molinier's attempts to justify himself:

Molinier said: never did the Committee for the Third International, never did Lenin and Trotsky pronounce the word *split*; and he added demagogically: they never substituted their experience for the experience of the masses.

Frédéric recognized Molinier's policy for what it was, as his letter to Crux of September 14, 1935, shows:

> In the present situation . . . the perspective of slowly winning ground by collaboration with such backward, constitutionally cowardly elements as Marceau Pivert lacks all sense; rather it takes on a reactionary character. This first sentimental reaction of Pivert is a loquacious solidarity; his real political attitude, when the situation becomes serious . . . is to separate himself from the revolutionaries. *And we negotiate and negotiate*, as if nothing could happen without him.

However, the Molinier-Frank faction had its way with its line of perpetual negotiation (always increasing the concessions to Pivert), as against the Rous-Naville factions, because the latter were themselves ready—albeit after some hesitations—either to make concessions (for "maneuvering" reasons) or to be content, on the whole, with working out abstract analyses. *Their two factions were not able to join as allies for a serious offensive against Molinier's opportunism.* On September 15, Crux wrote to Rous:

> For us to believe that it is possible to become reconciled with Pivert and the others through concessions would be very naive. On the contrary, they will respond to every step we take in their direction by a step in the direction of Zyromsky.

But as early as the following day he announced the need for a radical change of posture:

> The more I consider it, the more I am persuaded that P(ivert)'s latest article is a wretched and ignoble retreat before the pressure of social patriotism. In reality, he already has carried out the same function in relation to Léon Blum that Zyromsky carried out before him.

However, for Molinier-Frank there were no more preliminaries. They had made up their minds to go all the way down the road of negotiations and concessions. Argument and discussion no longer helped. Molinier, if we may be blunt, only spoke in order to dissimulate his real designs. The principal means of combat against their own organization became more-than-doubtful maneuvers, which Molinier-Frank knew well enough how to use, as the following resolution proves:

> The Political Bureau adopted the following resolution *unanimously* at its July 3 meeting: "The Political Bureau notes that Comrades Molinier and Frank have systematically abstained from participating in the meetings of the organization leadership since the Mulhouse congress, while occupying positions of major responsibility. Comrade Molinier, having deserted the leadership without giving any political reason, and having asked for a leave of absence, nevertheless continues his activity in the ranks of the organization and in the SP. Comrade Frank, having returned from a leave of absence, refused to participate in the Political Bureau of July 3 under the pretext that 'it was not serious.'
>
> "Since these comrades . . . have responsibly directed the policy of the tendency with the support of the majority of the Central Committee, since they give no political reason, since it turns out that at an excellent moment for the activity of the tendency they plan to act outside the leadership, i.e., to practically break up the tendency;
>
> "The Political Bureau energetically condemns their *attitude of desertion*. . . ."

Rous commented on this resolution in a letter to Crux, July 5:

> The leave of absence requested by Raymond turned out to be simply a pretext in order to be able to continue factional work in the ranks of the organization in peace. . . .

Again, in connection with the national conference of September 21, 1935, Molinier used a method which is not exactly irreproachable. The pretext was a draft of a keynote report drawn up by Rous for this conference. On this subject, Naville wrote to Crux August 27:

> This draft was drawn up just before the Mulhouse congress. In the discussion in the Central Committee, Raymond and Frank rejected it as a basis of discussion. . . . Finally it was decided that Raymond would make amendments and modifications, without modifying the spirit of the report.

But let us listen to Rous:

> . . . Raymond, instead of limiting himself to a few additions, completely remolded it in violation of the decisions and agreements,

profiting from my absence. This is completely disloyal and totally miserable. (Rous to Crux, September 3, 1935)

And in fact not a single sentence from Comrade Rous's keynote report was kept. All the clear and unequivocal points were carefully replaced by abstractions, empty of meaning but high-sounding, such that the organization was not pointed in any direction. Several examples will illustrate. Rous's report says:

> The branch groups, i.e., the fraction of Bolshevik-Leninist militants from the same branch, should not limit themselves to internal work (!), which inevitably turns around and runs up against the social composition of the section, but should organize to carry their work to the exterior. . . .

In Molinier's:

> If it is observed that one of the characteristics of the SFIO party is the very small percentage of active members (one-fifth at the most), our propaganda quickly won the most sympathy and our influence was expanded by our relationship of forces in this percentage. . . . It was necessary to give a boost to certain branches (!) through a systematic action toward the masses.

That is called smuggling. The concrete analysis of the social composition of the SFIO was replaced by the abstraction of "activity." The invitation "not to be limited to internal work" was replaced by the contrary, though expressed in an imprecise way: "to give a boost to certain branches," i.e., obviously, branches of the SFIO.

On the other hand, a completely hypocritical "self-criticism" follows—a feature of all Molinier's organizational writing—which *always falls only on the shoulders of others*. But it gives Molinier the false halo of honesty:

> Despite our immediate decision, because of the chaotic character of our central leadership, our numerical weakness, and also the inertia of the apparatus of the branches, we are still only taking the first steps along this path (of giving certain SFIO branches a boost).

If therefore the successes in mass work did not make themselves felt, it is not because the possibilities were limited by the social composition of the SFIO; but because work in the SFIO had not really begun. Molinier's hidden intentions are made clear in the chapter on "our press." Rous's report says:

It is obvious that the propaganda tool of this work should be *La Vérité*, which will only become a mass paper to the degree that the Bolshevik-Leninists themselves orient to mass work.

And Molinier's:

It is sufficient to note that the editorial responsibility for the newspaper fell . . . on four or five members of the leadership . . . in order to explain the at once hasty and routine character of our press. There is little or no serious study (!?) of an issue. . . . No central documentation (?). . . . Thus *La Vérité* does not succeed in being readable (?!), not only for the masses, but for the ordinary member of the present workers' organizations.

Who could fail to recognize even here the plotter of *La Commune* who sacrifices *La Vérité* and its program to the centrists?

We limit ourselves here only to a confrontation of the most significant chapters: "International Work" (in Rous):

Too many Bolshevik-Leninists take no interest in international questions. However . . . the problem of the Fourth International is posed with the greatest sharpness, and must be discussed in all the propaganda of the tendency. The GBL must be the organizer of the resistance to the sacred union and for the Fourth International, inside and outside the SP. . . . Having let itself be absorbed by discussions on questions relating to the SFIO . . . the Central Committee has not accorded time to international questions (!!).

After raising the need for international work and support to the IS, he continued:

The international question should be taken into the SFIO through the newspaper and the conference. *The manifesto of the Fourth International should be the point of departure* for a campaign of this type. (Rous's emphasis)

Molinier had already practically abandoned his international-ism. To "international activity," he devoted . . . eight lines!

. . . The French section thus had to make a special effort for this neighboring body (the IS). On the whole, during the past year, by its rather broad external activity (what excuses!) the section showed an equally great interest in the problems of the sister sections; the distribution of the international bulletin proves it.

And that is all. The words served only to hide the fact that the author had abandoned internationalism.

The "revised" draft was published immediately as the keynote report of the Central Committee in the internal bulletin before Rous had a chance to oppose its publication. The reaction to this surprise attack by Molinier is itself characteristic of the unbelievably soft attitude held during the acute stage of the crisis. The IS said, in the minutes of September 16, 1935 (draft):

> The keynote report . . . is unanimously considered insufficient. This keynote report, in this form, was in fact inserted against the decisions of the Central Committee, on the responsiblity of one comrade (Molinier).

Rous protested in his letter to the Central Committee, September 3, 1935:

> Raymond had not respected the decisions of the Central Committee any more than the agreement reached in the commission (Gérard, Raymond, Rous), . . . which provided that the parts of Report No. 1 concerning the organizational questions and leadership questions should be reproduced without change.

It is clear from this that the Central Committee permitted *political* changes, i.e., it was ready to make *political* concessions. In the "organizational questions and leadership questions" it was less conciliatory. Rous "does not see" the political disfigurations made by Molinier. He wrote on September 3, 1935, to Crux:

> I had to protest for the record (!), but all efforts will be made with Gérard-Naville so that this manuever will not have the effect (perhaps "desired"), i.e., to open up personal quarrels on the occasion of the National Conference, instead of seriously examining the situation.

Similarly, Naville saw only the personal side of the dispute. In a letter to Crux of August 27, 1935, he wrote concerning the discussion on the keynote report:

> Personally, I did not intervene in this discussion, which took place in the internal life of the GBL in a period when I was absent from it. . .

The case described here confirms what Crux said:

> In any case, the most serious mistake was to oppose the systematic

campaign in favor of the new party and the Fourth International. It
was confusion over that question that opened the way for the
Molinier-Frank scheme. (Crux to Rous, December 26, 1935)

The Fourth National Conference

After the Lille expulsions, the banning of *La Vérité,* the
suspension of Molinier for three years, etc., . . . there was no
doubt that a new party was soon going to come into being. The
conference of the GBL therefore had the task of preparing the
separation from the SFIO and independence. Crux wrote to Rous,
September 16, 1935:

> You are not yet proclaiming the new party, but you are in effect
> preparing the groundwork for it. A serious break in the CP, or the
> split of the Pivertists with the SFIO, or even an important local
> development, like Doriot's open betrayal, could serve our purposes if
> we present ourselves all at once as a new party.

But how could the conference carry out this preparatory work,
inasmuch as this conference was itself only improvised, although
it had already been put off once because of insufficient
preparation? Frédéric described the state of the conference in his
letter of September 26, 1935:

> A number of basic necessities, such as the timely distribution and
> discussion of documents decided upon by the different tendencies for
> *all* the questions, the draft resolutions, etc., were neglected before and
> during the conference. Thus we see the spectacle that in the heated
> debates on perspectives (and the tasks that are derived from them),
> on the question of the newspaper, neither of the two main tendencies
> was able to present a precise document. The delegates—for those who
> came from the provinces these problems only became clear at the
> conference itself—were therefore obliged to trust only their ears and
> orient themselves according to their personal impressions. The vote
> was on the basis of documents read out loud and more or less
> improvised, presented by third parties. . . .

What was the reason for this unbelievable negligence?
With Molinier-Frank, it is not hard to understand. A poorly
organized conference which could not make clear decisions was
in their interests. The center faction was weakened by Rous's
illness and Comrades Bardin and Boitel were quite absorbed in
trade union work. Naville and his faction contented themselves

with drawing up documents. Their organization spirit was in complete default.

The *true* cause of the problem was the absence of revolutionary will and political clarity. None of the three factions wanted a truly revolutionary offensive under the banner of the Fourth International and that is why the work of preparation for the conference was only of minimal interest to them. Organizational negligence as a result of political inadequacy can be clearly recognized here.

Under the circumstances, there is no point in going into the details of Naville's political resolution, twenty-one points in all, adopted unanimously (!). Considering the absolute lack of organizational work, it is at best only of literary interest. What good is it that everyone voted to prepare for the independent organization, if at the same time Molinier was allowed to go his way unimpeded? Moreover, the latter was designated responsible for mass propaganda—work that he could do without any supervision,* without caring in the least later on about Naville's twenty-one points (just like Naville himself, moreover!).

The fact that the personal dissensions were apparently overcome ("Naville greeted Molinier's desire for an understanding," as Frédéric relates in his report of September 26, 1935) and that the new leadership was elected by an overwhelming majority of votes served only to mask the serious conflict which was to come. Molinier at first tried to hide his real intentions. Frédéric wrote on September 26, 1935:

> Molinier made one of his pathetic and senseless speeches. . . . He spoke of the fundamental necessity, which no one contests, of daily work of a rank-and-file and mass character, and this in the guise of a response to the perspective of the independent party!

But his real intentions nevertheless did not remain obscure

---

*Jeanne Brissack wrote in the internal bulletin, December 13, 1935, under the title, "Some Explanation of the Present Conflict":

> Propaganda work among the masses—in charge of this work, Comrade Molinier had propaganda material printed: posters, leaflets, flyers—all outside the organization. He personally keeps this material . . . he pays for it, sells it, distributes it, without any supervision and without its being recorded in any account of the organization.

A truly shameful situation!

anymore, as the minutes of the IS show (reported by Rous), October 20, 1935:

> On the National Conference—Molinier, speaking for the comrades who still had illusions about the possibility of further cohabitation with the reformists . . . recommended remaining a tendency of the SFIO without letting our turn toward the independent organization, whose time has not yet come, be proscribed by the bureaucracy. . . . But he nevertheless limited himself to abstaining (!!!) in the vote without presenting countermotions.

This abstention on a resolution that expressed directly the opposite of Molinier's opinion was probably a new ruse of Molinier's and an element in his scheme. Despite this, one cannot excuse oneself, as Rous tries to do in the internal bulletin of December 13, 1935, in his article "On the Molinier Adventure," as follows: "Comrade Molinier is always ready to vote for and write anything at all."

If the dangerous intentions of a group or faction are known, a really good resolution should be worded in such a concrete (and, if necessary, personal) way as to allow no dodging. In the September 26, 1935, report, already quoted several times, Frédéric gives a characterization of the tendencies that had manifested themselves at the conference, and hits the nail on the head:

> What the two tendencies boil down to is: *a course toward the new party* (Naville, Gérard, Rousset, Rigal, Craipeau) and *remaining a faction in the SFIO* (Molinier, Lille, etc.). But in reality . . . both are wrong. The former, because they are unable to take hold of the policy of Molinier at its root, because they are not yet able to draw the concrete real conclusions from their perspective, because they want to use the unity-split demagogy. . . .

Thus it turns out that, despite the sharp conflicts, all the resolutions were adopted *unanimously* with a *single* exception: 131 votes were cast for *Révolution* as a "mass paper," and 118 for *La Vérité* as a "mass paper." On this question of third-rate importance, *falsely posed by both tendencies,* the fictitious character of the "unity" and "conciliation" of the Fourth National Conference of the GBL became evident. Precisely because the divergences were momentarily "surmounted" an all the more violent collision was prepared.

Vain Attempts to Form Blocs

In the fight against the SFIO bureaucracy, the Bolshevik-Leninists did not run up directly against Blum and his associates, but against his retinue of servants, headed by Marceau Pivert. The latter, after the split with Zyromsky, had formed—from some of the debris of *Bataille Socialiste*, from the last gasps of *L'Action socialiste*, from the "CASR" and from SAP-Spartacus—the Revolutionary Left, which constituted a centrist faction of the SFIO without any program. Its only "principle" was not to separate itself from the SFIO under any circumstances. For that reason even its revolutionary slogans took on a reactionary content. Its only serious "action" was the neutralization of the influence of the Trotskyists in the SFIO.

On September 29, 1935, the Political Bureau had *unanimously* adopted a resolution presented by Naville on the Revolutionary Left. Here is how the latter is described:

> The Political Bureau considers (1) that the GR, through its split from *Bataille Socialiste*, may contain progressive elements; (2) that the GBL should publicly present its position vis-à-vis this left wing, explaining its centrist character and calling for people to join the GBL; (3) the GBL should organize, especially in the sections and in the ranks, common action and discussion with the elements of the left wing.

On October 4, 1935, Naville wrote as a comment on this resolution:

> The present resolution was introduced by me against a document of Comrade Molinier which left the door open to a surreptitious fusion with the "Pivertist left." The Political Bureau adopted it; it must (!!?) therefore be applied.

Unfortunately, the adoption of the document did not yet mean its application—not even on the part of the one who had presented it.

Rous voted for Molinier's pseudo-radical resolution on the Revolutionary Left, presented by Molinier to fool the conciliators. He tried to justify his attitude in his letter of October 7, 1935, to Crux:

At the last Political Bureau it was Raymond himself who presented the most radical (?) resolution on the question of the firm attitude toward the left wing. . . . We adopted this resolution in order to be better able to hold him to his word (!) and demand actions in accord with it.

Just as Naville was led by literary-bureaucratic considerations, Rous was led by formal-juridical considerations.

La Vérité, which appeared several days after the National Conference, overturned in practice all the fine documents that had been adopted there. Although the conference had decided to prepare an independent organization, the line of adaptation to the SFIO was continued—and in a still more extreme way— because of the Revolutionary Left. Instead of preparing the consciousness of the radical members of the SFIO for the split, which was absolutely necessary, *La Vérité* said: "Against a policy of harmful split (!)," with the result that the second slogan, "For revolutionary unity," took on a meaning that was perfectly acceptable to any opportunist. Instead of carrying on "merciless criticism of opportunism," as the conference had decided, *La Vérité* recommended a bloc, in reality centrist, of the youth: "We must reinforce the revolutionary bloc." Not a word against Marceau Pivert in this issue of *La Vérité.* The response to the threats of expulsion was not a political offensive against the social patriots, but a "resumé of unquestionable facts," drawn up in a bureaucratic style and hidden on the last page, in which an attempt was made to prove the "injustice" committed toward the Bolshevik-Leninists. It was recalled that the party leadership "does not trouble itself with formal questions" vis-à-vis the right wing; and as a, so to speak, supreme expression of protest it was stated: "The leadership wants a split." It is difficult, alas, to ascertain now who the authors were.*

----

* In *La Vérité,* no. 242, June 8, 1935, the editors explained why the articles are not signed:

The explanation is simple: we wanted to stay in the Communist tradition. Read the old Bolshevik newspapers. The articles were rarely signed. For us a newspaper is a collective piece of work. It is the expression of the policy of the whole tendency.

We find a similar explanation also in the first issues of *La Commune.* The SAP editors of *Neue Front* also gave such a motivation for a similar attitude. All three editorial staffs wish to create an appearance of complete homogeneity. But who could fail to see that behind this type of

Soon opportunism will not show itself only in *La Vérité*. When M. Pivert convened a meeting to prepare the GR, the Central Committee sent as its representative . . . Molinier. Obviously, there was no criticism of Pivert from him. Frédéric reported to Crux, September 28, 1935:

> Yesterday the great assembly of the 15th arrondissement was held. . . . The formation of the Revolutionary Left was mentioned only in passing, and Molinier was the only one to do so, declaring that we were ready to participate on the basis of public opposition to national defense and public propaganda for revolutionary defeatism.

The contrast between the speech by F. Zeller, non–Bolshevik-Leninist at the time, and that of the "Old Bolshevik" Molinier,

---

"collective spirit" the fiercest infighting of groupings and cliques goes on? Of course, in this way it can better remain hidden from the members; in this way, too, it is possible for a certain time to avoid clearly differentiating the ideas by radically solving the differences. The daily work of problem-solving thus impeded, it becomes possible for the elements of conflict to accumulate, with the result that the inevitable crisis will be accompanied by explosions of an all the more violent character and will come crashing down on an insufficiently prepared rank and file.

In the interests of a healthy selection of the leaders, too, it seems more indicated at the present time to abandon the complete anonymity of the newspaper. Young and capable new elements from the provinces and from the capital will thus more easily be made known to the whole organization. Internal bulletins are not enough for this because the articles printed there are not given enough attention. Furthermore, it will no longer be so easy for the leading comrades to escape their responsibility. If Molinier had had to sign all his opportunist articles, he would not be able today to permit himself the impertinence of shifting onto others the responsibility for the opportunist course steered since Mulhouse and Lille.

It is correct that the best Marxist and Bolshevik newspapers, in their best periods, were anonymous. That was based on the fact that they were the product of a fully developed tendency with a distinguished leadership, whose authority was recognized by all and which took responsibility, before the party and before the outside world, for what was published. But this situation was arrived at only through a sharp struggle. In the present situation, where the creation of a young and authoritative leadership is still to be accomplished, it seems more appropriate to sign all the articles that are not editorials. The ranks will thus have a chance to more easily examine the different nuances. That will contribute to putting an end to the situation of cliques as soon as possible and to preparing the unity of the party on a higher level.

according to the report in *Révolution* (beginning of October, no. 13), shows clearly that the Central Committee representative was already playing the role of a reactionary brake.*

The non–Bolshevik-Leninist Zeller:

> Not the Bolshevik-Leninists but our opponents in the party are the ones we must distinguish ourselves from! . . . Whatever happens, if in this discussion we must remain alone against everyone, we will remain alone against everyone.

The "Old Bolshevik" Molinier:

> Molinier: He affirms the desire of his friends to remain in the party as long as possible in order to struggle fraternally alongside the members who are evolving toward the correct positions.

Opportunism in this period was expressed in the crudest fashion in *Révolution,* on which the Bolshevik-Leninists already exercised a preponderant influence. Here Pivert's centrist bloc was greeted with, "Long live the Revolutionary Left!" The front page was given to Marceau Pivert for an article filled with phrases. Naville characterized the situation as follows, in a "Note for the Central Committee," October 1, 1935:

> Thanks to R. Molinier's demagogy, the problem of the Revolutionary Left becomes further tangled. . . . At the informational meeting our representative made a scandalous speech. . . . Semi-private conversations in the corridors are still being held with Pivert, etc., instead of working on grouping militants *around* us. Tricks are being used, parliamentarism is being practiced, members are being confused. This is the first result of the decisions of the National Conference on the press (??).—*In practice,* Molinier acts as if to politically *liquidate* the GBL. He follows, in actual fact, the line used before the National Conference: he had proposed to the Central Committee stopping the publication of *La Vérité* as the newspaper of the organization. He wants to fuse us at all costs with the SAP-Pivert amalgam, to camouflage, to deceive. He proposes to the Political Bureau to have Balay and Henri join the Revolutionary Left. . . . Zeller is told to have young comrades join the Revolutionary Left, etc. . . . We do not need optical-illusion resolutions and two-faced resolutions. It is necessary to pass over to application, to the work:

---

*It goes without saying that here, as elsewhere in this article, only those passages are quoted which are *characteristic,* and the meaning of the quoted passage is strictly taken into account.

Orient all our forces around the branch groups. Call on sympathizers to join the ranks of the GBL; shake up Pivert's left, lead it into action without confusing ourselves with it. Stop the little game of six points or seven points, this document or that, journalistic quibbles over a common platform. We have our platform; it must be published, commented on, explained, and applied.

Naville's trenchant words are surprising. But they were for private use; for it is equally surprising to see, in the following three issues of *La Vérité, appearing under the responsibility of Naville as editor in chief,* a continuation of the shameful policy of adaptation to the Revolutionary Left, uninterrupted and even more emphasized; and *in these issues the question of the Fourth International is not even touched.* In *La Vérité* of October 11, 1935, we can read in a report on the founding meeting of the Revolutionary Left:

Comrade Pivert is a firm (?) opponent of the expulsions. . . . He showed . . . that the offensive by the CAP was motivated by our Marxist position on the problems of war and the People's Front. However, he only opposes expulsions on the grounds of formal democracy, demanding the same right to existence in the party for the right wing as for the proletarian left. . . .

There is not a word in *La Vérité* on the fact that the Revolutionary Left included even members who had voted for the expulsion for the Bolshevik-Leninists. On the question of the new party, this issue says:

As for ourselves, we fight for the revolutionary unity of the proletariat, and therefore for separation from the avowed supporters of capitalism in our ranks, social imperialists, and others.

The pacifists and the centrists of the Revolutionary Left, who are much more dangerous to the radical workers than the social imperialists are, were left unnamed.

This was because in the meantime the Revolutionary Left had formally proposed a fusion. Of course, the Central Committee could not accept the fusion proposal, because there was not even a trace of a common programmatic basis. But through the common resolution proposed for the Seine congress (see *La Vérité*, October 25, 1935), it went over *in practice* to the centrist position of the Revolutionary Left. But, as can be seen in the *Vérité* commentary, Pivert was more "consistent." There we read:

Read this motion. It contains nothing that a militant adhering to the Revolutionary Left has not (!) accepted or could not accept. However, at the meeting last Sunday, October 20 . . . the Executive Committee of the Revolutionary Left informed us that it did not want to make a common motion with our tendency and that the Revolutionary Left would have its own motion. We stressed the importance of our two tendencies' confirming our common action (?) in a motion at the congress.

Despite the refusal that was received, they continued to flatter Pivert. In a report on the assembly of the Revolutionary Left we read:

We cannot but be pleased to see . . . these comrades defend a platform which seals the definitive breakup of *Bataille Socialiste* (*La Vérité*, October 25, 1935).

Then regret once again:

He (Pivert) could not explain why the members of the Revolutionary Left accepted a common motion with Zyromsky for Mulhouse when they disagreed with him, but refused to make a common motion with the Bolshevik-Leninists, now that they had adopted a similar (?!!!) position on important points.

Without doubt the policy we have been speaking of is the work of Molinier-Frank. But the two other factions are also fully responsible because they tolerated this policy. Not only Rous, with his lack of perseverance, but also Naville, whose "notes" have no other meaning than a literary "alibi." At the moment when he should have changed the situation, instead of interpreting it, he recoiled before the practical consequences required by harsh reality. To be able to fight the opportunists—inside and outside the organization—would have required deciding on a political offensive *against the bureaucracy* under the *banner of the Fourth International*. But that is exactly what Naville and his faction did not want. The same Naville who made an excellent criticism of Molinier's opportunism is himself the main author of Motion C for the Federal Congress of the Seine (November 1935), which constitutes, so to speak, the culminating point of the opportunist curve of the GBL: not a word on the need for a new party; the question of the International is not even touched upon. On the contrary, we find that its final chapter is "New federal methods of work are needed"; a whole series of proposed administrative modifications, as if one wanted to install oneself forever in the SFIO. The hope was to win over the members of the Revolutionary Left with this centrist motion, but all that was achieved was the opposite. This time, fewer votes were obtained than at the Mulhouse congress. Frédéric reported to Crux, November 8, 1935:

> Marceau Pivert immediately canceled the memberships in the Revolutionary Left of all those who had voted Bolshevik-Leninist. Many only voted for the Revolutionary Left to observe discipline . . . and because they did not view the differences between the Revolutionary Left and the Bolshevik-Leninists as very important.

A report by Rous for the Central Committee, November 11, says:

> It is a fact that in the present situation the GBL solicited collaboration and obtained only refusals. It is a fact that the Revolutionary Left has further isolated us and, above all, has "encroached" on our positions in the party.

IV. The Split

The Beginnings of the Split

After the National Conference of September 21-22, 1935, the Molinier-Frank faction in practice dictated and directed the policy of retreat. The question is posed: How was this faction able, against the decisions of the congress, and against the Naville-Rous factions, to win over to its purely centrist policy a considerable part of the organization, among which we find old Bolshevik-Leninist members, and to accomplish the split?

With the retreat of the Molinierists before Pivert consisting of the abandonment of one principled position after another, Naville's criticism—even if there had been at that time the desire and the strength for action—had to remain without effect inasmuch as it did not begin with the defense of the *whole Bolshevik-Leninist program.* Only in that way could the best elements have been assembled and encroachments made on the conciliators' camp. But we have seen that Naville left the slogan of the Fourth International, which is the most concentrated expression of the Bolshevik-Leninist program, in the background as much as possible. That this was not simply because he was opposed to "superfluous" repetition of an "abstract" slogan, as was claimed, but was in practice a departure from the positions of internationalism, is shown by the fact that Naville resisted in the same silent and surreptitious way discussing a very concrete international question, the persecution of the Bolshevik-Leninists in the Soviet Union.

Solidarity with the Russian Bolshevik-Leninists does not, of course, make life easy and comfortable for the sections of the Fourth International. But this difficulty is inevitable; it is in the nature of things. No workers' organization in the world, even if it sometimes violently criticizes the Communist Party of its own country, as in the case of the SAP, the ILP, etc., has ever been as heinously slandered as the "Trotskyists," characterized as the "vanguard of the counterrevolutionary bourgeoisie," etc. . . . This is not explained—as some philistines believe—by "old personal recriminations," or even by the principled sharpness of our criticism, but by the existence of tens of thousands of Bolshevik-Leninists in the Soviet Union itself, who represent a direct danger to the Soviet bureaucracy. *To Stalin they are the principal enemy,* and Stalin fights the "Trotskyists" in Western Europe to the degree that, in the international arena, they create the premises for the victory of the Bolshevik-Leninists in the Soviet Union and solidarize with them.*

But here Naville's conservative sectarianism can be seen. Naville prefers to make correct but abstract analyses in his study, in order to be able to display them later as alibis, but he never takes nearly enough interest in what is going on in the working class. He is satisfied to develop certain ideas, to be the conservative preacher of abstract truths, but he also desires to be left alone on other matters. Hence his exasperated resistance to the entry into the SFIO in the summer of 1934, which disturbed his peace; hence also his indifference toward internationalism on the Russian question.

Another side of the same malady is his constant effort to use his "Trotskyism" as discreetly as possible so as not to "provoke" anyone.

Even the centrists often accept our slogans, such as the workers' militia, arming of the proletariat, revolutionary defeatism, etc. But when it comes time to draw the final conclusions, as "Trotskyism" demands, they recoil. These conclusions are none other than the organic linking of revolutionary slogans in a Marxist program. Without this linking, we can see exactly "in numerous comrades (even on the Central Committee)" this

> particular cretinism: the sterile repetition of formulas (defeatism, militias) without any actual content (see the keynote report for the Central Committee of November 10, 1935)

which Naville describes but which he does not pursue to its roots.

The cretinism of many centrists comes from the fact that their political physiognomy lacks a programmatic backbone. The essential difficulty for those who move toward us is the audacious leap from centrism to Marxism. The fear that this leap inspires is veiled by sophisms directed against "Trotskyism." Immediately Schwab and Company intervene here, saying (in complete agreement with the Stalinists) that it is "demonstrated in

---

*It is no accident that throughout its existence the reactionary SAP has never written a word on the persecution of the revolutionaries in the USSR. It, too, tries in this way to avoid the vicious attacks of the Comintern.

practice" that the Trotskyist line is wrong because . . . otherwise Trotsky and not Stalin would have come out victorious. To an ordinary person or an inexperienced youth, this "argument" has a hundred times more effect than all the others. That is why the conscious Stalinist crooks and the miserable centrist dilettantes are able to have success with their sophisms from time to time. They are further helped by the powerful attractive force of victory associated with the prestige of the October revolution.

That is where the greatest difficulties are for us, difficulties which we will conquer *definitively* only by a victorious October in another country. But to get there, we must at least educate our young cadres in the understanding of victories and defeats. It is necessary to tell the workers who approach us that one doesn't win whenever one wants to; in other words, that even the most correct policy in the world cannot guarantee victory in each historical situation. This problem of the historical dialectic is personified in the question of why Stalin triumphed. Since only by finding the correct answer to this question can our epoch be completely understood, Trotsky devoted to it, on the occasion of a visit from Zeller, an article especially for the youth, who were just on the verge of making that last leap from centrism to Marxism.

But here Naville's sabotage began. With the help of his friends, he has prevented this article from appearing in French to this day. He and the conservative sectarians like him objected sometimes that it was a "historical," "personal," or "separate" question, which "was not needed"; and sometimes that it was necessary not to publish too many articles by Trotsky, because . . . "the youth will complain."

But in reality they wanted to avoid talking about "Trotsky-ism," they wanted to hide their ideas, in order to avoid embarrassing attacks from all sides. But it is just this evasion that weakened our organization enormously and made it accessible to all the bad influences. In avoiding speaking and writing on the subject of "Trotskyism," in reality they neglected to educate and to win over sympathizers as well as youth in the spirit of the whole program of the GBL. They thought it was enough to win people to the most important slogans of the action program. It was only for this reason that Molinier-Frank could even think of making *Révolution,* until then the semi-Pivertist organ of Naville-Rous-Rousset-Craipeau, into a purely centrist organ of Pivert-Molinier-Frank. Given that none of the three factions of the GBL truly defended the whole program, their struggle had to appear to the youth as purely a clique struggle.

The sabotage of Trotsky's articles continued after the split. To a question from Braun, Rous replied on February 23, 1936 (!!):

> . . . the same reactionary state of mind is what is involved, in the last analysis. They think that the masses are not interested in long articles concerning these questions, despite daily evidence to the contrary (Stakhanov, etc.).

The most diverse kinds of "vague excuses" covered up political uncertainty in some, fear of embarrassing attacks in others. The latter preferred to introduce "Trotskyism" to the youth as a false category, so as not to be disturbed in their tranquillity. But the *enemies* do not allow the question of "Trotskyism" to be eluded. To study it with the youth is the first requirement for the *education* of our cadres. It must be stated openly that our ideas are correct and we must know how to prove it despite the defeats. But to openly propagate "Trotskyism" is the first thing to do to *temper* our cadres, because that requires struggle and courage and permits no cowardly evasion. Moreover, the creation of educated and tempered cadres is the most crucial task in France. *Without resolving it the French section of the Fourth International cannot be built and the French proletariat cannot be led to victory.*

The question of "Trotskyism" becomes the most important touchstone for the young generation. When Marceau Pivert in a moment of lucidity says that the struggle against "Trotskyism" is the sign of a reactionary conception, it can also be said that *a lukewarm adherence to "Trotskyism," the tendency to leave this question in silence, characterizes centrism in our own ranks.*

The SFIO Carries Out the Expulsion

If the wavering character of the Naville-Rous faction on the question of the program of the Fourth International represented the fundamental precondition for Molinier's adventurist plan, the perplexity in the ranks of the GBL created by the blows of the SFIO bureaucracy provided the best conditions for its success. In his report of November 10, 1935, Naville described the situation as follows:

> We are witnessing . . . a veritable rout: no political line (no consistent view of the People's Front or the Croix de Feu "coups d'état"; no propaganda for a program of action (!); TPPS actions out of all

control of the Bolshevik-Leninists; agrarian and trade union
questions never examined). . . . On this point we cry out: Beware!

It is true that in this report Naville had proposed a detailed
plan for the creation of independent organizations. But the
political foundation for this plan was missing. There was not a
word calling for an offensive for the Fourth International.
Naville is content with . . . the program of action. But that is just
what Molinier promised to defend with considerably greater
means than others had at their disposal. That is why Naville's
plan could not have any appeal. On the contrary, it increased the
confusion; for, at the precise moment when Molinier had
abandoned his plan of transforming *Révolution* into a "mass
paper" in favor of a third paper, the future *Commune*, precisely
then did Naville (supposedly in order to take the sabotage into
account) seize upon Molinier's old plan for his own use, the same
plan against which he had always furiously protested. He
proposed therefore to downgrade *La Vérité, which represented
the Bolshevik tradition and the Leninist program in France*, into
a bulletin—and to make *Révolution* the "mass paper." At that
time no one could understand the struggle between Molinier and
Naville any longer. In these conditions, Naville could neither
defeat the conciliators (Rous, etc.) nor unite with them against
Molinier-Frank. Rous wrote to Crux, November 15, 1935:

> Unfortunately, each time that we thought it useful to resist
> Raymond's improvisations (when a circular on mass work was sent
> out, or on the pretext of mass work, he would want to carry on a direct
> and personal correspondence with the groups; at the Central
> Committee before last, when Raymond proposed a paper other than
> *Révolution* and *La Vérité*, which he and his friends would publish
> implicitly "outside the organization"), each time that it proved to be
> indispensable to put the weight of the organization against the
> personal policy of Raymond, Naville took no interest in the question,
> thus playing Raymond's game, abstaining or just attacking me,
> saying that all the trouble originated in the center.

While Naville did not fight energetically against political
conciliationism, the center did indeed write against Molinier, but
in reality acted with Molinier, naturally, so as to . . . "maneuver." A striking example: Rous wrote to Crux, Nov. 15, 1935:

> However, in the political field, we have not accepted any false coin.
> Raymond, whose more or less official policy, very difficult to expose,
> is to try to "do something" . . . is sufficiently skillful when he

proposes a document to make it look very radical and in conformity
(?) with the opinion of the comrades of the Political Bureau. Thus, to
tie him to his own documents, we voted for and amended one of his
documents in which he showed the need for an implacable firmness
(?) toward the Revolutionary Left at the same time that he himself
lacked this firmness in relations with the Revolutionary Left.

That is how the Rous faction always, in the last analysis, acted
during the crisis. When the task was to expose an opportunist like
Molinier, this faction thought it could "tie him" to his own
resolutions. When Naville's "traditional" struggle against Molinier became a positive factor, a rotten compromise with Molinier
was approved instead of concluding a necessary compromise with
Naville. Crux wrote to the Political Bureau concerning the Rous
faction, December 3, 1935:

> . . . The center group of Rous played an entirely positive role to the
> degree that what was involved were clique and personal struggles.
> But the spirit of conciliation became a serious fault once the
> capitulationist and centrist tendencies were clearly manifested inside
> the Molinier group.

The Central Committee, divided into three factions without any
clear political perspective, could no longer offer any resistance to
the blows of the bureaucracy which began to fall just at that
moment. As anyone could expect, the expulsions of the thirteen
leading Bolshevik-Leninist comrades were ratified November 17,
1935, by the National Council, thus becoming definitive.

But instead of utilizing the expulsion proceedings at this time
for broad propaganda for the Fourth International, they let
themselves be pushed around on the false terrain of statutes,
discipline, etc. . . . The bureaucracy did not want to limit itself to
the statement that the expelled promised "not to resort to insults"
in political questions and to be disciplined in action as they had
been up to then. They demanded a much more complete
declaration of loyalty and created hope that in that case the
expulsion could be avoided. The Central Committee accepted the
"loyalty" document by nine votes to four (Naville, etc.). . . . In
his letter to Crux of November 18, 1935, Rous tried to justify his
attitude in the well-known manner:

> In order to better show how the reformists want a split, we signed this
> promise, to the applause of the Revolutionary Left. Today, as a result
> (!), the Revolutionary Left can do nothing (?) against solidarity with
> the expelled.

Molinier, on the other hand, no longer concealed in the slightest his disposition toward complete capitulation, as can be seen from Frédéric's letter to Crux, November 17, 1935:

> In yesterday's general assembly Rous defended this decision. Molinier and Frank were walking on air. . . . Molinier sees in the signing of this document a first step and demands that we go *"all the way."* He once again points to the absolute necessity of hanging on to the party. . . . Blasco asked: "And if they demand that we give up *La Vérité,* what will Molinier do?" Molinier: "I have always said that *Vérité* can be given up. It's a problem of bringing our ideas to the masses. How? With a mass paper."

Despite the most sizable concessions the reformist inquisitors were not appeased. We read in the Bolshevik-Leninists' protest leaflet:

> The reply of the bureaucracy was: expulsion nevertheless, despite the promises which were made.

Molinier Executes the Split

After the November 17 expulsions, Crux wrote to Zeller:

> The National Council in any case has the merit of having created a clear situation. In the last few weeks too much time and energy have really been spent on illusory and sterile maneuvers. . . . It is a serious lesson for the future! In any case, now the way is clear. Political progress is possible only through a ferocious offensive and through openly denouncing not only León Blum but also Marceau Pivert, albeit in different tones.

But the GBL continued its retreat. It still wanted to cling to the SFIO. Crux again raised his voice in a warning:

> Your memorandum concerning the expulsion . . . contains two lines on the demand for readmission! These lines are scratched out with a pen! However, there were voices in favor of a new attempt to be readmitted, even after the National Council meeting. Incredible! You could do excellent things with the forces you are now wasting on these sterile and demoralizing maneuvers.

Still they did not go on the offensive: although the thirteen expelled comrades no longer had punishment to expect, they held on to the centrist language and attitude. Instead of calling for a new party, they protested "against the reformist (!) split (!)." In a leaflet addressed to the adherents of the SFIO they say, ambiguously:

> You will reply with us: Revolutionary politics . . . for the creation of a continuous (!!) revolutionary leadership.

The Revolutionary Left was still not criticized, as Crux wrote in his letter of November 25, 1935: "*La Vérité* is silent about the Revolutionary Left. It is unbelievable! Permit me to use the right word: it is scandalous!"

In the youth organization a healthy reaction appeared against the weak-kneed attitude of the GBL, but this was limited to young Bolshevik-Leninists. Many old Bolshevik-Leninist members, on the other hand, defended a frankly opportunist line, whereas comrades coming from the SFIO often had a more radical attitude. But the opposition did not have a *principled political* character. A violent conflict did occur over whether the same declaration of loyalty should be made as the adults had made, with or without amendment; but on the question of the International, agreement was reached without difficulty on . . . a centrist basis.

Frédéric wrote to Crux, November 30, 1935:

> Internationally, it was decided to maintain relations with the left of the Socialist Youth International and to enter relations with all the organizations of independent young revolutionaries (in particular with our own in Holland, America, Chile, Canada, Switzerland, etc.).

This decision shows once again the political confusion resulting from the absence of an ideologically and organizationally coherent Bolshevik-Leninist fraction. Despite this attitude of the youth, who without being solid in principles were nevertheless more radical, the centrists were this time obliged to capitulate *to the lefts*. Frédéric wrote to Crux, November 20, 1935:

> Spartacus fell apart. This tendency, after violently attacking the "provocative" policy of the present leadership toward the party . . . finally approved the line of absolutely refusing to capitulate politically. This was done—and how could it be otherwise?—so as not to be isolated from the masses: this time . . . from the great mass of Young Socialists ready for independence.

This incident at the youth congress shows with absolute certainty the important successes that could have been obtained with the adult organization, if only we had shown our teeth a little to the treacherous Revolutionary Left, not to mention a consistent policy in favor of a "Trotskyist" program.

*   *   *

But Molinier determined the policy of the GBL. He had already stated that he would go all the way along the road on which he had entered. That meant that he was ready to sacrifice not only *La Vérité* but the whole Bolshevik-Leninist program and the organization itself, only to be able to execute his plan of the "mass paper" embracing everything. He made the preparations that he considered appropriate, as Rous's letter of November 15, 1935, tells:

> Raymond has Frank (who carries out only half of his responsibilities) conduct a whispering campaign against the "conservatives" of the organization and for the need, at "historic" moments, to leap over the organization and its conservatism.

Having abandoned his plan for *Révolution*, following the ill will which his "third paper" raised against him, Molinier could therefore permit himself the following demagogy. Rous wrote to Crux, November 15, 1935:

> Raymond defends himself as if from a low and abominable slander on our part concerning the dangerous idea of entrusting co-ownership of *Révolution* to the Revolutionary Left.

Added to this deception, which was unfortunately not without its results, was the blackmail which also, unfortunately, was successful. Rous continues in his letter:

> Since he (Molinier) gives none of his financial or other means for *La Vérité* and since he is disposed to get *Révolution* under way (?) . . . we have instructed Raymond to concern himself with that question.

Molinier took charge of this as he usually does. He used the undisciplined attitude of some young comrades as a pretext to impose on the organization the third paper, *La Commune*, which he had prepared with great secrecy. He himself described the accomplishment of his attack on the organization in his pamphlet *La Crise de la Section Française.* There we read:

> The majority of the Central Committee showed itself incapable of applying the decisions of the National Conference (?); there was no perspective of putting out the mass paper very quickly. Eight Paris Central Committee comrades . . . decided to take the initiative to work out a complete plan for this newspaper. A leaflet, an office, and posters were prepared in less than three days (?).

The "plan" was in reality an ultimatum. Crux wrote on the subject of the methods which were employed here in his letter to the Political Bureau, December 4:

> I would like to draw your attention once again to the absolutely intolerable methods of the *Commune* group. Here is how Frank himself describes them: "Having made the decision to launch *La Commune,* having taken the first steps, we turned toward the existing organizations (GBL, the Young Socialists, the Social Front minority, the Revolutionary Action Groups), telling them: 'Your discussions are going on dangerously long. We have gotten a newspaper under way for you; go ahead, take it!'" Now, it was the so-called Bolshevik-Leninists themselves who launched *La Commune,* and who afterwards, from the heights of the position they had attained, addressed the simple mortals of the "various tendencies and organizations" thus: "Go ahead!" What have these audacious initiators thus created? *La Commune.* And what is *La Commune?* A doctrine, a program, some slogans, a banner? Nothing of the kind. It's a headquarters, some posters and . . . the cashbox. . . . No, our organization cannot be led by such methods.

*   *   *

The Central Committee of November 23 was faced with an accomplished fact. It would be ridiculous to suppose that the eight splitters of *La Commune* would give up their plan—which had already demanded great financial means—after a vote of some kind. But the vote is instructive in spite of everything, as much in its distinguishing factors as in the common factors which are revealed:

The Molinierist splitters knew what they wanted: the eight voted unanimously for *La Commune,* the mass paper; ten voted against.

Rous remained faithful to his credulous conciliationism. The

Rous-Craipeau motion was formulated in this way:

> The Central Committee instructs Comrade Molinier (!) to undertake
> the launching of *Révolution* as a mass paper for revolutionary
> regroupment under the political control of the JS and the GBL
> according to the plan (!) and proposals (!) of Comrade Molinier,
> accepted by the JS.

The resolution meant in practice: Molinier is accorded *every-thing* he demands. Molinier is refused only . . . the name (*La Commune*); in return they are ready to put at his disposal the whole apparatus of *Révolution* for his opportunist policy. The Rous resolution received four votes, the eight from *La Commune* voted against, and Naville's supporters abstained. The attitude of *Naville* in this vote is no less characteristic than that of the center. Only twelve days earlier he had proposed: *Révolution—* mass paper; *La Vérité—*bulletin. But now when this decision would have produced a majority against Molinier, suddenly he insisted again that *La Vérité* become a mass paper. Five voted for his resolution; against, the eight of *La Commune*; and Rous's supporters abstained.

That is how Molinier was able to go home with a plurality (eight to four to five) for his proposal, naturally trying in that way to justify his hostile attitude toward the organization.

An even more essential characteristic for judging the conflict in general as well as for assessing the principled positions of the three factions in particular, is what all three have in common: *they all voted for the creation of a "mass paper," each having a centrist paper in mind.*

Molinier made no secret of it.

Rous wanted to let the youth paper be transformed "according to the plan and proposals of Comrade Molinier."

Naville was prepared to transform *La Vérité* into a mass paper, i.e., a centrist paper. He admitted this in his resolution on the transformation of *La Vérité*. There we read:

> It (*La Vérité*) should have its polemical content reduced considerably
> (i.e., nothing on the Russian Bolshevik-Leninists) and its theoretical
> content cut (i.e., nothing on the "Trotskyist" program).

The correctness of this interpretation is fully confirmed by Naville's *practice* toward *Révolution,* later elevated into the "mass paper."

However, the *decisive* difference between Rous-Naville and

Molinier-Frank is this: the first two committed their errors in the framework of the national and international organization; the latter two pushed their opportunism to the limit at which it would have to be characterized by the severe term of treason.

Conciliationism

The days following the November 23, 1935, vote were filled with practical preparations by the *Commune* people for the launching of their paper and with . . . conciliatory negotiations inside the Central Committee.

As early as November 21, 1935, Crux, learning of the conciliatory attitude of the Central Committee in the National Council of the SFIO, had used a more severe tone:

> Are there comrades among you who wish at all costs to remain cooped up in the SFIO? . . . If someone among you says, "Outside the SFIO we will be isolated, we will sink into futility, etc.," we should answer, "Dear friend, your nerves are shot; take a four-week vacation, and then we'll see!" At the same time we must engrave in our memory the attitude of these comrades in this moment of crisis: we will know more formidable crises in the future, and the same faint-heartedness can recur on a much vaster scale. Let us not forget that the attitude of Zinoviev and Kamenev in October 1917 was not accidental. . . .

From this it can clearly be concluded that it was necessary not to be conciliatory any longer toward the capitulators.

However, the "Conciliation Commission" which met after Molinier's ultimatum, composed of Rous, Hic, Molinier, Frank and Craipeau, thought otherwise. It tried to arrive at a compromise *at any price*, even after the *Commune* people had announced the publication of the third paper in their November 24 letter to the members of the GBL.

The *Commune* people obviously did not take the negotiations and decisions seriously, as we can see from a letter from Rous to Crux, November 26, 1935:

> Raymond broke off several times, then returned saying that he accepted our document without reading it (!). . . . We took note of this (!!).

Out of these long negotiations of conciliation finally came an eclectical and extremely contradictory mixture of various fragments of the old proposals. On the decisive political questions

Molinier was allowed to have his way completely. The resolution of the "Conciliation Commission" contains the decision to launch a newspaper on a *centrist* basis:

> The newspaper will be launched by the existing organizations on the basis of an *elementary* political agreement for regroupment (the slogan of communes (!!), a militia, and revolutionary defeatism).

The Political Bureau meeting of November 26 *unanimously* adopted this resolution and a considerable majority of the Central Committee was won over to it (Naville abstained). Thus they began to give in on the important organizational questions: Frank, the most faithful partisan of Molinier and chief preacher of opportunism, was elected editorial secretary of the future "mass paper." On the other hand, Molinier "gave in" on . . . the name of the paper. Here is the decision on that: "The new mass paper will from the first issue be called *Révolution*, with a special page on the 'Commune.'"

The "mass paper" projected was to be put out on a basis corresponding exactly to Molinier's desires and anticipated the composition of the editorial staff of *La Commune*, which was created by Molinier later:

> In sum: *Révolution* will come out December 5 as a mass paper based principally on the politics and organization of the Bolshevik-Leninists and Young Socialists (Seine Alliance) with the participation of the GAR and Desnots (a leader of the petty-bourgeois "Social Front").

Molinier wrote demagogically to the Political Bureau on November 30, 1935, about the November 26 "conciliation":

> You accepted all our draft documents and voted for them; *La Commune* was a title more suited to this work, but it was better to give it up than cause a crisis.

The decisions for which a four-day struggle had been waged lasted less than twenty-four hours. On November 29, 1935, Frédéric reported to Crux concerning the attitude taken by Molinier two days before:

> Under the pretext that the resolution of the Central Committee on the question of the newspaper meant "*Commune* equals *Révolution* plus *Vérité*," Molinier did not destroy his posters but on the contrary had

them stamped and posted by a company on the walls of Paris, with a notice pasted over them saying "Beginning December 6." I saw Frank distributing the leaflets which you know about and organizing sales of *La Commune* with sympathizers. *That means split.*

The breaking of discipline on the part of *La Commune* was thus accomplished. The Political Bureau found itself obliged on November 29 to withdraw the concessions which had been abused by Molinier-Frank.

*   *   *

Crux could only follow all these negotiations with a delay of several days. The first news was moreover extremely vague. After the first report, he wrote (November 25 to the Political Bureau): "If a hermaphroditic newspaper is actually in the works, I wish to announce in advance that I am not responsible."

After learning of the ultimatum of the *Commune* people, he telegraphed to Rous (November 26, 1935): *"All concessions to Raymond would be fatal."*

At the same time he demanded the intervention of the International Secretariat, demanding an immediate dissociation of the sharpest character from the new paper and an energetic political offensive under the banner of the Fourth International, in common with the youth organization. On November 28, 1935, in his letter to the IS, Trotsky authorized the French comrades to publish the following statement:

> The new paper *La Commune* uses, among other names, the name of L. Trotsky. Comrade Trotsky must state that he has nothing to do with *La Commune,* the paper of "various tendencies" (moreover, anonymous ones). L. Trotsky belongs to one tendency only, which has a name, a program, and a banner—that of the Fourth International.

The next day arrived a "programmatic" letter from Frank, dated November 28, 1935 (postdated two days), which clearly demonstrated that what was involved was not "deviations" by the *Commune* people—however serious they might be—but a complete "abdication of principles." Crux telegraphed right away: "Frank letter reveals centrist demoralization. I consider split preferable to concessions."

Crux's insistence and all the open propaganda by the

Commune people finally led the Political Bureau to break with Molinier's people. It declared on November 29, 1935, that the new newspaper was an organ of struggle against the GBL and removed Frank from the post of editorial secretary of the "mass paper" even before he had begun to make use of it. On December 1, Molinier demanded of the Executive Committee of the JSR that the newspaper *La Commune* be published in common. The youth unanimously refused to discuss the proposal. It was then that the Political Bureau (circular of December 2, 1935) decided it had to end the negotiations with Molinier.

The long hesitations in Paris had convinced Crux to propose the following severe action to the IS on December 3:

> Comrade Raymond Molinier continues to be formally a member of the plenum. I do not believe that his political attitude allows us to keep him even formally inside the leading body of our international organization.
>
> *Politically,* Molinier has gone over to centrist positions.
>
> *Organizationally,* he has made a bloc with the centrists against our tendency. He has not consulted the International Secretariat about his "turn." He allowed himself to present ultimatums to our organization, relying on semicapitalist methods of "surprise attacks." His activity becomes more and more demoralizing. I propose to invite the Central Committee of the French section to recall Comrade Molinier. At the same time, I propose the convening of an international control commission, to investigate the activity of Comrade Molinier and possibly that of other comrades associated with him.

On December 4—before this letter arrived—the IS demanded

> a response from Comrade Molinier within twenty-four hours saying that he submits to the discipline of the organization, i.e., that he renounces the publication of *La Commune.*

This letter changed nothing. Molinier replied the same day:

> I have never been expelled without being heard; if I had been you would be better informed and you would know that we are executing a decision of the Central Committee of our GBL.
>
> Fraternally: Molinier

Two days later—December 6—the first issue of *La Commune* appeared.

*   *   *

All the concessions made by the Central Committee to avoid a split were shown to be not only in vain but also dangerous.

The promoters of the conciliatory bargaining were Rous and his group. The conciliatory role played by him and his friends earlier was completely justified. It will always be necessary. But this method must not be applied to great decisive questions. Since what was at stake were the program and the physiognomy themselves, it could not but be dangerous.

If the immediate attitude toward Molinier on the *decisive* questions had been implacable, he would not have dared to go so far, and perhaps the split could have been avoided. Only after getting the impression that he could obtain one concession after another, even in the questions which put the fate of the party in question, did Molinier push his opportunist demands to the extreme, launching him finally on his criminal adventure.

The law of all conciliationism was thus verified: it avoids conflicts over small questions; but in connection with large ones it provokes splits.

V. La Commune

Before going into the details of the content of *La Commune*, it is necessary to answer the question of how it was possible for a few founding members of the French Communist League to fall into the worst opportunism, which later led them to split.

The fear of becoming isolated played the decisive role. In a letter dated September 13, 1935, Crux wrote:

> It is possible that the two bureaucracies, with the aid of the two governments, will succeed for a certain period in making our existence quite precarious. With the approach of war, the situation of revolutionists can be neither easy nor pleasant. Lenin and Liebknecht began by "isolating themselves" from the mass organizations. Neither Marceau Pivert nor anyone else will be able to come up with any other method.

Still earlier, in a letter dated August 23, 1935, to Comrade Schmidt, Crux had written of the great test to which all working class organizations are subjected in this critical period:

> Why did de Kadt betray your party? At the critical moment, under violent pressure from bourgeois and reformist public opinion, he completely lost his small ration of courage. Greater and more important examples exist: Zinoviev and Kamenev before October 1917, Brandler and Walcher in 1923. It would be fatal not to notice the similarity of these deeds, despite their different appearance. We are marching toward great events, great tests, toward the greatest pressure of patriotic bourgeois "public opinion."

In less than four months Crux was to assert in his letter of December 3, 1935, to the Central Committee, at the time of the Molinier enterprise:

> It is a capitulation to the social-patriotic wave. Whoever doesn't understand this is not a Marxist.
>
> The approach of the war has (temporarily) given the social patriots a powerful weapon against the internationalists. Hence the expulsion of the Leninists. Hence Pivert's cowardly capitulation. . . . Hence, finally, the fear felt by the unstable elements in our own ranks of "isolation" and their tendency to go with the centrists at all costs and to be differentiated from them as little as possible. There is no

other political content in the attitude of Molinier and Frank. They are capitulating to the social-patriotic wave.

Anyone who knew the situation would not be surprised to see that it was precisely Molinier and Frank who became the leaders of the capitulation. On December 3, 1935, Crux wrote to the Political Bureau:

> Molinier's opportunist tendencies were not born yesterday and are no mystery to any of us. Molinier's participation in leadership work has been justified only to the degree that other comrades, more solidly grounded in Marxist principles, supervised and corrected him. From the moment Molinier escaped from national and international control . . . he immediately fell into the swamp of opportunism. . . .

As for Frank, he made himself sufficiently famous through his pamphlet about the February 6, 1934, events, in which he characterized the slogan of arming the proletariat as "romantic."

The organization was ripe for the Molinier-Frank adventure only until it became clear that the policy of adaptation to the SFIO and formation of a bloc with Pivert was fruitless. Molinier's promise to "act quickly and firmly" attracted many comrades. The good elements among the *Commune* people really believed that Molinier-Frank had now discovered the philosopher's stone for attracting the masses. They did not realize that Molinier-Frank had found their miraculous stone in the alchemists' laboratory of Schwab and Company.

The Five Points

The "plan" for winning over the masses was presented, naturally, by Frank, with his letter to Crux dated November 28, 1935. This plan's simplicity is breathtaking: the masses don't accept the program of the Bolshevik-Leninists? Well then, to hell with the program! However, the masses must also hear from us somehow. It is very simple: we create a "mass paper," that is, "financial resources, an administration, a big promotion, etc." And since it is necessary to do something with the masses won over in this way, "Revolutionary Action Groups" are created with the snap of your fingers, a hybrid of the party and the soviet following the Molinier-Frank style. But since one is an "Old Bolshevik," one does all that . . . in order to create a new party. One is thus covered in the eyes of naive Bolshevik-Leninists.

The "Old Bolshevik" also knew how to historically "ground"

the program of his lack of a program. In his November 28 letter he wrote:

> The GBL, or any currently existing group, cannot claim organizational domination. In 1917, the Bolshevik Party absorbed and assimilated different revolutionary formations . . . not so much through the doctrinal capital (!) which it had accumulated as through the revolutionary force which it unquestionably represented in everyone's eyes and by its authority among the masses, which increased every day.

How Frank's "theory" was announced in practice we can see in the first appeal by *La Commune*. It is completely anonymous. It simply says: "*La Commune* is inaugurated by members of various (?) tendencies."

The name "Bolshevik-Leninists" was downplayed and the wishes of Pivert and all the petty-bourgeois elements were thus fulfilled. Along with the name, the program had disappeared as well. Crux wrote, in his November 30 letter:

> What the masses can demand of a newspaper is *a clear program and a correct orientation*. But precisely on this question the appeal (of *La Commune*) is utterly silent. Why? Because it wants more to conceal its ideas than to express them. It accepts the SAPist (centrist) recipe: in seeking the line of least resistance *do not say what is*. The program of the Fourth International, that's for "us," for the big shots of the leadership. And the masses? What are the masses? They can rest content with a quarter, or even a tenth, of the program. This mentality we call elitism, of both an opportunist and, at the same time, an adventurist type. . . .
>
> But here is where the most important part begins: "*La Commune* is not going to add itself to the multiplicity of tendencies in the workers' movement. . . ." What does that mean? If all the tendencies are wrong or insufficient, a new one must be created, the true one, the correct one. If there are true and false tendencies, then the workers must be taught to distinguish among them; the masses must be called on to join the correct tendency in order to fight the false ones. But no, the initiators of *La Commune* . . . place themselves "above the battle." Such a procedure is absolutely unworthy of Marxists.

The *Commune* people reduced the role of the party to that of an advertising agency for revolutionary slogans. Frank "justified" abandoning the program in his November 28 letter, declaring: "No organizational ultimatism." Trotsky replied in his December 4, 1935, letter to the Political Bureau:

What a revolting distortion of the Leninist formulation! No ultimatism whatsoever in relation to the masses, the trade unions, the
workers' movement; but the most intransigent ultimatism in relation
to any group that claims to lead the masses. The ultimatism that we
are talking about is called the *Marxist program.* . . . In place of this
program, however, we find an adventurist type of devil-may-care
attitude. Nothing more.

The first appeal of *La Commune,* already mentioned, which
most faithfully reflects the ideas of Molinier-Frank, was characterized as follows by Crux in his letter to Naville, November 28,
1935: "The appeal is a total abdication of everything we have
proclaimed and taught in France since 1929."

This appeal is in itself sufficient proof that the *Commune*
people have absolutely no understanding of Bolshevism. Their
political lightmindedness cannot be expressed more crudely. The
"Old Bolsheviks" very simply yielded all their "Bolshevism" to a
few petty-bourgeois muddleheads.

One critical letter from Crux was enough to completely shake
up the primitive foundations of *La Commune.* The first appeal
was quickly abandoned and replaced by a new one. The
anonymity was maintained. What use was there in propagandiz-
ing for a party, the "Old Bolsheviks" thought? A few hastily
improvised points with a purely conjunctural significance
"replaced" the program. Only the "elected communes" were
original. On December 6, 1935, Crux wrote to the Political Bureau:

> *La Commune*'s second appeal contains nothing of interest except an
> attempt to confuse the slogan for committees of action with the
> slogan for "elected communes." But what was the [Paris] Commune?
> It was the *municipal government* elected *after the seizure of power.*
> How can you call for the election of "communes" (outside the
> framework of bourgeois legality) before seizing power? It is absolutely
> incomprehensible. The *committees of action* are formations for the
> conquest of power and not at all "elected communes." Naturally, we
> want to support the tradition of the Commune, but not by imitating
> its organizational forms and especially not by imitating its con-
> fusion. . . . This juxtaposing of committees of action with "com-
> munes" was invented specifically to justify the name of the
> newspaper, while spreading confusion.

Alongside the slogan of "elected communes" we also find:
"armed popular militias," "the arming of the workers," "preparation for the general strike," and "a government of the workers
and peasants," as the "platform" of the second appeal. But this

"foundation" did not last either. The first issue of *La Commune* proves that these points were exchanged, reduced, and finished off in a few days. In addition, the newspaper no longer appeared anonymously. It was placed under the patronage of a "Sponsoring Committee." On December 16, 1935, Crux wrote to the Political Bureau:

> A friend has written to me about that lamentable *Commune:* "But it is no longer anonymous tendencies that are involved. Everyone has signed up." Is that so? Then that only makes the situation worse. When I spoke of "anonymous tendencies," I meant that neither their past record nor their program were known to anyone. But what do we see now before us? Defectors from different tendencies: the Bolshevik-Leninists, the Revolutionary Left, the Social Front.
>
> The Bolshevik-Leninist group is not anonymous at all; the Revolutionary Left is not revolutionary at all, but all the same everyone knows what it is. The "Social Front" is a somewhat ambiguous enterprise, but everyone can nevertheless form an opinion of that formation. But the defectors from these three groups, who have come together not on the basis of principles but on the basis of "parity"—What do they represent? What is their political character? What is their program? "Bolshevik-Leninists" who found it necessary to launch an actual conspiracy against their own national and international organization . . . must have had decisive reasons for acting as they have acted. What are these reasons? In other words, what is the *new* program of those former Bolshevik-Leninists who so brutally abandoned their own organization? No one knows anything about this.

The *Commune* people renounced any program, because they hoped to have the whole world come to them. In reality, the *Commune* people succeeded in grouping only those they prevented from joining the GBL as well as . . . the "Social Front" people, whom Frank himself, in his November 28 letter, characterized as follows:

> I do not yet know these comrades well (!). According to their leaders (some of whom are former CP members) (?), there are a little over a hundred active petty-bourgeois (!!) militants (sales of newspapers, street fights) who have revolutionary tendencies. . . .

These unknown petty-bourgeois people were thus the "masses" in whose name they pawned the program and turned their back on their national and international organization, in order to be satisfied on a few still-changing points. With the appearance of the first issue of *La Commune* there was finally agreement (for a period of two weeks!) with the petty-bourgeois elements on the following points:

1. The creation of workers' committees and communes (??).
2. The formation of popular militias and the arming of the workers.
3. Revolutionary defeatism.
4. A government of the workers and peasants.

And, as an entirely new point: 5. Reconstruction of a revolutionary party.

That was what made the *Commune* people finally feel that they could rest their "Bolshevik consciences." However, the "reconstruction of a revolutionary party" is also a "programmatic point," given exactly the same abstract and ambitious formulation, of the centrists Schwab, Maurín, Maxton, etc. Crux wrote December 23 to the members of the GBL:

> The "political basis" of *La Commune* is approximately that of the Revolutionary Left. This basis is tested by experience. Its political result is the betrayal of the Bolshevik-Leninists and a servile attitude toward the social-patriotic apparatus.

"The Mass Paper"

If the centrist sickness of the GBL came from "lukewarmness" on the question of "Trotskyism"—in other words, from neglect for program and for the Fourth International—the confusion around the "mass paper" was the unfailing symptom making it possible to recognize this sickness. The discussion on the mass paper had already started.

In his "Perspectives and Tasks" mentioned above, the "theoretician" of opportunism, Frank, demanded as early as June 1935 a newspaper on a purely centrist basis which he later realized with *La Commune*.

> *A mass newspaper, a weekly of popular struggle, ought to be launched within a few weeks*. This should not be a Bolshevik-Leninist paper, but a paper bringing together, for example, those who are: (1) against national defense; (2) for the militia, against fascism.*

---

*But again, it was not Frank who originated this idea, but his cohort Molinier (see Molinier: "Present Tasks and Past Tasks," April 12, 1935):

La Vérité . . . should little by little be transformed into a larger

Crux replied on July 3 to a question asked by Rous:

> The idea of counterposing to *La Vérité* a mass paper that arises from
> the will of one group or another like a *deus ex machina* is absolutely
> false. I have observed similar attempts several times in Russia and
> elsewhere: they led either to failure or to the camouflaged formation
> of a new faction.

On July 26, Crux again explained to Naville:

> . . . I want to dwell especially on the question of a "mass newspaper."
> I do not at all consider this question to be "secondary"—quite the
> contrary. It is because I see all of its gravity that I cannot indulge in
> easy solutions. To create a mass paper apart from *La Vérité* would be
> a criminal adventure; you will quickly compromise both papers and
> end up at the same time with two factions.* You must try to
> transform *La Vérité* into a mass paper *without depriving it of its
> character as the paper of a tendency.* That is the only possible
> solution.

A few days later, on August 1, 1935, the Central Committee
unanimously passed a resolution "to inaugurate a mass newspaper." The main vehicle for this newspaper should be the Young
Socialists. The essential condition of safeguarding its *unequivocal character as a tendency paper* was completely put aside in
this resolution. In it we already find the embryonic ideology of *La
Commune.*

1. Collaboration with the centrists without criticizing them. It
was decided to invite Pivert (as an individual) to be a collaborator, without a single word to distinguish ourselves from him.

2. The denial of the GBL's leadership role. Here is a quotation
from the resolution:

> weekly, a mass weekly of a revolutionary vanguard. It should change
> completely (!) and in the coming months it should be a mass
> newspaper. *La Lutte de classes* should become our theoretical organ
> at this time, the organ of the Bolshevik-Leninist tendency (!).

* That obviously had nothing in common with Naville's conception of
the mass paper, as expressed in the resolution of November 23. Naville
conceived the mass paper—he proved it in practice—as a semi-centrist
paper (nothing on the Fourth International, nothing on "Trotskyism,"
etc.). Crux demanded a newspaper saying *everything,* but in a form
comprehensible to the masses (see letter from Crux, November 30, 1935).

Whatever the conceptions of the revolutionary tendencies may be, or their differences on the means for accomplishing the recovery, . . . they should regroup.

For the *Commune* people that was later called "no organizational domination," "parity of tendencies," etc. . . .

3. The complete absence of a programmatic basis for the newspaper. In the resolution we do not find a single word concerning a program. Instead it says, in Molinier's style:

> Situate ourselves in events: war and fascism. Express the living reality: a good deal of space for news reports, investigations, proletarian life, trade union life. Attach to doctrine no disordered literary articles; continuity in the production of theoretical documents.

Nothing but empty phrases!

On August 27 Naville informed Crux that the radical-opportunist partisans of the "mass paper" were committing themselves further:

> Now concessions are being considered which will weaken our position instead of improving it, among others the abandonment of *La Vérité* and the publication of *Révolution* (or something else) as the only newspaper of the new unified tendency, on a "broad" basis. . . .

In mid-September, in his article, "To Begin Mass Work We Need a Mass Newspaper," Frank expressed perfectly his opportunism—as it appears in the question of the press—and definitively acquired renown as the "theoretician of centrism." His ideas are without doubt a vulgar cliché of Martynov's economism. They are of absolutely the same origin as the platitudes of a Gilbert (SAPist of Spartacus), but they surpass it. It will be enough to reproduce a few passages:

> But first of all, what is this mass work which everyone agrees on? . . . Mass work, as distinguished from cadre work, is that which aims at making the accumulated experience of the whole class live in the consciousness of the militants, making slogans developed by these cadres live for sections of the class in proportion to their experience and to the situation, . . . a newspaper destined to bring revolutionary slogans to life by taking account of the political level of its readers. And the political level of the masses is at present very low (political level is not to be confused with combativity). . . . A newspaper which will therefore respond to such an aspiration will in

this way find much greater resources than might be suspected (?) (purely financial) and also resources in terms of sellers, propagandists, collaborators; its existence will depend especially on well-done promotion, presentation, and administration. . . . (internal bulletin of the GBL, no. 8)

For the theoretician of *La Commune*, the whole of Marxism is reduced to: "promotion, presentation," etc., and naturally "financial resources." The role of the party is reduced to that of an advertising agency.

The important role played in the conflict by the absence of an opportune, deep, and broad analysis of the question of the press, which could have once and for all radically freed the best elements of the GBL from opportunism on this question—this appears in the following lines written by Frédéric to Crux on November 27, 1935:

Many comrades say "Molinier has not acted correctly." However, he has done something good: without his initiative, however factional it was, we would have been in a sterile discussion of the mass paper for years.

Crux drew the conclusion for everyone from these decisive lessons in his letter of November 30, 1935, to the members of the GBL:

What is a "mass newspaper"? The question is not new. . . . It is the elementary duty of a revolutionary organization to make its political newspaper as accessible as possible to the masses. This task cannot be effectively accomplished except as a function of the growth of the organization and its cadres, who must pave the way to the masses for the newspaper—since it is not enough, of course, to call a publication a "mass paper" for the masses to really accept it. But quite often revolutionary impatience (which becomes transformed easily into opportunist impatience) leads to this conclusion: The masses do not come to us because our ideas are too complicated and our slogans too advanced. It is therefore necessary to simplify our program, water down our slogans—in short, to throw out some ballast. Basically, this means: Our slogans must correspond not to the objective situation, not to the relation of classes, analyzed by the Marxist method, but to subjective assessments (extremely superficial and inadequate ones) of what the "masses" can or cannot accept. . . . A mass paper is distinguished from a theoretical review or from a journal for cadres not by the *slogans* but by the *manner in which they are presented*. The cadre newspaper unfolds for its readers all the steps of the

Marxist analysis. The mass paper presents only its results, basing itself at the same time on the immediate experience of the masses themselves. *It is far more difficult to write in a Marxist manner for the masses than it is to write for cadres.*

The "Revolutionary Action Groups"

The *La Commune* people stated in their first appeal:

> *La Commune* is not a new tendency, it is a paper where all those who fight for the above program (the five points—Braun) have a place.

It appeared from the very start, however, that no newspaper could exist without an apparatus. The *Commune* people had to create it if they did not want to disappear from sight along with their newspaper.

The primitive idea of Molinier-Frank was to make their newspaper an instrument of the so-called "elected communes." This designation is only a vulgar disfigurement of the "action committees" which Crux conceived as an embryonic form of French soviets. But as the "communes" did not exist and the newspaper could not exist without the adequate bodies, another base was sought. This was found in the centrist groups, which were created as transitional bodies during the detachment of revolutionary elements from the SFIO and which Van described in his letter to Crux, November 21:

> In the ordinary branch meetings there were about a hundred present, including all the "B" comrades (Pivertists—Braun) and "C" comrades (Bolshevik-Leninists—Braun), who then again became the majority. These comrades, moreover, are now organized in a Revolutionary Action Group (Bolshevik-Leninist, Revolutionary Left, and those without a tendency), which now has its own headquarters (!). Two branches are forming, more every day, and in a few weeks all that will remain will be to cut the umbilical cord.

It is obvious that the GBL had to work for the Fourth International inside the transitional groups which were formed by the separation from the SFIO and that by this means it could rapidly win over for the new party some rather sizable groups.

But it was necessary to firmly distinguish between (1) the action committees, which must be created *in the struggle* for particular objectives and be embryonic soviets; (2) the centrist political groups composed of people who no longer submit to the old parties but who nevertheless cannot make up their minds for the new party. By working on them *according to correct guidelines,* we can turn these groups into cells of the new party.

Crux showed the dialectical link between the party and the soviets in his letter to Rous (at the beginning of November):

> It is repeated that it is a race between fascism and us. But it is very necessary to analyze the content of this formulation from the point of view of the revolutionary party. Will we know how to give the masses a revolutionary framework before the fascists wipe them out? It would be absurd to believe that we will have enough time to create an omnipotent party that would be able to eliminate all the other organizations before the decisive conflicts with fascism or before the outbreak of the war; but it is quite possible in a short time—with the help of events—to win over great masses, not for our program, not for the Fourth International, but for these committees of action. But once created, these committees of action would become a magnificent springboard for a revolutionary party. . . .
>
>   Here it is not a matter of one question or another; it is *the* question of life and death.

So as not to leave any room for misunderstanding, Crux further clarified the question with the help of another example:

> But when revolutionary action is set in motion by the masses themselves it is necessary to know how to counterpose to the opportunist apparatus an apparatus of revolutionary action created "ad hoc" by the masses to fill the needs of their action, and elected by the masses in struggle. If at the moment of the explosion in Toulon there had been a group with a sufficiently correct orientation to launch the clear and simple call, "Every hundred workers send one delegate to the Toulon Committee of Action," the masses would certainly have responded to this appeal. This committee of action would have had quite exceptional authority, not only in the eyes of the masses themselves, but also in the eyes of the local authorities and in the eyes of the rest of France and of the purged traditional organizations. (Crux to Rous, beginning of November)

Despite the numerous explanations given by Crux on the questions of the "action committees," they were not understood by the GBL, as is proven by Motion C (November 1935) calling for "committees led by the masses," which was criticized by Crux November 13, 1935, in his letter to Rous:

> The actual relations [between committees and masses] are the

opposite. The committees of action are necessary precisely to lead the masses. You do not say that these committees must emanate from the masses in struggle, and be elected by them (!) and that the delegates must be accountable and subject to recall. . . .

Molinier concretized this confusion in his Revolutionary Action Groups. In his incomprehension of the nature of the thing, he tried to *mechanically* link the tasks of a cell of the party with those of the action committees through the GARs. After two weeks of long discussion on the GARs, agreement was finally reached on the following basis (see *La Commune,* no. 3):

> The GARs are a grouping of comrades who agree on a minimum basis of action (?) and who want to act quickly and forcefully: (1) through propaganda in the working class inside and outside of its organizations; and (2) through effective direct action (!) against the class enemy.

Here appears, in a quite abstract form, the hybrid character of the GARs. However, it appeared quite soon that the latter could carry out neither the tasks of "action committees" nor those of the party cell. At this point, the idea of replacing the "action committees" by the GARs was again abandoned and the GARs were instead given the task of *propagating* the action committees. But this was a task incumbent on the party. The need for a political platform was at once felt. What was chosen—after interminable and absolutely sterile debate and experimentation—was *the five points of La Commune*, and organizational cells for a *new* tendency were finally created to help them. Thus, what was done was just the opposite of what was claimed to have been done.

The Collapse

It was not difficult to foresee the approaching end of the adventurist enterprise. Opportunist impatience, together with political superficiality, based on a panicky evaluation of the situation, had led Molinier to throw overboard all the teachings of Bolshevism on the education and concentration of revolutionary forces. That is the irrefutable proof that he had never seriously absorbed these teachings. Now he wanted to win over the masses all at once with conjunctural slogans and with the so-called "mass paper." The masses, who have a justified distrust of any new organization, in any case did not show the least inclination to put their confidence in the hodgepodge of *La Commune* with its unknown banner and its unknown program (which was not a program and which changed every day).

The whole enterprise proved to be a complete and miserable fiasco. Only then, when they felt the cruelest disappointment, did the initiators of the *Commune* adventure begin to appreciate the meaning of the teachings of Bolshevik-Leninism in relation to the party and the program. Like drowning men, they looked around for the lifeboat and found it in the Fourth International, which they had abandoned, not to say betrayed.

A brief glimpse with the aid of the newspaper will illustrate the political collapse:

The Bloc with the Petty Bourgeois
(December 6, 1935–January 7, 1936)

The *Commune* people gave up, a few days after the appearance of the first leaflet, the complete anonymity and absence of program, and the adventure laid itself out in all its poverty. They had exchanged principles for a few constantly changing points, and the organization itself, rich with traditions, for a doubtful alliance with the so-called "revolutionary minority of the Social Front," with people whom Frank himself had characterized as petty bourgeois and whom he did not even know exactly. To this bloc were added sincere revolutionaries, mostly coming from the SFIO, who had lost their organizational home because of their opinions, or who were threatened with losing it. To the degree that they were won to our ideas and not impeded by the Molinier people from joining the GBL, they would have come unfailingly to the GBL as the only consistently revolutionary organization in France. Among the youth, the *Commune* enterprise had practically no partisans. . . .

Externally, this centrist bloc was represented by a "Sponsoring Committee" which brought together: nine Bolshevik-Leninists, four Social Front members, seven members of the GAR, four members of the Revolutionary Socialist Youth (unaffiliated).

However, the revolutionary elements did not take long to feel deeply disappointed. The fundamental idea of winning the masses by the influx of all those "who hesitate to leave the parties but do not hesitate to support a newspaper expressing their desire for action" (the letter of the *Commune* people, November 24, 1935) turned out to be completely false. All the parties considered the *Commune* group as a new organization, particularly hostile, and threatened to take severe measures against dual affiliations. The GBL expelled the *Commune* people. Bergery, leader of the "Social Front," disavowed its supporters and directly threatened to resort to the Press Law (concerning the distribution of false information), because the "revolutionary minority" was not at all a minority of the "Social Front" but had been expelled long ago. Marceau Pivert declared in the Executive Commission of the Seine Federation (December 27, 1935):

> that the Revolutionary Left is neither in solidarity with the GAR, whose indiscipline is clear, nor in solidarity with the party's repression.

He considered the *Commune* people as his most dangerous rivals and tolerated without protest the expulsion of GAR members from the SFIO.

The petty-bourgeois elements of the "Social Front" felt the most tricked. Of the four signers of the first appeal, two had withdrawn by the first week. Their signatures were replaced in silence with two others. The same procedure was followed with one of the youth. Number 4 of *La Commune* announced only a single one of the four brave Frontists of the "Sponsoring Committee." In spite of that, the "overall balance sheet" remained the "same" because a new "alternate" was quickly found for the deserters. The number of signatures therefore never changed.

In number 3 of *La Commune* the Frontist Biron gives us some interesting information on the serious differences that had already arisen in the first two weeks of honeymoon with the petty bourgeois. He starts with the avowal: "If (!) the goal of *La Commune* is to become a mass paper, etc. . ."

Thus it seems that it was still very far from Frank's ideal. Then he continues with commendable sincerity:

> Something I consider more unfortunate is a certain (?) lack of unity which was revealed from the first and which makes it impossible to clearly pinpoint the political line. . . .

Two weeks after the conclusion of the alliance that had cost the Bolshevik-Leninists their program, it turned out that even the pitiful five points were too much for the petty bourgeois. Biron writes:

> . . . But for me one thing goes beyond all the secondary criticisms,

and this is the absolute certainty that the second and third slogans—arming of the workers and revolutionary defeatism—are badly formulated (!) and represent at this time a political error. At this time the slogan of "arming the workers," formulated in this way is incorrect because it is premature. As for bald "revolutionary defeatism," this is ultraleft schematism. . . .

Let us see how Biron gives lessons to the theoreticians of the "mass paper" of Molinier-Frank:

I must clearly formulate my opinion because I believe that if *La Commune* does not wish to perish, it needs to take a correct position which takes into account the exact situation. Only on this condition will it become a mass newspaper. . . .

Biron was on target. He also showed himself to be a clairvoyant prophet:

If in four or five weeks, *La Commune* has not succeeded in touching and interesting a certain number of people, it is done for.

The first thing Biron said to the *Commune* people was in a very disillusioned manner: "*La Commune* is becoming an organ of a tendency again in spite of the wishes of its founders. . . ."

The Frontists also drew conclusions from their convictions. They passed a resolution on January 7, 1936 (unanimously except for two votes) which said, among other things:

The Frontist minority, as such, cannot at present be organizationally represented on the editorial committee responsible for *La Commune,* nor can it be integrated into its political orientation.

With that—after exactly four weeks—the adventure of *La Commune* was finished *politically.*

The Suppression of the Collapse and Hastening Toward the Fourth International (January 7-31, 1936)

The following weeks were filled with maneuvers to calm the faction supporters, whose hopes had vanished. At this time, Comrade Van turned his back on the *Commune* people. It was only because of the bad tactical errors of the GBL leadership (to which we must devote a separate chapter) that the first desertions were not followed by an actual split in the ranks of the former Bolshevik-Leninists.

At first Molinier-Frank, in their very precarious position, tried to cover up the bankruptcy on the surface, in order not to be totally discredited politically. The resolution of the Frontists, marking their separation from the ex-Bolshevik-Leninists, was kept secret. (Exactly four weeks later, when they came over to advocating the Fourth International, they were obliged to publish it, however; but at that time it was no longer dangerous.) The signatures of the "Sponsoring Committee" disappeared. The readers were deceived; in number 6 of *La Commune* the editors made an excuse of an "abundance of copy"; in number 7 it was a lack of space because of the "special character of this issue, in which two pages are devoted to Lenin, Liebknecht, and Luxemburg." These three names had to serve to cover up the collapse.

At the same time a half-turn was made toward the Fourth International. So that the turn would not appear too abrupt, right after the break with the Frontists they started a "survey" on "organic unity and the new party" in which most of the former supporters of the Fourth International spoke. The retreat to the old positions was supposed to appear as a turn and the turn was supposed to appear to be not the result of the collapse but the result of discussion.

While *La Commune* still kept a "supra-party" external appearance, we find in number 7 (January 17) that a "Committee for the Fourth International" intended to publish a monthly magazine under the title *Quatrième Internationale*. The promise was never kept. That is explained by the whole character of the Molinier group. There are groups which have ideas but not financial means; this one had the means but not the ideas. Frank-Molinier could launch *La Commune* if need be, since it was possible there to live on what remained of the old times and fill up the gaps with photomontage. But in a theoretical magazine it would have been necessary to express their views in depth and they were not capable of that. This was proof of ideological bankruptcy.

On January 31, 1936, we read at last that *La Commune* is no longer an organ of "different tendencies," but one of the "Committee for the Fourth International." This put an end to "the mass paper" formally as well.

"Preparation" and Proclamation of the "New Party" (February 1-March 7, 1936)

In the appeal of the new editorial committee of *La Commune,* we read:

> Regroupment is not a simple thing to do, a thing that depends on one or another person's will: to achieve it, it is necessary to arrive at a doctrine responding to the fundamental problems of the historical period in which we struggle.

One would have thought that this was the beginning of a self-criticism. But not in the least. As an introduction to the new Fourth International policy, there appeared at the end of January the pamphlet *La Crise de la Section Française de la Ligue Communiste Internationaliste,* published by the "Committee for the Fourth International in France," which must be considered one of the most hypocritical documents in the literature of the workers' movement. To give themselves the appearance of honesty, Molinier-Frank reproduce in it among other things a series of harsh letters from Trotsky, which were directed against *La Commune,* but which were already common knowledge. On the other hand, all blame was disavowed:

> Among the reproaches which were made of us . . . is that of combinations from the top with the Pivertists. In reality, the only (!) combinations from the top which we accepted were those with the leadership of the GBL, without the organization knowing about it. (page 4)

Molinier-Frank fell "victim" to their "conciliation" because they . . . had given their agreement to the personal composition of the Political Bureau. Listen to the "self-accusation" in the pamphlet (what follows deals with the period of the Fourth National Conference in mid-September):

> Finally, Molinier and Frank accepted the proposed Political Bureau and the keynote report as amended; the political differences did not appear to them to be clear enough (?) at that time and they feared that if they rejected an agreement, the discussion . . . might have looked like a personal quarrel. They accepted this organizational compromise at the top and as a result they could not carry the

political discussion to the ranks without the risk of destroying the
agreement which they had accepted. . . . After the National
Conference, the same error was committed: in the Central Committee
one agreement was made after another . . . and we left the
organization uninformed of what was going on.

Such (!) is our part of the responsibility (!!).

In other words: the great error of Molinier and Frank was not
that they plotted with the centrists against the Bolshevik-
Leninists, but that they came to agreement with the members of
the Central Committee on several disputed questions.

But it would be naive to think that this was the high point of
the hypocrisy.

On every page the responsibility for the split is put solely on
the Bolshevik-Leninists. The pamphlet was published for this
purpose alone. The method used is very simple: (1) the formal
aspect of the question was distorted; (2) the past was falsified; (3)
a complete abstraction was made of the political content of the
conflict.

That is the basis on which the *Commune* people built the "new
party," founded March 7 at their conference, which they called
the "Internationalist Communist Party, section of the Fourth
International."

Molinier-Frank, who for years had thundered against nonexis-
tent people who wanted, it seems, to immediately create a new
party, launched into the immediate proclamation of the "new
party" as if they wanted to regain lost time and wipe out the
memory of their past crimes.

It is not worth the trouble to analyze the "program" of the "new
party." It bears all the traits of an improvisation. Its most
striking trait is its abstract character. But the value of a program
is not determined by the more or less correct formulations on the
need for a new party, for the Fourth International, etc. . . .

After the collapse of the adventurist enterprise it could not
suffice to "save" the situation through a Stalinist half-turn. *If the
Commune people had learned anything from their experience,
they should have considered it their first duty to make a sincere
accounting*, as Van did—though not publicly—writing:

Personally, I have left the *Commune* group. The hypotheses and
ideas of its initiators largely vanished and ran dry; experience laid
them to rest. This was as true for the "mass paper" as for the GARs.
The whole *Commune* tendency (which was mine) is foreign to
Marxism in its conception of the party, its education, and its relations

with the masses. All that is clear now. (Van to Crux, January 16, 1936)

The Commune people preferred to present a false balance sheet and they thus proved their bureaucratic dishonesty. Such methods are intolerable in our ranks.
A REVOLUTIONARY ORGANIZATION WHICH SUPPRESSES ITS OWN PAST OR TRIES TO LIE ABOUT ITS SERIOUS MISTAKES AND CRIMES HAS NO FUTURE. IT WILL NEVER BE THE PARTY OF THE PROLETARIAT AND THE PARTY OF THE WORLD REVOLUTION.

VI. The Policy of the GBL

The harm done to the cause of the Fourth International by the Frank-Molinier adventure is immense. A situation which was unprecedentedly favorable for the creation of the new party was allowed to escape. But now it was necessary to save what was still left to be saved, to repair at least part of the damage.

The weighty *political* attacks directed by the GBL against the centrism of Molinier produced very positive results:

> Politically a complete victory was attained in a few weeks (wrote Crux to Fischer on March 4, 1936) since *La Commune* gave up all its windfalls and was converted quite simply to the Open Letter.

Frank's letter of November 28, 1935, the programmatic basis of *La Commune*, turned to dust. *But this victory was only half a victory. The problem was posed: who will profit from the victory, i.e., who will transform the victory into an organizational victory?*

Instead of Political Intransigence . . .

The first task after the split was to again "act as Bolshevik-Leninists," i.e., to be politically unrelenting and to have an offensive spirit. However, instead of that, the Naville-Rous factions persevered—and now without Molinier, who could no longer be an "excuse"—in their old lukewarm manner. The publication, even the discussion of the "Open Letter of the GBL and JSR for a Revolutionary Party," ran up against the resistance of Naville, who did not want to admit that the correction was being carried out "ultimatistically and suddenly," without taking into account the present state of the organization and the JS. The Crux-Zeller plan for winning the youth to the Fourth International was sabotaged. Crux wrote to Rous, November 29, 1935:

> You had stressed the need to win Zeller over definitively for the Bolshevik-Leninists. Now that is an accomplished fact. But the Bolshevik-Leninists are attacking him and it seems to me that you are not supporting him. . . . Zeller left here with a certain plan,

which appeared to me to follow from the whole situation: *to win the Youth Alliance for the Fourth International* (without that you are leaving the door open to all sorts of adventures). . . . To ignore the interests of your own tendency is the greatest crime imaginable. You are completely silent on that question.

Rousset and Rigal, Molinier's fiercest adversaries, proved that their struggle did not result from a principled political attitude. On December 9, Frédéric informed Crux:

Things are going badly concerning the question of the Fourth International. Rousset-Rigal still do not think the time has come to put this question up for discussion in the youth. They would have had the great majority of the organization for joining the Fourth International. . . . What good is it to fight Molinier's centrism if pretty much the same things are done or tolerated in our own camp?

A few weeks later, Zeller tried in vain to push forward. He wrote to Crux on December 24, 1935:

Yesterday in the Central Committee I asked for a prompt discussion in the organization on the manifesto of the Fourth International, which was signed by the Spartacus Youth, by the Young Leninist Guards of Holland, etc. . . . As a result, in the next issue of *Révolution* we will start a major survey: for or against the Fourth International? This survey will end with a definitive vote on accepting the manifesto of the Fourth International. This will be the most important step we will have taken since the expulsions.

But the survey was never taken.

Révolution maintained its centrist and "national" character after the split (under the editorial direction of Rous): instead of taking a principled position on the question of the International . . . it carried rare, defective, and even partly false international reports; and nothing on the Russian Bolshevik-Leninists.

Although Marceau Pivert, at the youth congress of December 8, 1935, had taken an openly traitorous position and was hissed, he was treated with kid gloves in *Révolution:*

We regret that instead of fully supporting us in this struggle, Comrade Pivert prefers not to take a position (?). . . .

It had not even been decided to put an end to the vain clinging to the SFIO, since the decision was made—six months after the Lille expulsions—to participate in the youth congress of January

5, which was manipulated by the SFIO bureaucracy. In his letter to Crux of December 24, Zeller gave the following "reason":

> Certain comrades think, and it is an error, that by not participating we would cut ourselves off from a great number of comrades who can still follow us.

The decision to boycott was only made December 24 at the insistence of Crux and some young comrades.

. . . Obstinacy and Prestige Politics

The Central Committee of the GBL had shown evidence of being in too much of a hurry to give in at the time the crisis broke out. Only very late, only under the impact of Molinier's breach of discipline and Crux's incessant exhortations by letter and telegram, did it understand the need for a sharp change of course. Its task was now to win all the members, or at least the greater part of them, to this turn. But the same Central Committee thought—and this gives a certain indication of bureaucratism or its embryonic literary form—that the turn, which it finally understood and sharply applied, was therefore "obligatory" for the whole organization. "As for me, I have understood," the Central Committee members said to themselves, "so the others only have to follow, whether they have understood or not." But *they themselves* had understood so "quickly" only because they found themselves at the center of events, whereas the members on the periphery were still under the influence of the old arch-conciliatory policy of the Central Committee. It was thus inevitable that the Central Committee would spread confusion among a great part of the members (particularly in the provinces) if everything were not immediately done to achieve the closest contact with the ranks. The best means would have been: *an ample political discussion,* in which it might have been necessary to let Molinier or his supporters speak as well, since the members had the full right to consider for themselves whether the organizational measures taken by the leadership were justified. Further: *the immediate organization of a national conference* on a broad democratic basis. This was the direction in which all the proposals of all the conciliators tended and the *Commune* people were skillful enough to exploit this state of mind. They unceasingly repeated:

> A political discussion is needed right away, ending with an enlarged

Central Committee or a council or a national conference. . . . (Letter of the nine *Commune* members, December 13, 1935, "To all the members of the GBL, to all the members of the ICL")

Seeing that the Central Committee was persisting in its bureaucratic passivity, Molinier-Frank dared to go quite far in their demagogy. After a short (and false) exposition of their politics, they continued in their letter to the members of the GBL:

We ask that these views be discussed instead of being simply characterized as capitulation to the wave of social patriotism. . . . If a political agreement is reached, then the matter of merging the two papers will be easy. We commit ourselves to acting with all our might to get the non–Bolshevik-Leninist comrades collaborating with us on *La Commune* to accept whatever solutions the GBL may adopt. ("To all the members of the GBL," letter of the nine *Commune* members, December 13, 1935)

And what policy was counterposed to this demagogy? None!— unless we want to consider as a policy the refusal to meet with Molinier, the ultimatum to his supporters and their expulsion, and the refusal to call an enlarged Central Committee and a national conference. The urgency of a conference was shown by a letter from Rous dated December 17, 1935, concerning the Lyons conciliators:

The Lyons group still hesitates on the expulsion. . . . What are its arguments? (1) You did not prepare us for this dramatic move; (2) Molinier is "a bit headstrong," but does not have fundamental differences; (!) . . . (3) a national conference is needed to find out whether or not Molinier should be expelled (!!). . . .

In spite of this, the group refuses to distribute *La Commune* and has called on Molinier to cease its publication.

But Rous rejected a national conference, which had been suggested by Crux as well, with these words: "A national conference at the present stage would settle nothing."

The *entire* Central Committee's lack of understanding of the needs of the organization in its critical situation should not be attributed only to their bureaucratic obstinacy and their illusions about the coming financial collapse (!) of *La Commune*; to these two considerations are added totally false considerations of prestige.

To be able to carry on a broad discussion and call a national conference, the Central Committee should have had the courage to say: "We made opportunist errors in the past and in doing so we facilitated Molinier-Frank's work against the organization." If the Central Committee had then added: "We went too far in our conciliatory dealing and we made inadmissible concessions; we ourselves had a false conception of the 'mass paper,' etc., but . . . we see our error, while Molinier is pursuing his toward betrayal," then every rank-and-file member would have had respect and a new confidence in the Central Committee. But in its statement of December 11, 1935, the Central Committee said that the responsibility for *all* the past errors, since Mulhouse and Lille, fell on the Molinier group. Only

> Molinier directly reflected the pressure of the capitulationist centrist currents of Pivert and Company. Through him (!) this pressure was felt even in the Central Committee, which was able to escape its influence only quite recently.

So: the Central Committee was only a "victim" of Molinier. There was complete silence on the arch-conciliatory attitude and the absolutely impermissible concessions which had been made during the outbreak of the crisis. It is true that they now stated that "a mass newspaper is a newspaper written in a simple manner but presenting all our views," but there is no mention that on November 23 the motions of all three factions (Molinier-Naville-Rous) on the question of the "mass paper" reflect the same confusion on this question. As a result of this attitude on the part of the Central Committee Molinier won at his game. One example:

The Central Committee of the GBL correctly designated and condemned *La Commune* as a centrist paper. However, Molinier proved, on the basis of a conciliatory resolution *proposed by Rous* and *adopted by the Central Committee,* that *La Commune*, except for the title, corresponded exactly to this resolution. But since Rous's text was, for "reasons of prestige," not admitted to be false in any way, it was natural that the confusion increased and that the authority of the Central Committee diminished. It was precisely false considerations of prestige, as we see it, that destroyed prestige.

Because of the lack of frankness, even the correct points made in the statement had a negative result. The following example proves it. The resolution of December 11, 1935, states, of course, that even a mass paper should fight for a "definite program": "That is what *Révolution* should be," it says. But comparing *La Commune* with *Révolution*, a member of the organization found this "definite program" in neither one nor the other. Many people then said to themselves: "The difference in political content is not so great. So why wouldn't a conciliation be possible?" Conciliationism and confusion mounted again. And Molinier fished in these troubled waters. Conciliators, like the Lyons group, for example, who at first condemned Molinier's *La Commune*, after that refused to distribute *La Vérité* and finally went over to the side of the "most dynamic" ones.

*   *   *

After Molinier's expulsion by the IS on December 4, the Central Committee satisfied itself, in the resolution on December 11, 1935, with inviting his supporters

> to respect the discipline of the GBL by giving *Révolution* and *La Vérité* their cooperation. Persisting in their attitude would put them outside the GBL.

After the turn, the Central Committee did nothing until December 23. Then it sent a three-day ultimatum, without result; they were finally obliged to resort to expulsion. It then appeared that its bureaucratic measures had already split its own ranks. The expulsions passed by a five-to-four vote.

The Central Committee, trusting in its correct political position, thought it could be satisfied with bureaucratic measures against the *Commune* people and simply wait for the collapse of *La Commune*. Crux energetically criticized this attitude in his January 14, 1936, letter to D., in which he wrote:

> If each one had been invited separately and dealt with in an official meeting with minutes, it would have been possible to get to know the different groupings and tendencies and to become thoroughly familiar with the differences among them.

Molinier solidified his ranks by launching a big campaign "against the splitters," "for reunification," etc. The editorial board of *La Commune* stated December 20 with excessive kindness:

> To our friends of *Révolution:*
>   We think that in the first place it would be extremely desirable to merge our two papers. . . .

Crux, in his letter of January 4, 1936, to the Central Committee of the GBL, proposed to parry the blow as follows:

"You propose that we merge our newspapers? Very well. We are quite ready to prepare for and facilitate this task of revolutionary groupment. But the Marxist newspaper cannot be based on a few slogans that are deliberately vague or conjunctural and transitory. A mass newspaper is the instrument of the Marxist party in preparation. A newspaper must have a complete program. We consider a discussion of this draft, and especially of the slogans of the new party and the Fourth International, to be a preliminary condition . . . for the fusion of the mass newspapers, that is, for organic unity, these two things being equivalent. . . ."

From the same point of view, *Révolution* could very well respond to the sugary and hypocritical proposition of *La Commune* in this sense: "The four paragraphs of *La Commune*'s platform—which moreover change every week—are absolutely insufficient to guide a mass newspaper. . . . The Youth Alliance is now in a discussion preparing its program, which will at the same time be the program of our mass newspaper. We, *Révolution,* will be very pleased if you will adopt the same Marxist program, which is the only condition on our part for the fusion of the two papers."

This clear and sound attitude will necessarily destroy once and for all the machinations of Molinier and Company, which are directed not only against the GBL and the youth but also against the sincere and naive members of *La Commune* itself.

But the Central Committee did not dare to reply in this way and remained passive. In the guise of a "reply" to the proposal for fusion, *Révolution* published the following statement on January 1, 1936:

The enlarged Central Committee of the GBL met. . . . The expulsions of those in charge of *La Commune* were approved and their politics unanimously condemned.

Despite all the faults of the Central Committee, the opposite side was hardly reassured, since it had to note that after only two weeks, when the disaster with the petty-bourgeois elements of the "Social Front" took place, its "platform" slipped from under its feet. It was thus *obliged* to maneuver. Crux wrote, January 14, 1936:

Molinier wanted to demonstrate his "goodwill." People will learn only through their own experience that behind that "goodwill" is hiding ill will.

An excellent occasion presented itself when, at the beginning of January, a group of more than twenty conciliators from both camps proposed to send Molinier and a representative of the Central Committee of the GBL to Crux. Crux, of course, in his reply to the conciliators, did not neglect to point out to this group the inconsistency of their political viewpoint, but he did not refuse the proposed visit. In his letter to D., January 7, 1936, he explained his position:

> Why not accept this proposal?. . . The trip can be mutually informative. This *outward* concession to the conciliators will achieve the best results, because Molinier will obviously gain nothing from it, but on the contrary, when he returns his situation will be much more difficult. The Central Committee will thus definitively demonstrate its goodwill toward the conciliators. To round off an essentially firm policy by such "concessions" of form has always had its advantages.

But the Central Committee obstinately opposed this proposal. Those who did not reject it categorically reasoned: We have nothing against a trip by Molinier and we would like to believe that the results can be somewhat favorable, *on the condition that they are negative.* The question would present itself in another light if Molinier promised certain things (the liquidation of *La Commune*) and then misused Crux's words; then the trip could only be harmful. Finally, a trip by the Central Committee is not realizable. That is why it must be given up. But at any rate (!), there was not much belief that it would be good, because in this case the interview would have the atmosphere of arbitration, while there was and could be no question of that being the case.

Crux replied to these objections and other similar objections in his letter of January 14, 1936:

> Your worst enemy appeals to a person who is entirely on your side. What should you reply? "Very well! Crux's opinion is important to you. It is important to us also. Let's go listen to him. . . ." What could be wrong—not from the point of view of bureaucratic pigheadedness but from the point of view of reason—with listening to the opinion and advice of an older comrade, before making a final decision? . . . But the . . . bureaucrat . . . replies: "We cannot accept any arbitration." What has this got to do with arbitration? . . . This formal side of the affair is not worth an eggshell (all the more so inasmuch as Crux had already written to the conciliators before: "Naturally it can only be a matter of personal explanations that could in no way alter the decisions made by the responsible bodies"—

Braun). . . . This proposal by Raymond's supporters should have been seized with both hands and exploited thoroughly."

Most of the comrades nurtured the illusion that *La Commune* would somehow collapse by itself. Crux replied to them: The correct policy would have shown Molinier to be bankrupt a long time ago,

> But as it is, his bankruptcy will not be demonstrated for months, because you are helping him with all your might.

Ostrich Politics

The situation changed from the moment Molinier suddenly made a 180-degree turn and to his new policy in favor of the Fourth International added ultraconciliatory proposals toward the GBL. A new organization for the Fourth International had come onto the scene and *by that fact the Central Committee of the GBL had lost the advantage of its correct political position vis-à-vis La Commune*. At that moment it was necessary to recognize the new situation immediately and draw all the necessary conclusions from it. The GBL Central Committee should have immediately taken the initiative for the unification and said: "See, the turn of *La Commune* proves that we were right. The split was all the more unjustified. It must be ended immediately."

However, the attitude toward *La Commune* did not change at all. To the degree that they deigned to take any notice of it at all, it was characterized simply as an adventurist enterprise typical of Molinier, which the Amsterdam secretariat of the Fourth International ought to simply disavow with a declaration. Crux warned Rous in his letter of January 31, 1936:

> You see only Molinier, whereas on the political plane what exists is a *new* organization for the Fourth International. This organization is the product of earlier political and organizational mistakes. But that doesn't matter. It exists.
>
> A "statement" by the Amsterdam secretariat would be a gesture of bureaucratic powerlessness. What can they say? That Molinier is an adventurer? That *La Commune* should change its orientation? But everyone now will judge *La Commune* according to its *new* orientation, based on the Open Letter for the Fourth International. How is it possible not to see that there is a new situation (created by

the old mistakes) that demands a somewhat more serious intervention and one that is more comprehensible to the outside world than a
futile statement?

At the close of this letter, to emphasize the importance, Crux
repeats:

> Politically a new grouping for the Fourth International exists and
> demands a clear and flexible attitude on our part if we want to avoid
> accumulating more difficulties by bureaucratic obstinacy. (Letter to
> Rous, January 31)

Crux was not content with pressing exhortations, but supple-
mented them with concrete organizational proposals, taking the
new situation into account. But in Paris there was silence. After
more than four weeks, Crux insisted most energetically in his
letter to Fischer, March 4, 1936:

> It is not a political program . . . to say "We don't want to have
> anything to do with Molinier." Because it is not a matter of Molinier
> but of an important group, *La Commune*. This group came into
> existence because of the errors of our section. It is possible to change
> an incorrect policy, but the material consequences of the past period
> do not disappear with this change: they continue to block the way. It
> is incontestable that Molinier has been more harmful to our
> movement in the last few months than he could be useful in several
> years. . . . By your whole policy in the past period you have only
> helped him. . . . There is talk of a congress of the new party but you
> proceed as though *La Commune* did not exist. If you want to wipe it
> out you must declare a holy war, in words and on paper. . . . But to
> simply remain silent about *La Commune* is certainly the most inept
> and dangerous policy imaginable.

The *La Commune* people were not idlers and they exploited the
favorable situation at will. The demagogy of unity was something *they* could use:

> See, we have the same ideas as the Bolshevik-Leninists. Why were we
> chased off? Can't we have immediate unity? On essentials our ideas
> are the same. (Quoted in the letter from Van to Crux, February 23,
> 1936)

Since the Central Committee was putting its head in the sand,
the thieves could cry "thief" with impunity.

In the Tow of "La Commune"

By refusing to take *La Commune* into consideration despite its recent conversion to the Fourth International, the Central Committee placed itself in reality politically in its tow.

The *Commune* people had clearly announced their turn from the time of the resolution passed at their enlarged Central Committee of January 12, 1936. It said:

> The formation of a new revolutionary party is becoming . . . the essential task on the agenda for the Bolshevik-Leninists. . . . The Bolshevik-Leninists are passing from the phase of proclaiming the need for the new party to the phase of proclaiming the party.

What was still needed, however, was the *official constitution of the "Committee for the Fourth International"* (January 16) before the GBL would decide to publish in its press the "Open Letter for the New Party." *Révolution* still kept its limited national character. The "Fourth International" was hidden in the text. Now it was the *founding of the Internationalist Communist Party (section of the Fourth International),* accomplished March 7, 1936, which dealt a strong blow to the editorial board of *Révolution*. Some days later, on March 13, 1936, *Révolution* put the "Fourth International," as its main slogan, on the front page.

As for the question of solidarity with the Russian Bolshevik-Leninists, this was handled no better than the question of the International. The *Commune* people, once the turn toward the Fourth International had been accomplished, had not been slow to again take up propaganda for the Russian revolutionaries. But it was still necessary for them to announce a special pamphlet in order for the editorial board of *Révolution* to remember the Russian Bolshevik-Leninists.

Navillism showed itself to be the most obstinate of all in rejecting the articles by Trotsky on this question. From December 7, 1935, to February 28, 1936, the editorial board of *Révolution* cast aside all articles by Trotsky. On March 27, D. wrote to Crux:

> On what you wrote on the question of the article "How Did Stalin Defeat the Opposition?" the same idiotic spirit can be noted as Well and Company had in Berlin (the latter prepared their capitulation to the Stalinists in this way—Braun): "We don't need to publish too

many articles by Trotsky." This spirit we (i.e., the International Secretariat) are not tolerating passively but are combating energetically. The article on Stalin's victory will appear in the next *Révolution.*

However, this article has not yet appeared to this day in the French language. Navillism was not extirpated from the GBL. The final result of this policy was that a few isolated individuals left *La Commune,* not *because of* but *in spite of* the policy of the GBL. Van is an example of this. After turning his back on *La Commune,* he wrote to Crux on January 1, 1936:

> I can only judge the policy of the GBL at present through *Révolution* and a few rare personal conversations. *Révolution* does not at all have the offensive attitude that would befit it. . . . And I have been told from different sides (I give you the information with this reservation) that one of the Bolshevik-Leninists with the highest authority and the fiercest attitude says it is not good psychology to speak of the Fourth International. No, thank you, I have had enough of *La Commune.*

Politics and Methods

All politics, by the very nature of things, has its own methods. In the period of the wavering political course, an unbelievable negligence reigned in all the technical, administrative, and financial questions. However, there were people who did not even notice this. Immediately after the split, Crux raised with Naville by letter the question of how the financial and administrative side of the press was doing. The latter replied on December 17 (more than three weeks after the split):

> *Révolution will come out every week* (!). Financially we live from week to week. But there is a serious mobilization by everyone. . . . Now the subscriptions will start again. . . . *The life of La Vérité is assured* (!!).

In reality, *Révolution* appeared only quite irregularly and later only once a month in two pages. *La Vérité* appeared only . . . twice. The reason was organizational negligence and incompetence. These qualities are always the consequence of lack of theoretical clarity and political will. *If one seriously wants something that one has clearly understood, then one also looks for the means.*

For a leadership that means finding in the organization the comrades best suited for organizational purposes. A healthy and active organization raises the most capable organizers to its head by means of a correct selection process. Unfortunately, Naville, in spite of his knowledge and talents, possesses none of this important side of the revolutionary movement. This can be seen in the big questions as well as in the small ones. Under the pressure of Molinier's radical-adventurist policy, Naville tried to repair in one blow all the errors he had made through negligence. He who had always excused the past policy by the fact that it had been necessary to take into account the "state of mind" of the youth, that it was necessary not to be "brusque" with them or treat them in an "ultimatistic" way, was now forced to set up the worst bureaucratic command in order to "recapture" *La Commune* at a gallop.

This policy was described in a letter from Corvin to Crux in mid-March (signed by several other young comrades).

The Naville faction, as is known, held up the discussion of the "Open Letter" [for a Revolutionary Party] for months. At present it functions as follows:

> The "Open Letter" was signed for the JSR by Comrade Hic, in the name of the Political Bureau, without this body knowing at the time that the previous Central Committee of the JSR had decided that it should be discussed in the organization first. (Letter from Corvin to Crux)

In the same way, the Crux-Zeller plan for a fusion conference with the youth on the basis of the "Open Letter" had been undermined. On the other hand, they now see themselves as forced to resort to the following methods:

> The National Conference preparatory to the new party was announced in *Révolution* without any comrade (even the Bolshevik-Leninists) or any organized body knowing about it in advance; however, at this moment the JSR congress was decided upon and Naville knew very well that these two simultaneous conferences would be difficult to hold and that it was necessary to at least have an understanding in advance with those responsible for the JSR congress. . . .
>
> To explain these two abuses of power, we were told that time was pressing (!) and that nothing else could be done; but in reality the "Open Letter" and the preparatory conference had been discussed for months and the discussion dragged on, the documents did not appear,

nothing was prepared, and suddenly they rushed into it, without taking time to announce in advance what would be done, the comrades were not prepared and they were given the impression that they had an incoherent leadership that did not know what it wanted, that first hesitates and then rushes in recklessly. This impression is all the more striking when it is borne in mind that neither Comrade N(aville) nor anyone else spoke of the immediate need for a preparatory conference fifteen days before announcing it, but they brusquely made up their minds when R. M(olinier) announced the formation of his "party." . . . In other less important areas the same method is followed, consisting of doing nothing for a long period and then suddenly, without warning anyone, and in an extremely short time, organizing some kind of demonstration. . . . This idiotic work has for its inevitable corollary the necessity of making decisions (political and practical) in an airtight chamber without warning the competent comrades or bodies and naturally the result is the aborting of the projected enterprises.

The Naville faction had for a long time prided itself as a champion against the antidemocratic methods of Molinier-Frank. Now it suppressed party democracy itself:

I must state to you on this subject that in regard most particularly to the political decisions thus taken it is the central bodies of the Bolshevik-Leninists which are trying to forcibly drag along the JSR movement (especially those who are not Bolshevik-Leninists), thus putting the leaders in a ridiculous position in the eyes of the ranks. The result of all this is now being felt. The ranks lose confidence in their leadership and complain that there is no democracy. . . .

The disastrous consequences of these methods could not be long in manifesting themselves. A deep dejection momentarily seized the organization and especially the youth. Rous wrote to Crux, February 23, 1936: "The flower of pessimism and impressionism is blooming." And nevertheless this state of mind was completely unjustified.

When at the beginning of June the fusion, which had become inevitable, took place between the two organizations supporting the Fourth International, it turned out that the *Commune* group, which had left in order to win the masses, was already at the end of its rope organizationally and held onto its supporters only with great trouble. The GBL, despite all its grave errors, had been not weakened but strengthened. Why? The Central Committee of the GBL had not separated from the national and international organization, but had acted in their framework. Its international affiliation had in the last analysis protected the GBL from decomposition.

Under certain conditions any organization can reveal the seeds of disintegration, just as any living organism can become sick. But the illness will not be fatal for the young sections of the Fourth International, and it will disappear as soon as the organization returns to the true Marxist policy. There is no reason for pessimism in the ranks of the Fourth International.

Afterword

This work was almost finished when the two groups unified at the Pentecost congress. Although this does not yet repair the major errors of the past, it has changed and improved the situation. Doubts about whether it is still today a good idea to publish this work may arise. Some will say: "A new chapter has begun in the history of the French section of the Fourth International. The gigantic wave of strikes by the French proletariat tells us that we are on the threshold of revolution. Today there is no time for old stories."

But it is precisely because our French comrades have the gigantic task of winning the masses for the revolutionary path that the question of the education of new tempered cadres has become a vital question. The best method for achieving it is through implacable and daily criticism, in light of the experiences and lessons of the past. It is this task to which the present article aims to contribute in the first place.

The French comrades were the ones who cleared the way for an entry into as well as a departure from an alien party. To make use of the French experience internationally is the second and not lesser aim of this work.

That I was able to set myself up as a "critic," I owe mainly to a series of external circumstances: I worked until mid-September in the International Secretariat and I participated in Comrade Crux's correspondence with the French comrades as his technical aide. I considered the opportunity for access to the archives of the critical period as an obligation to make this rich and still fresh material accessible to the whole international organization. As for the logical and chronological order and the use of numerous quotations, I tried to make the facts and the documents speak for themselves. As a member of the German section of the ICL, I hope I have made a useful contribution to internationalism on behalf of my organization.

June 17, 1936

Appendix B:
Comments
by Pierre Frank

On the split among the French Trotskyists in 1935-36, here are some general ideas. . . .

1. The Trotskyist movement was formed only in 1929, not as the result of a struggle by a tendency within the Communist Party but as a regroupment of militants who had been expelled from the party at various times and for various reasons. As a result, there was a great heterogeneity among the leaders from the very start and this heterogeneity had certainly not been overcome when the war broke out in 1939, much less in 1935.

2. On several occasions, the French section of the Trotskyist movement was in the forefront when it came to new tactical maneuvers by our international movement. That was the case when we entered the SFIO. In those days, when the possibility of entrism in other countries was discussed, this was referred to as the "French turn." At the time of the entry into the SFIO, an initial break occurred; some, like Naville and a tendency that followed him, fought against the entrist tactic within the [French Communist] League; they did not follow us when the majority decided to enter, but they entered so soon afterwards, and we were reunited so quickly, that the split, an episodic one, is hardly ever mentioned.

3. The development of the Bolshevik-Leninist Group—which is the name we took in the SFIO—was uneven. Progress was more rapid and substantial in the Young Socialists, and slower and less substantial in the adult party, although more workers were recruited there.

4. Having been the first to practice entrism, we in France were also the first to have to decide on another tactic—one to confront

---

Notes written in the mid-seventies for a comrade preparing a class on the history of French Trotskyism, and provided to the editors by Pierre Frank. Translated by Gerry Foley.

the expulsions by the SFIO leadership. In this latter case, also, we had no prior experience that might have prepared us.

The leadership of the Socialist Party took the offensive, having one tendency, the JSR, expelled from the Young Socialists. These youth, who were attracted by our Trotskyist activity in the SFIO and in the Young Socialists, were ready, even anxious, to leave the Socialist Party.

The GBL tendency organized around Molinier and me included primarily comrades active among the adults. At that time the situation in the party was complicated for us by the fact that, almost at the exact same time as the expulsion of the youth, Marceau Pivert broke away from Zyromsky and the *Bataille Socialiste* tendency within the party to form his own tendency, the Revolutionary Left. This slowed down the movement toward us by a good number of Socialist Party members. That was the reason that we (that is, Molinier and I) wanted to try to counter the Pivertist maneuver by staying in the SFIO for a while longer and by launching the journal *La Commune,* to try to attract more hesitant elements as well to the Fourth International.

The split occurred in practice, then, on the basis of a difference in tempo that was a result of working in different milieus.

5. But once the split was accomplished, deeper political differences were quick to appear. It is, however, necessary to explain all the manifold nuances. The POI was composed for the most part of young people from the Young Socialists, thus without much political education and with hazy notions about organization. The PCI of the prewar period had a higher average age and included more than a few former members of the CP, who were politically more rigid. If a careful study is made of the POI and of the PCI during this period, it will be seen that the POI leaned frequently toward opportunism, while the PCI often showed sectarian traits. All this is an overall judgment.

In retrospect, in my opinion, the meager gains that Molinier and I made in the SFIO by our tactic were insignificant in comparison with the problems that would have been avoided, or at least reduced, especially on the eve of the war, by maintaining unity.

I do not believe there is any reason to reply to the argument that was put forward at the time, that with the appearance of *La Commune* we abandoned Trotskyism. Today, this accusation raised by Rous and others seems grotesque.

6. Trotsky, who opposed the PCI very vigorously, supported the POI without closing his eyes to its frequently opportunist policies.

Even in *L'Organe de masse*, Nicolle Braun's pamphlet against the PCI written largely under Trotsky's inspiration, this can be seen. Trotsky's support to the POI can be explained, in my opinion, by the fact that he saw the world war coming and he thought that only youth, even if they were politically confused, could enable the movement to survive and grow during the war. In substance, he explains this idea in an interview that he had around this time with C.L.R. James. It fact, it was above all the youth, those who were in the POI and also those who were in the PCI, who made it possible to maintain the continuity of the movement during the war.

7. Concerning the breakup of the POI on the eve of the war, what I know on that subject from outside is too general. I was familiar only with the broadest tendencies of the different groups that took shape then. It would be necessary to see the people concerned and to read the documents that they wrote at the time. I have never had occasion to read these documents.

Notes

1. The **Chinese** revolution of 1925-27 was crushed because the Chinese Communists, under order from Moscow, entered the bourgeois nationalist Kuomintang (Nationalist Party), which was led by Chiang Kai-shek, and subordinated the revolution to the interests of their coalition with the Kuomintang. The **German** Communist Party, following an ultraleft policy dictated by Moscow, played into the hands of the Nazis by refusing to apply the Leninist tactic of the united front toward the Social Democratic Party, thus permitting Hitler to divide and conquer the German working class without any effective opposition. In February 1934, the workers of **Austria** rose in a heroic insurrection against repressive measures of the right-wing regime of Engelbert Dollfuss but were defeated, in part because of the vacillation of their Social Democratic leaders. The Austrian Social Democracy had previously refused to lead a serious struggle against the Dollfuss regime, "tolerating" him as a lesser evil to the Nazis. These policies enabled both Dollfuss and the Nazis to consolidate their strength and smash the powerful Austrian labor movement.

2. **The Unitary Federation of Teachers, Friends of the New Age,** and **Communist Youth of St-Denis** were among those who solidarized with the expelled Bolshevik-Leninists.

3. The Molinierists later cited Trotsky's remark about a possible **Pivertist split from the SFIO** to support their contention that Trotsky had illusions about Pivert.

4. In May 1935, Stalin signed a Soviet-French nonaggression pact with French Foreign Minister Laval. A final communiqué attached to the pact by Stalin "fully approved" France's policy of national defense. Trotsky's point here is that the Comintern had turned from Stalin's official policy (support for France's rearmament) to the pacifism and support for disarmament promoted by the Blum leadership in the SFIO, as a way of clearing the obstacles to a bloc or merger between the two parties.

5. See "The ILP and the Fourth International," in *Writings of Leon Trotsky (1935-36)*.

6. After the Italian attack on Ethiopia in October 1935, the British Labour Party and CP called for a campaign of pressure on the Conservative government to force the Italians to stop their aggression through a policy of **"sanctions"** (coercive measures, such as blockade or boycott) by members of the League of Nations. The European workers' movement was divided over whether to call for League of Nations sanctions, sanctions by the workers themselves, or no sanctions at all.

7. "Motion C," prepared by the GBL for the SFIO's Seine congress (held in November), advocated "committees led by the masses." Trotsky criticized that formulation in this excerpt from a letter to Rous. As a result, the section of Motion C was rewritten before the motion was published.

8. **Zinoviev** and **Kamenev**, prominent Bolsheviks, opposed the October 1917 insurrection and published a statement to that effect in a semi-Menshevik paper. Lenin condemned them as strikebreakers and called for their expulsion from the Bolshevik Party. This proposal was dropped after the insurrection, when they returned to the Bolshevik leadership. Lenin's **testament**, giving his final evaluation of the other Soviet leaders, was written in December 1922 and January 1923. It is included in volume 36 of Lenin's *Collected Works*.

9. **No resignations!** refers to a custom among leaders of the French section in the 1930s. When they wanted to give emphasis to their disagreement with a decision, they sometimes would submit their resignations from the committee or bureau to which they had been elected, and sometimes even from the French section itself. Since the true meaning of such actions was understood by everyone and since these resignations were rarely accepted, they were soon retracted or forgotten, and everything went on as before. At the time of Trotsky's letter there had been such resignations from the Central Committee, the Political Bureau, and the Paris Regional Committee, along with a number of resignations by youth leaders from the GBL at a Seine Young Socialist congress.

10. This refers to a peculiarity of French electoral procedures, consisting of two "rounds" of voting. On the second round, in many cases, the Communist and Socialist candidates withdrew in favor of the Radical candidates.

11. **Bonapartism** was a central concept in Trotsky's writings during the thirties. He used the term to describe a dictatorship, or a regime with certain features of a dictatorship, during periods when class rule is not secure; it is based on the military, police, and state bureaucracy, rather than on parliamentary parties or a mass movement. Trotsky saw two types—bourgeois and Soviet. His most extensive writings on bourgeois Bonapartism are in *The Struggle Against Fascism in Germany* (Pathfinder Press, 1970). His views on Soviet Bonapartism reached their final form in the essay "The Workers' State, Thermidor and Bonapartism," reprinted in *Writings of Leon Trotsky (1934-35)*.

12. In **1848**, struggles for bourgeois democratic rights, national independence, and constitutional reforms took place throughout Europe.

13. In its attempt to be popular, *La Commune* adopted a lighthearted tone. It opened a **"Chameleon Contest"** featuring caricatures of various French political figures, with quotations from their speeches, the point being to guess the identity of each figure. The choice for a mascot of the chameleon, an animal that is notoriously adaptable to its surroundings, appears to be unintentional humor.

14. **Kurt von Schleicher** (1882-1934), was Hitler's predecessor as

chancellor of Germany. He and **Ernst Röhm** (1887-1934), a prominent Nazi leader, were murdered by the Nazis during the "blood purge" of June 1934. **Heinrich Brüning** (1885-1970), chancellor from 1930 to 1932, issued a decree in April 1932 banning the Nazi paramilitary forces, the SA and the SS. This led to his ouster soon after. His successor, von Papen, rescinded the ban on the SA in June, which led to a resurgence of Nazi terror and provided a lesson for France in 1935 about the transience and unreliability of "antifascist" measures by capitalist governments. **Wilhelm Groener** (1867-1939) was minister of defense during Brüning's regime.

15. In December 1935, a French law was passed to dissolve all paramilitary organizations. The fascists responded by reorganizing themselves in the form of political parties.

16. Relations between Trotsky and Molinier deteriorated after this meeting in June 1935. Molinier later published an excerpt from a letter Trotsky sent him on October 24, 1935: "Your letter reveals the mental state of someone who makes his presence felt in a very dangerous way in political life. You make a number of gratuitous charges based on nothing but your imagination, and I wonder with some apprehension how you must present the same things to the young comrades if they are so distorted in your consciousness. Let's proceed systematically. You say: 'If you intend to eliminate me, there was no need to urge me to go to the North a year ago, and then to the South.' That verges on paranoia . . ." (*La Crise des Bolcheviks-Léninistes*, 1939).

17. A reference to **Problems of Civil War**, Trotsky's 1924 pamphlet, now in English in *The Challenge of the Left Opposition* (1923-25) (Pathfinder Press, 1975).

18. Chiang Kai-shek carried out a military **coup d'état in Canton** on March 20, 1926, arresting Communists and establishing a military dictatorship. Despite this development, Stalin insisted that the Chinese CP remain inside the Kuomintang and collaborate with Chiang.

19. **Pierre Frank's pamphlet** was entitled *La Semaine du 6 au 12 février. Pour l'alliance ouvrière! Pour l'alliance internationale!*

20. **Feodor Dan** (1871-1949), a Menshevik leader, was a pacifist during World War I and an opponent of the Bolshevik revolution. He was expelled from the Soviet Union in 1922. In 1935, he, Zyromsky, and Otto Bauer, a leader of the Austrian Social Democracy, issued joint **theses,** entitled "Socialism and the War Danger," calling for support to the national bourgeoisie in order to defend the Soviet Union and defeat Hitler. The theses were the Second International's equivalent to the Comintern's People's Front policy and its quid pro quo for organic unity.

21. The Provisional Contact Committee proposed at the end of the Open Letter for the Fourth International became known as the **Amsterdam secretariat.** It was in charge of issuing the ICL's bulletin in 1935-36.

22. "The Decisive Stage" and "The French Revolution Has Begun" are in *Leon Trotsky on France* (Pathfinder Press, 1978).

23. The **"third period"** was the name by which the Stalinists

designated the ultraleft and sectarian policies they followed internationally from 1928 to 1934, before switching to People's Frontism. Trotsky uses it here for the Molinier group because it developed sectarian tendencies in 1936, possibly out of an overreaction to Trotsky's characterization of it as opportunist in November and December 1935.

24. **200 families** refers to the financial elite controlling France's government.

25. Trotsky's next article was "Before the Second Stage." It is in *Leon Trotsky on France.*

26. **The February revolution** in Russia in 1917 overthrew the czar and established the bourgeois Provisional Government. The **July days** in Petrograd were a period of spontaneous upsurges and bloody repression. The Bolsheviks were declared responsible, their leaders arrested, and their papers shut down. In **April,** Lenin arrived from Switzerland and attempted to orient the Bolshevik Party toward taking power. This precipitated a crisis in the Bolshevik Party, which had been following a conciliatory policy toward the Provisional Government. Lenin's call for a dictatorship of the proletariat was at first opposed by virtually the entire Bolshevik leadership.

27. An account of the takeover and running of a candy factory in **Lille** by the workers, called "How the Delespaul-Havez Workers Ran the Factory," was in *Lutte ouvrière,* July 11, 1936.

28. The June 23, 1936, issue of *L'Intransigeant,* a bourgeois paper, carried an article speculating about "outside" forces that had allegedly instigated the labor upsurge, and containing predictable errors and distortions about the new party, its recent congress, its internal differences, etc. Molinier took the article to be an attack on his group, an attack that must have had the collaboration of his factional opponents, and demanded that the Political Bureau name a commission to investigate the identity of the culprits. Meanwhile, at his cell meeting and elsewhere, he charged that "Rous and his friends" were responsible.

29. Rous's pamphlet was entitled *Où va le gouvernement Blum?* (Where is the Blum government going?) (1936).

Glossary

The persons, newspapers, organizations, and events in this glossary are French, unless otherwise specified.

Action Socialiste Révolutionnaire (ASR): Journal of the left wing in the Belgian Labor Party (POB), under the influence of the Trotskyists, 1935-36.

Adolphe: see Klement, Rudolf.

Attlee, Clement (1883-1967): Head of the British Labour Party from 1935; in Churchill's cabinet, 1940-45; prime minister, 1945-51.

Bakunin, Mikhail (1814-1887): Russian founder of anarchism.

Baldwin, Stanley (1867-1957): British Conservative prime minister, 1935-37.

Bardin, Alexis (1905-   ): A young trade unionist recruited to the GBL by Trotsky.

Bardin, Joannès ("Boitel") (1909-   ): Administrative secretary of the POI, 1936.

Bataille Socialiste group: The "traditional" left wing in the SFIO. Divided into a right, led by Zyromsky, and a left, led by Pivert.

Bergery, Gaston (1892-1958): Left the Radical Party to found the petty-bourgeois Social Front group in 1933.

Blanqui, Louis-Auguste (1805-1881): Developed the theory of armed insurrection by small groups of conspirators, as opposed to the Marxist concept of mass action.

Blum, Léon (1872-1950): Head of the SFIO in the thirties and premier of the first People's Front government, 1936.

Boitel: see Bardin, Joannès.

Bolshevik-Leninist Group (GBL): The name used by the French Trotskyists, September 1934 until June 1936.

Bolshevik-Leninists: The name by which the Trotskyists designated themselves in all countries in the thirties.

Brandler, Heinrich (1881-1967): A central German CP leader, expelled in 1929 as a supporter of Bukharin's Right Opposition in the USSR; maintained an independent organization until World War II.

Braun, Nicolle; see Wolf, Erwin.

Briand, Aristide (1862-1932): Ex-Socialist; organized the bourgeois Republican Socialist Party in 1911 and was head of the wartime coalition cabinet, 1915-17.

Cachin, Marcel (1869-1958): A right-wing Socialist and supporter of World War I. Went into the CP with the SFIO majority in 1920 and became a CP leader.

CAP: Permanent Administrative Commission, a leading body of the SFIO.

CASR: Committee for Revolutionary Socialist Action, the successor to Action Socialiste, a leftist tendency in the SFIO.

CGT: General Confederation of Labor, the major union federation in France, dominated by a reformist leadership. Split in 1921, resulting in the formation of a smaller and more radical rival, the Unitary General Confederation of Labor (CGTU). Reunited in March 1936.

Chochoy, Bernard: Became the new national secretary of the Young Socialists after helping to expel the Bolshevik-Leninist youth at the Lille congress.

Collinet, Michel (1904-   ): A leader of Pivert's Revolutionary Left in the SFIO, and former Left Oppositionist.

Comintern: see Third International.

Committee for the Fourth International (CQI): The name taken by the Molinier group in January 1936.

Commune, La: "Mass paper" started by Molinier group, December 1935.

Communist International: see Third International.

Communist League: The name of the French Trotskyist movement, 1930-34.

Corvin, Mathias (1911-   ): A leader of the Young Socialists of the Seine; expelled in July 1935 and joined the GBL.

CP: The Communist Party.

CQI: Comité pour la Quatrième Internationale, see Committee for the Fourth International.

Craipeau, Yvan (1912-   ): A leader of the Bolshevik-Leninist youth, expelled from the JS in July 1935.

Crux: A Trotsky pseudonym.

D: see Sedov, Leon.

Daladier, Edouard (1884-1970): Radical Socialist premier of France, 1933-34; resigned after an attempted fascist coup d'état. Minister of war under Blum. As premier again in 1938, signed the Munich pact with Hitler.

Dauge, Walter (1907-1944): A member of the *ASR* group who became a leader of the Belgian Trotskyists, 1936-39.

DeKadt, Jaques: A leader of the Dutch OSP's right wing; expelled in 1934.

De la Rocque, Casimir (1886-1946): Chief candidate for fascist dictator, 1934-37; founder of the French Social Party, 1936.

Delbos, Yvon (1885-1956): A Radical deputy; minister of foreign affairs several times between 1936 and 1940.

Dimitrov, Georgi (1882-1949): A Bulgarian Communist tried by the Nazis in 1933 on charges of having set the German Reichstag on fire; acquitted. Executive secretary of the Comintern, 1935-43; chief proponent of the People's Front policy at the Comintern's 7th Congress in 1935.

Doriot, Jacques (1898-1945): CP leader and mayor of St-Denis, a left-wing industrial suburb of Paris. Advocated a workers' united front against fascism early in 1934. When the CP would not discuss his proposals, he made them publicly and was expelled. Swung to the right and formed a fascist party in 1936.

Doumergue, Gaston (1863-1937): Former president of France. Came out of retirement to replace Daladier as premier after an attempted fascist coup d'état in 1934, promising a "strong" government and restriction of democratic liberties.

Engels, Frederick (1820-1895): German revolutionary and founder, with Marx, of scientific socialism; also a leader of the First International.

Ercoli (pseudonym of Palmiro Togliatti) (1893-1964): A leader of the Italian CP and a member of the secretariat of the Comintern's executive committee.

Faure, Paul (1878-1960): Leader of SFIO minority that opposed affiliation to the Comintern in 1920; headed its apparatus until World War II.

Fischer, Ruth ("Dubois") (1895-1961): Former central leader of the German CP, expelled in 1927. Member of the IS, 1934-36.

Flandin, Pierre-Etienne (1889-1958): Left Republican premier, 1934-35. Minister of foreign affairs in Blum's first government.

Frank, Pierre (1905-   ): A founder of the French section and a member of the IS during the thirties. Trotsky's secretary in Turkey, 1932-33. Was allied with Molinier in 1935-36 and was expelled with him.

Frankel, Jan ("Werner Keller"): A Czech Oppositionist who served as Trotsky's secretary in Turkey, Norway, and Mexico, and also worked in the IS.

Frédéric: see Klement, Rudolf.

French section: Communist League, 1930-34; Bolshevik-Leninist Group, 1934-36; Internationalist Workers Party, 1936-39.

Frontists: see Social Front.

GARs: Groupes d'Action Révolutionnaire, see Revolutionary Action Groups.

GBL: Groupe Bolchevik-Léniniste, see Bolshevik-Leninist Group.

Gilbert, Bertrand (pseudonym of Boris Goldenberg): A German refugee and SAP representative; a founder of the Revolutionary Left in 1935.

Godefroid, Ferdinand: Head of the Belgian Young Socialist Guards (JGS), the POB youth group.

GR: Gauche Révolutionnaire, see Revolutionary Left.

Guesde, Jules (1845-1922): Founder of French Marxism and a cofounder of the SFIO. Supported World War I and served in the cabinet, 1914-16.

Held, Walter (1910-1941): A German Trotskyist who emigrated to Norway when Hitler came to power; was one of Trotsky's secretaries in Norway.

Henderson, Arthur (1863-1935): Labour Party leader and supporter of the British war policy in World War I. President of the Second Internation-

Herriot, Edouard (1872-1957): A leader of the Radical Party and president of the Chamber of Deputies, 1936-40.
al, 1925-29.

Hervé, Gustave (1871-1944): An outspoken antimilitarist before World War I, became an ultrapatriot in 1914, organized a profascist movement in 1927.

Humanité, L': Newspaper of the French CP.

IAG (International Labor Community): Predecessor of the London Bureau, established in 1932. A loose association of centrist parties not affiliated to either the Second or the Third International, but opposed to forming a Fourth Internatior al.

International Communist League (ICL): The name of the international Trotskyist movement from 1933 until July 1936, when it changed its name to the Movement for the Fourth International (MFI).

Internationalist Communist Party (PCI): The name taken by the *Commune* group in March 1936.

Internationalist Workers Party (POI): Formed by a merger between the PCI and the POR in June 1936.

International Secretariat (IS): The administrative leadership of the Trotskyist movement. Composition in spring 1935: R. Fischer, Leonetti, Rous, Sedov, Wolf; also Sneevliet and Trotsky, who functioned mainly by correspondence; and Klement as administrative secretary.

Jaurés, Jean (1859-1914): A founder of the Socialist Party of France and a pacifist. Assassinated at the start of World War I.

JGS: Jeunes Gardes Socialistes, see Young Socialist Guards.

Jouhaux, Léon (1870-1954): General secretary of the CGT, 1909-40, 1945-47. A supporter of both world wars and an opponent of the Russian revolution.

JS: Jeunesse Socialiste, see Young Socialists.

JSR: Jeunesse Socialiste Révolutionnaire, see Revolutionary Socialist Youth.

Kamenev, Leon (1883-1936): A prominent Russian Bolshevik; helped Stalin initiate the crusade against Trotskyism, then blocked with Trotsky, 1926-27. Capitulated when expelled from the party. A victim of the first Moscow trial.

Keller, Werner, see Frankel, Jan.

Klement, Rudolf ("Adolphe," "Frédéric") (1910-1938): German secretary to Trotsky in Turkey and France; administrative secretary of the IS. Killed by the GPU.

Lagorgette, Louis: The SFIO representative who spearheaded the attack on the Bolshevik-Leninists at the Lille youth congress.

Lansbury, George (1859-1940): A Labour member of the British Parliament and a founder of the Labour Party paper, *The Daily Herald.*

Laval, Pierre (1883-1945): Conservative Republican foreign minister, 1934-35; signed nonaggression pact with Stalin. Premier 1935-36 and 1942, when he collaborated with the Nazi occupation forces. Executed for treason.

Lebas, Jean-Baptiste (1878-1944): A Socialist deputy, 1932-40; a minister in Blum's government.

Lenin, V.I. (1870-1924): The leader of the Russian Bolshevik Party and October revolution, and founder of the Comintern. Prepared a fight against the bureaucratization of the Russian CP and Soviet state, but died before he could carry it out.

Liebknecht, Karl (1871-1919): A left-wing German Social Democrat, the first to vote against war credits for World War I. A leader of the Berlin uprising of 1919; assassinated by government soldiers.

Lille congress of Young Socialists (July 1935): The congress that expelled thirteen youth leaders, including Bolshevik-Leninist youth and left centrists.

Longuet, Jean (1876-1938): Marx's grandson, leader of the pacifist minority in the SFIO in 1915. Remained in the SFIO after the majority affiliated to the Comintern in 1920.

Louzon, Robert (1882-1976): A syndicalist who left the CP to found *Révolution prolétarienne* and the Syndicalist League.

Lutte de classes, La: The theoretical review of the French Trotskyists, 1929-35, edited by Naville.

Lutte ouvrière, La: Newspaper of the POI, June 1936–July 1939.

M: see Molinier.

MacDonald, James Ramsey (1866-1938): A founder of the British Labour Party and prime minister in the first two Labour governments, 1924, 1929-31. In 1931 he led a minority of the Labour Party into a coalition with the Conservatives; prime minister of this "national" government until 1935.

Martynov, Alexander (1865-1935): A right-wing Menshevik who joined the Russian Communist Party in 1923 and became a major apologist for Stalinist policy in China.

Marx, Karl (1818-1883): German revolutionary and founder, with Engels, of scientific socialism; also a leader of the First International.

Maurín Julia, Joaquín (1897-1973): Leader of the Spanish Workers and Peasants Bloc, which fused with the former Bolshevik-Leninists to form the POUM. Elected to Parliament in 1936.

Maxton, James (1885-1946): The principal leader of the British Independent Labour Party in the thirties and a pacifist.

Meichler, Jean ("Mèche") (1896-1942): A founder of the French section and a leader of the PCI, executed by the Nazis as a hostage.

MFI: see Movement for the Fourth International.

Molinier, Henri (1898-1944): A member of the French section and Raymond's brother, killed in the fighting for the liberation of Paris.

Molinier, Raymond (1904-   ): A cofounder of the French section and one of its leaders until his expulsion in December 1935 for publishing his own newspaper *(La Commune)*. Founded the PCI, which merged with the former GBL majority. Expelled again in July 1936.

Monatte, Pierre (1881-1960): A syndicalist who left the CP to found *Révolution prolétarienne* and the Syndicalist League.

Monmousseau, Gaston (1883-1960): Had been a revolutionary syndicalist before World War I; became a leader of the CP and CGTU.

Mot-Dag: A Norwegian centrist youth group that supported the Norwegian Labor government and endorsed Stalin's statement approving French rearmament.

Motion C: Prepared by the GBL for the SFIO's Seine congress, held November 1935.

Movement for the Fourth International (MFI): The name of the international Trotskyist movement from July 1936 until September 1938.

Mulhouse congress of SFIO (June 1935): High point of GBL influence in the SFIO. The Bolshevik-Leninists had three delegates whose vigorous activity forced the other tendencies to debate their views, but they were politically isolated at the congress, which was largely devoted to hailing the People's Front.

Naville, Pierre (1904-   ): A founder of the French section in 1929 and a member of the IS through most of the thirties. His group split when a majority of the section voted to enter the SFIO in 1934, but entered shortly thereafter; he was one of the GBL spokesmen at the Mulhouse congress although the two groups were not formally reunited until September 1935.

Neo-Socialists: The right wing of the SFIO, which left the party in 1933.

Neue Front, Die: Newspaper of the German SAP.

Open Letter for the Fourth International: An appeal signed by representatives of the Dutch RSAP, Workers Party of the U.S., Workers Party of Canada, GBL, and IS, published in July 1935.

Organic unity: A movement term for a CP-SFIO merger.

Paul-Boncour, Joseph (1873-1972): A right-wing Socialist until 1931; premier, 1932-33; minister of foreign affairs in Blum's second government.

Paz, Magdeleine: A former Left Oppositionist, active in French civil liberties work in the thirties.

Paz, Maurice (1896-   ): Broke with the Left Opposition in 1929, joined the SFIO and became part of its leadership.

PCI: Parti Communiste Internationaliste, see Internationalist Communist Party.

People's Front: Coalition of the SFIO and CP with the Radical and other bourgeois parties, formed in July 1935. Won the parliamentary elections in May 1936 and held office 1936-38.

Pioneers: Those too young to join the Communist Youth.

Pivert, Marceau (1895-1958): A leader of the Seine (Paris) Federation of the SFIO and Zyromsky's lieutenant in the *Bataille Socialiste* group. Founded the Revolutionary Left in the SFIO in 1935; condemned the expulsions of Bolshevik-Leninists but urged them to avoid provoking the SFIO leaders. Served as an aide to Léon Blum in the first People's Front government. Left the SFIO and founded the PSOP (Workers and Peasants Socialist Party) in 1938; returned to the SFIO after World War II.

Plenum: The highest body of the ICL between international conferences. Included members of the IS and other ICL leaders. Composition in spring 1935: Cannon, Craipeau, R. Fischer, Leonetti, Lesoil, Molinier, Schmidt, Sedov, Sneevliet, Trotsky, Vereecken.

POB: Parti Ouvrier Belge, the Belgian Labor Party.

POI: Parti Ouvrier Internationaliste, see Internationalist Workers Party.

Populaire, Le: The official SFIO newspaper.

POR: Parti Ouvrier Révolutionnaire, see Revolutionary Workers Party.

Proudhon, Pierre Joseph (1809-1865): An early theoretician of anarchism.

Que faire? (What is to be done?): Began in 1934 as a small centrist group distributing a bulletin advocating a united front with the SFIO. Later joined by ex-Trotskyists. Published a magazine until 1939. Its chief leaders were expelled from the CP in 1936. Most of its members joined the SFIO in 1938 and supported organic unity.

Radicals (Radical Socialists): The principal party of French capitalism between the world wars, comparable to the Democrats in the U.S.

Rakovsky, Christian (1873-1941): An early leader of the Russian Left Opposition and the last known to capitulate to Stalin, in 1934. A defendant in the third Moscow trial.

Révolution, La: The newspaper of the Seine (Paris) Alliance of the Young Socialists, under the influence of the Bolshevik-Leninists; later became the paper of the JSR.

Revolutionary Action Groups (GARs): Amorphous bodies formed in October 1935 including Bolshevik-Leninists, Pivertists, and other left-wingers. Seen variously as embryos of a new revolutionary party or of soviets.

Revolutionary Left (GR): Organized by Pivert in the SFIO in September 1935. Repeated many of the slogans the GBL had popularized in the SFIO, but remained equivocal on the People's Front and the new International.

Revolutionary Socialist Youth (JSR): Officially formed in January 1936 by the revolutionary Young Socialists expelled from the JS, although the name was used earlier. Later became the youth affiliate of the POI.

Revolutionary Workers Party (POR): Short-lived party formed in June 1936 by the majority of the former GBL and the JSR, for the purpose of merging with the PCI to form the POI.

Révolution proletarienne: A syndicalist journal published by former members of the CP.

Rigal, Louis (1911-   ): A leader of the Bolshevik-Leninist youth and the Seine Young Socialists, expelled from the JS in July 1935.

Rolland, Romain (1866-1944): A French novelist; lent his name to Stalinist literary causes and supported the Moscow trials.

Rosenthal, Gérard (1903-   ): A political ally of Naville and Trotsky's attorney in France.

Rosmer, Alfred (1877-1964): A revolutionary syndicalist, then a member of the Left Opposition until 1930.

Rote Front, Die: The publication of a German-speaking Trotskyist group in Czechoslovakia.

Rous, Jean (1908-   ): A lawyer and former SFIO member who joined the Communist League in 1932. National secretary of the GBL and a member of the IS.

Rousset, David (1912-   ): A leader of the Bolshevik-Leninist youth, expelled from the JS in July 1935.

Sacred union: The French expression for wartime class collaboration.

Salengro, Roger (1890-1936): Blum's minister of the interior in 1936.

276 *Crisis of the French Section (1935-36)*

Tried to halt factory occupations during the strike wave and persecuted the POI and its press.

SAP: Sozialistische Arbeiterpartei, see Socialist Workers Party of Germany.

Schwab, Jim (1887-   ): Also called Jakob Walcher; a founder of the German CP, expelled as a supporter of the Right Opposition. Became a leader of the SAP in 1932.

Second International: From 1889 to 1914, a loose association of labor and Social Democratic parties, uniting both reformist and revolutionary elements. Its major sections supported their own imperialist governments in World War I. Fell apart during the war, but was revived in 1919 as a completely reformist organization.

Sedov, Leon ("D") (1906-1938): Trotsky's son and chief collaborator; a member of the IS.

Seine Alliance: The Paris section of the Young Socialists.

Seine congress of the SFIO (November 1935): Notable because Pivert voted for Blum's political resolution and declined to speak against the expulsion of the Bolshevik-Leninists.

Seine Federation: The Paris section of the SFIO.

Séverac, Jean-Baptiste (1879-1951): Administrative secretary of the SFIO.

SFIO: Section Française de l'Internationale Ouvrière (French Section of the Labor [Second] International), the official name of the French Socialist Party before World War II. In 1920 a majority of the SFIO left to form the French CP; the reformist minority retained the name.

Social Front ("Frontists"): A petty-bourgeois group founded in 1933; some former members participated in Revolutionary Action Groups.

Socialist Party: see SFIO.

Socialist Workers Party of Germany (SAP): Formed from a split in the German Social Democracy in 1931. Joined with the International Left Opposition in 1933 in signing the Declaration of the Four, for a new International, but moved rapidly to the right, endorsing a People's Front for Germany.

Spartacus group: A small centrist group in the left wing of the SFIO and JS that was ideologically close to the SAP.

Stalin, Joseph (1879-1953): General secretary of the Soviet CP from 1922 until his death, a post he used to bureaucratize the party and state apparatuses and eliminate all opponents.

Syndicalists, revolutionary: Militants who relied on the trade unions instead of a political party to overthrow capitalism; before World War I they organized opposition to class collaborationist tendencies in the trade unions.

Théodor: Code name for the IS.

Third (Communist) International (Comintern): Organized by Lenin as a revolutionary successor to the Second International and turned by Stalin into a tool of the conservative Soviet bureaucracy before being dissolved in 1943. Its 7th Congress in 1935 adopted the People's Front policy.

Thorez, Maurice (1900-1964): General secretary of the CP. After World War II became a minister in the Gaullist government.

TPPS (Toujours Prêts Pour Servir—Always Ready to Serve): SFIO defense guard, organized primarily by GBL members and Pivertists in the Seine Federation of the SFIO to protect meetings and literature sales against fascist attacks.

Treint, Albert (1889-1972): A former leader of the French CP and briefly a member of the Communist League. Became a syndicalist.

Vandervelde, Emile (1866-1938): Belgian Labor Party leader and president of the Second International, 1929-36.

Van Heijenoort, Jean ("Van") (1912-   ): Served as Trotsky's secretary in all four countries of his last exile. Briefly a supporter of the Molinier tendency in 1935.

Vérité, La: The newspaper of the French Trotskyists, 1929-36.

Wels, Otto (1873-1939): A leading functionary of the German Social Democratic Party. As military commander of Berlin, crushed the uprising of 1919. Later led his party's delegation in the Reichstag.

Wolf, Erwin ("Nicolle Braun"): A Czech Trotskyist and member of the IS; Trotsky's secretary in Norway, where he wrote *L'Organe de masse* (The Mass Paper). Killed by the GPU in Spain.

Young Socialist Guards (JGS): The Belgian Labor Party's youth group.

Young Socialists (JS): The SFIO youth group.

Zeller, Fred (1912-   ): The leader of the Seine (Paris) Alliance of the JS, expelled in July 1935. Belonged to the Revolutionary Left before joining the GBL. Visited Trotsky in Norway and wrote a pamphlet on the lessons of the SFIO expulsions, *The Road for Revolutionary Socialists,* with an introduction by Trotsky. Became international youth secretary of the ICL and a leader of the French party until 1937.

Zinoviev, Gregory (1883-1936): A prominent Russian Bolshevik and head of the Comintern, 1919-26; helped Stalin initiate the crusade against Trotskyism, then blocked with Trotsky, 1926-27. Capitulated when expelled from the party. A victim of the first Moscow trial.

Zyromsky, Jean (1890-1975): Leader of the right wing of the *Bataille Socialiste* group in the SFIO. Advocated organic unity with the CP in the thirties and joined the CP in 1945.

Selected Bibliography

The following list of books and pamphlets, which does not exhaust the literature on this subject or the sources consulted in preparing this book, may help students of the period and other readers interested in delving more deeply into the history of the French section of the Fourth International.

Craipeau, Yvan. *Le Mouvement trotskyste en France.* Paris, 1971.
———. *Contre vents et marées: les révolutionnaires pendant la seconde guerre mondiale.* Paris, 1977.
La Crise de la Section Française de la Ligue Communiste Internationaliste (1935-36). Paris, 1936.
La Crise des Bolcheviks-Léninistes. Paris, 1939.
Danos, Jacques and Marcel Gibelin. *Juin 36.* Paris, 1972.
Deutscher, Isaac. *The Prophet Outcast. Trotsky 1929-40.* New York, 1963.
Documents of the Fourth International: The Formative Years (1933-40). New York, 1973.
Frank, Pierre. *La Quatrième internationale; contribution à l'histoire du mouvement trotskyste.* Paris, 1969. (Translated into English in *Intercontinental Press,* March 13–June 5, 1972.)
———. *La semaine du 6 au 12 février. Pour l'alliance ouvrière! Pour l'alliance internationale!* Paris, 1934.
Gras, Christian. *Alfred Rosmer et le mouvement révolutionnaire internationale.* Paris, 1971.
Guérin, Daniel. *Front populaire, révolution manquée.* 2nd ed. Paris, 1970.
Joubert, Jean-Paul. *Révolutionnaires de la SFIO.* Paris, 1977.
Marie, Jean-Jacques. *Le Trotskysme.* Paris, 1970.
Naville, Pierre. *L'entre-deux guerres. La lutte des classes en France 1926-1939.* Paris, 1975.
———. *Trotsky vivant.* Paris, 1962.
Quélques enseignements de notre histoire (supplement to *La Vérité,* no. 548). Paris, 1970.

Rabaut, Jean. *Tout est possible! Les "gauchistes" français 1929-1944*. Paris, 1974.

Rioux, Jean-Pierre. *Révolutionnaires du front populaire*. Paris, 1973.

Rosenthal, Gérard. *L'Avocat de Trotsky*. Paris, 1975.

Roussel, Jacques. *Les Enfants du prophète. Histoire du mouvement trotskyste en France*. Paris, 1972.

Serge, Victor. *Memoirs of a Revolutionary 1901-1941*. Oxford, 1967.

———and Leon Trotsky. *La Lutte contre le stalinisme*. Edited by Michel Dreyfus. Paris 1977.

Sinclair, Louis. *Leon Trotsky: A Bibliography*. Stanford (Calif.), 1972.

Trotsky, Leon. *Leon Trotsky on France* (includes *Whither France?*). (to be published 1978).

———. *Le Mouvement communiste en France 1919-1939*. Edited and annotated by Pierre Broué. Paris, 1967.

———. *Trotsky's Diary in Exile, 1935*. 2nd ed. Introduction by Jean van Heijenoort. Cambridge (Mass.), 1976.

———. *Writings of Leon Trotsky (1929-40)*. See particularly volumes written in France ("1933-34" and "1934-35") and in Norway ("1935-36"). New York, 1969-77.

Vereeken, Georges. *The GPU in the Trotskyist Movement*. London, 1976.

Zeller, Fred. *The Road for Revolutionary Socialists*. Introduction by Leon Trotsky. New York, 1936.

———. *Trois points c'est tout*. Paris, 1976.

Also consulted for this period were the following periodicals: *La Commune, Lutte de classes, Lutte ouvrière, New Militant, Quatrième Internationale, Révolution, Socialist Appeal, La Vérité;* international bulletins and the press service of the International Communist League; and internal bulletins of the Bolshevik-Leninist Group (GBL), the Internationalist Workers Party (POI), and the Internationalist Communist Party (PCI), all of France, and of the Workers Party of the United States (WPUS).

INDEX

Action française, l', 148
Action socialiste, l', 203
Adolphe, *see* Klement, Rudolf
Amsterdam secretariat (of Fourth International), 132-33, 134, 253
Anonymity, in politics, 95, 104, 111-12, 115, 204-05n, 228, 229, 239
"Antifascism," 128, 231
ASR group (Belgium), 76, 269g
Attlee, Clement, 65, 269g
Austria, 41, 265n.1

Bakunin, Mikhail, 130, 269g
Baldwin, Stanley, 65, 269g
Bardin, Alexis, 42, 159, 200, 269g
Bardin, Joannès ("Boitel"), 143n, 159, 169, 200, 269g
Bataille Socialiste group, 23, 24, 42, 176, 203, 208, 262, 269g
Bauer, Erwin, 21
Bauer, Otto, 124, 267n.20
"Before the Second Stage," 153
Belgium, 112, 142
Bergery, Gaston, 123, 269g
Biau, 180
Biron, 239-40
Blanqui, Louis-Auguste, 98-99, 269g
Blasco, 216
Blum, Léon, 203, 269g; engineers expulsion of Bolshevik-Leninists, 29, 64, 76, 117, 124, 185, 187; government of, 148, 150, 163, 166; and social patriotism, 41, 49, 52, 53, 58, 60, 62, 64, 85, 98, 103-04, 111-12, 120, 124, 193, 195; *see also* People's Front
Boitel, *see* Bardin, Joannès
Bolshevik-Leninist Group (GBL), 141-43, 144, 269g; activity in SFIO, 23-24, 53, 124, 175-79, 197; activity in spring 1936 strike wave, 135-36, 149-51; attempts to gain readmission to SFIO, 29-34, 43, 49-50, 51, 54, 75-76, 78-80, 181, 183-90, 216; and attention to CP, 139, 147-48, 154, 179; centrism in, 212, 213, 220, 222, 231, 233; and *Commune*

group, 95-96, 97-102, 102-05, 106-09, 115, 126-30, 218-25, 239, 245-59; conciliationism in, 87-88, 92, 130-32, 199, 213-16, 219, 221-25, 247-53; expelled from SFIO, 10, 11, 28-32, 34, 42, 43-44, 61-63, 75, 100-01, 184, 187, 215, 216, 221; fails to take offensive after Mulhouse, 29-35, 75-77, 78-80, l00-01, 124, 142, 147, 182-90; handling of crisis by, 90-91, 103, 132-33, 134, 144, 241, 245-59; Lyons group in, 248, 250; mass paper controversy in, *see* "Mass paper" controversy; and Molinier's call for national conference to discuss split, 247-48, 257; and Motion C, 208-09, 236; National Conference of (Sept. 1935), 27, 32, 33, 190, 196, 199, 200-02, 204, 206, 242-43, 257-58; new party controversy in, *see* Independent party; and Open Letter for FI, 26, 29, 30, 48, 183-85, 193, 198, 246, 253; and People's Front, 27-28, 148-51, 163; and Pivertists, 29-31, 33-34, 37, 48, 75, 78-80, 104, 203, 207-09, 215, 218, 246, 249; and proposed fusion with JSR, 34, 96, 101, 110n, 122, 220; and proposed visit by conciliators to Trotsky, 92, 130-32, 252-53; and unification with PCI (June 1936), 136, 141, 151, 152, 158, 160, 162, 258, 260; *see also* Communist League of France *and* Internationalist Workers Party
Bolshevik Party, 228; democracy in, 44-45, 47
Bolshevism, 56, 168
Bonapartism, 82, 85, 111, 266n.11
Brandler, Heinrich, 57, 226, 269g
Braun, Nicolle, *see* Wolf, Erwin
Briand, Aristide, 57, 269g
Brissac, Jeanne, 201n
British Labour Party, 65
Brüning, Heinrich, 111, 267n
Burnham, James, 170

Cachin, Marcel, 41, 49, 64, 85, 111, 269g

280

272g, 276g; on alliance with Revolutionary Left, 80; on *La Commune* adventure, 88, 95-96, 105, 223, 224, 250, 256; on Molinier's finances, 138, 157, 158, 159; on People's Front, 55-58; on PSOP, 169; on reunification of French section, 136
Intransigeant, l', 159, 268n.28

James, C.L.R., 167, 169-70, 263
Jaurès, Jean, 42, 272n
Jouhaux, Léon, 42, 49, 64, 65, 120, 272n
JS, *see* Young Socialists
JSR, *see* Revolutionary Socialist Youth

Kamenev, Leon, 76, 104, 165, 221, 266n.8, 272g
Keller, Werner, *see* Frankel, Jan
Klement, Rudolf ("Adolphe," "Frédéric"), 95, 128, 272g
Kuomintang (China), 50, 57, 116, 117, 265n.1

Lagorgette, Louis, 117, 272g
Lansbury, George, 63, 272g
Laval, Pierre, 23, 30, 49, 63, 82, 85, 111, 114, 272g; *see also* Stalin-Laval pact
League of Nations, 65, 265n.6
Lebas, Jean-Baptiste, 41, 62, 117, 272g
Lenin, V.I., 64, 100, 119, 241, 272g; on organization, 68, 70, 72, 123; on sectarianism, 69; testament of, 76, 160, 266n.8; on war, 52, 226
Liebknecht, Karl, 52, 63, 226, 241, 273g
Lille affair, *see* Molinier, Raymond
Lille case (of workers' control), 153, 268n.27
Lille congress of Young Socialists, *see* Young Socialists, Lille congress expulsions from
Longuet, Jean, 46, 273g
Louzon, Robert, 67, 273g
Loyalty statement to SFIO bureaucracy, 34-35, 87, 215, 217
Lutte de classes, La, 18, 22, 52, 187, 232n, 273g
Lutte ouvrière, La, 136, 139, 144-45, 147-48, 160, 273g
Luxemburg, Rosa, 241
Lyons group of GBL, 248, 250

M., *see* Molinier, Raymond
MacDonald, James R., 65, 273g
Makarowski, 191
Maneuvers, 186, 188-89, 214-15
Martynov, Alexander, 273g

Marx, Karl, 99-100, 111, 119, 123, 273g
Mass Paper, The, see Organe de masse, l'
"Mass paper" controversy in GBL, 27, 31, 39, 40, 97-102, 117, 118, 185, 251; vs. cadre journal, 98, 234-35; character of, 27, 98, 131, 249; *La Vérité* vs. *Révolution,* 32, 77, 88, 198, 202, 212, 214, 222, 231-35; *see also Commune, La*
Matin, le, 149
Maurín Julia, Joaquín, 231, 273g
Maxton, James, 231, 273g
Meichler, Jean ("Mèche"), 158, 273g
Menshevism, 56, 57, 64
MFI, *see* Movement for the Fourth International
Molinier, Henri, 158, 160, 273g
Molinier, Raymond ("M," "R.M."): appeals to GBL for unity, 247-48, 249, 254; behavior of, in POI, 137-39, 146, 147, 151, 158-59, 165; "business affairs" of, 18-19, 138, 139, 152, 157, 159, 161; on entering SFIO, 20, 123; expelled from GBL, 90; expelled from plenum of ICL, 89, 105, 128, 151, 224, 250; financial pressure by, 152, 158, 168, 218; and GARs, 36, 111, 117; indiscipline by, 35, 196-97, 201, 216-21, 247; on leaving SFIO, 25, 29-32, 35, 100, 124, 125, 182n, 189, 190, 194-200, 202, 206, 210-16; and Lille affair, 157, 161; and mass paper, 36-37, 87-93, 212, 214, 218-25, 227; on new party, 32, 34-35, 202; organizes CQI, 92, 132-34, 241; organizes PCI, 93, 242-44; personal qualities of, 67-68, 105, 109, 113-14, 118-19, 146, 157, 170-71; and Pivertists, 31, 33, 101, 103, 113, 117, 192-93, 194, 203-06; program of, 89-90, 102-05, 106-08, 121-23, 126-30; proposes open Central Committee, 139, 146-47; proposes that conciliators visit Trotsky (January 1936), 130n, 132, 252-53; and PSOP, 169; suspension of, from SFIO, 187, 200; on *Vérité,* 31, 186, 194, 216, 231-32n; visits Trotsky (July 1936), 139, 156-62; and youth, 96, 116-17, 118, 218, 238
Monatte, Pierre, 67, 273g
Monmousseau, Gaston, 42, 49, 64, 65, 273g
Moscow trial (August 1936), 165
Mot-Dag, 273g
Motion C, 33-34, 78, 80, 208-09, 236, 266n.7, 273g

FOR FURTHER READING

The History of the Russian Revolution
Leon Trotsky
The social, economic, and political dynamics of the first socialist revolution. The story is told by one of the revolution's principal leaders writing from exile in the early 1930s, with these historic events still fresh in his mind. Unabridged edition, 3 vols. in one. $35.95

The First Five Years of the Communist International
Leon Trotsky
The early years of the Communist International, documented in articles and speeches by one of its founding leaders. Two volumes, $25.95 each

Imperialism: The Highest Stage of Capitalism
V.I. Lenin
"I trust that this pamphlet will help the reader to understand the fundamental economic question, that of the economic essence of imperialism," Lenin wrote in 1917. "For unless this is studied, it will be impossible to understand and appraise modern war and modern politics." $3.95

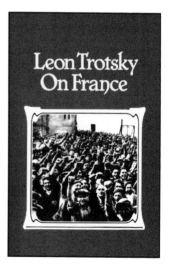

Leon Trotsky on France
An assessment of the social and economic crisis that shook France in the mid-1930s in the aftermath of Hitler's rise to power in Germany, and a program to unite the working class and exploited peasantry to confront it. $21.95

Write for catalog. See front of book for addresses.

Collected Works of V.I. Lenin

Writings of V.I. Lenin (1870–1924), the central
leader of the Bolshevik Party, the October 1917
Russian revolution, the young Soviet republic, and
the early Communist International. 47 vols.
$500.00

Alliance of the Working Class and the Peasantry

V.I. Lenin

From the early years of the Marxist movement in Russia, Lenin fought to
forge an alliance between the working class and the toiling peasantry.
Such an alliance was needed to make possible working-class leadership
of the democratic revolution and, on that basis, the opening of the
socialist revolution. $17.95

The Revolution Betrayed

What Is the Soviet Union and Where Is It Going?
Leon Trotsky

In 1917 the working class and peasantry of Russia carried out one of the
most deep-going revolutions in history. Yet within ten years reaction set
in. Workers and peasants were driven from power by a privileged
bureaucratic social layer led by Joseph Stalin. This classic study of the
Soviet workers state and its degeneration illuminates the roots of the
social and political crisis shaking the countries of the former Soviet
Union today. $19.95

Lenin's Final Fight

Speeches and Writings, 1922–23
V.I. Lenin

The record of Lenin's last effort to win the
leadership of the Communist Party of the USSR in
the early 1920s to maintain the political course
that had enabled the workers and peasants to
overthrow the old tsarist empire, carry out the
first successful socialist revolution, and begin
building a world communist movement. The
issues posed in that political battle remain at the
heart of world politics today. Includes several
items appearing in English for the first time.
$19.95

The Communist International in Lenin's Time

Workers of the World and Oppressed Peoples, Unite!
Proceedings and Documents of the Second Congress, 1920
The debate among delegates from 37 countries
takes up key questions of working-class strategy
and program and offers a vivid portrait of social
struggles in the era of the October revolution.
2-vol. set $65

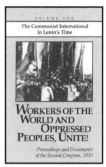

To See the Dawn
*Baku, 1920—First Congress of the
Peoples of the East*
How can peasants and workers in the colonial
world achieve freedom from imperialist
exploitation? By what means can working people
overcome divisions incited by their national ruling
classes and act together for their common class
interests? These questions were addressed by 2,000
delegates to the 1920 Congress of the Peoples of
the East. $19.95

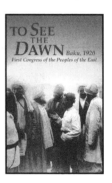

Lenin's Struggle for a Revolutionary International
Documents,1907–1916; The Preparatory Years
The debate among revolutionary working-class
leaders, including V.I. Lenin and Leon Trotsky, on a
socialist response to World War I. $32.95

The German Revolution and the Debate on Soviet Power
*Documents, 1918–1919; Preparing the
Founding Congress*
$31.95

Founding the Communist International
*Proceedings and Documents of the
First Congress, March 1919*
$27.95

AVAILABLE FROM PATHFINDER

Also from PATHFINDER

The Changing Face of U.S. Politics

Working-Class Politics and the Trade Unions
JACK BARNES

A handbook for workers coming into the factories, mines, and mills, as they react to the uncertain life, ceaseless turmoil, and brutality of capitalism in the closing years of the twentieth century. It shows how millions of workers, as political resistance grows, will revolutionize themselves, their unions, and all of society. $19.95

Woman's Evolution

From Matriarchal Clan to Patriarchal Family
EVELYN REED

Assesses women's leading and still largely unknown contributions to the development of human civilization and refutes the myth that women have always been subordinate to men. "Certain to become a classic text in women's history"—*Publishers Weekly*. $22.95

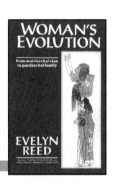

Episodes of the Cuban Revolutionary War, 1956–58

ERNESTO CHE GUEVARA

A firsthand account of the military campaigns and political events that culminated in the January 1959 popular insurrection that overthrew the U.S.-backed dictatorship in Cuba. Guevara describes how the struggle transformed the men and women of the Rebel Army and July 26 Movement led by Fidel Castro. And how these combatants forged a political leadership capable of guiding millions of workers and peasants to open the socialist revolution in the Americas. Guevara's *Episodes* appears here complete for the first time in English. Introduction by Mary-Alice Waters. $23.95

The History of American Trotskyism

JAMES P. CANNON

"Trotskyism is not a new movement, a new doctrine," Cannon says, "but the restoration, the revival of genuine Marxism as it was expounded and practiced in the Russian revolution and in the early days of the Communist International." In this series of twelve talks given in 1942, James P. Cannon recounts an important chapter in the efforts to build a proletarian party in the United States. $18.95

The Politics of Chicano Liberation

Recounts the lessons of the rise of the Chicano movement in the United States in the 1960s and 1970s, which dealt a lasting blow against the oppression of the Chicano people and the divisions within the working class based on language and national origin. Presents a fighting program for those today who are determined to defend hard-won social conquests and build a revolutionary movement capable of leading humanity out of the wars, racist assaults, and social crisis of capitalism in its decline. $15.95

February 1965: The Final Speeches

MALCOLM X

Speeches from the last three weeks of Malcolm X's life, presenting the accelerating evolution of his political views. A large part is material previously unavailable, with some in print for the first time. The inaugural volume in Pathfinder's selected works of Malcolm X. $17.95

Teamster Rebellion

FARRELL DOBBS

The 1934 strikes that built an industrial union and a fighting social movement in Minneapolis, recounted by a leader of that battle. The first in a four-volume series on the Teamster-led strikes and organizing drives in the Midwest that helped pave the way for the CIO and pointed a road toward independent labor political action. $16.95

The Communist Manifesto

KARL MARX, FREDERICK ENGELS

Founding document of the modern working-class movement, published in 1848. Explains why communists act on the basis not of preconceived principles but of *facts* springing from the actual class struggle, and why communism, to the degree it is a theory, is the generalization of the historical line of march of the working class and of the political conditions for its liberation. Also available in Spanish. Booklet $3.95

In Defense of Socialism

FIDEL CASTRO

Not only is economic and social progress possible without the dog-eat-dog competition of capitalism, Castro argues, but socialism remains the only way forward for humanity. Also discusses Cuba's role in the struggle against the apartheid regime in southern Africa. $13.95

The Struggle for a Proletarian Party

JAMES P. CANNON

In a political struggle in the late 1930s with a petty-bourgeois current in the Socialist Workers Party, Cannon and other SWP leaders defended the political and organizational principles of Marxism. The debate unfolded as Washington prepared to drag U.S. working people into the slaughter of World War II. A companion to *In Defense of Marxism* by Leon Trotsky. $19.95

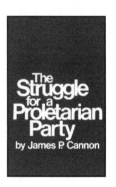

Nelson Mandela Speaks

Forging a Democratic, Nonracial South Africa

Mandela's speeches from 1990 through 1993 recount the course of struggle that put an end to apartheid and opened the fight for a deep-going political, economic, and social transformation in South Africa. $18.95

Write for a catalog

New International

A MAGAZINE OF MARXIST POLITICS AND THEORY

New International no. 10

Imperialism's March toward Fascism and War *by Jack Barnes* • What the 1987 Stock Market Crash Foretold • Defending Cuba, Defending Cuba's Socialist Revolution *by Mary-Alice Waters* • The Curve of Capitalist Development *by Leon Trotsky* $14.00

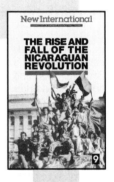

New International no. 9

The Triumph of the Nicaraguan Revolution • Washington's Contra War and the Challenge of Forging Proletarian Leadership • The Political Degeneration of the FSLN and the Demise of the Workers and Farmers Government $14.00

New International no. 8

The Politics of Economics: Che Guevara and Marxist Continuity *by Steve Clark and Jack Barnes* • Che's Contribution to the Cuban Economy *by Carlos Rafael Rodríguez* • On the Concept of Value *and* The Meaning of Socialist Planning *two articles by Ernesto Che Guevara* $10.00

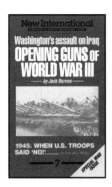

New International no. 7

Opening Guns of World War III:
Washington's Assault on Iraq *by Jack Barnes*
• Communist Policy in Wartime as well as
in Peacetime *by Mary-Alice Waters* •
Lessons from the Iran-Iraq War *by Samad
Sharif* $12.00

New International no. 6

The Second Assassination of Maurice Bishop
by Steve Clark • Washington's 50-year
Domestic Contra Operation *by Larry Seigle*
• Land, Labor, and the Canadian Revolution
by Michel Dugré • Renewal or Death:
Cuba's Rectification Process *two speeches
by Fidel Castro* $10.00

New International no. 5

The Coming Revolution in South Africa *by Jack
Barnes* • The Future Belongs to the Majority *by
Oliver Tambo* • Why Cuban Volunteers Are in
Angola *two speeches by Fidel Castro* $9.00

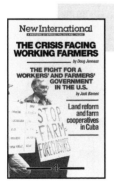

New International no. 4

The Fight for a Workers and Farmers
Government in the United States *by Jack
Barnes* • The Crisis Facing Working
Farmers *by Doug Jenness* • Land Reform
and Farm Cooperatives in Cuba *two
speeches by Fidel Castro* $9.00

New International no. 3

Communism and the Fight for a Popular Revolutionary Government: 1848 to Today *by Mary-Alice Waters* • 'A Nose for Power': Preparing the Nicaraguan Revolution *by Tomás Borge* • National Liberation and Socialism in the Americas *by Manuel Piñeiro* $8.00

New International no. 2

The Aristocracy of Labor: Development of the Marxist Position *by Steve Clark* • The Working-Class Fight for Peace *by Brian Grogan* • The Social Roots of Opportunism *by Gregory Zinoviev* $8.00

New International no. 1

Their Trotsky and Ours: Communist Continuity Today *by Jack Barnes* • Lenin and the Colonial Question *by Carlos Rafael Rodríguez* • The 1916 Easter Rebellion in Ireland: Two Views *by V.I. Lenin and Leon Trotsky* $8.00

Distributed by Pathfinder

Many of the articles that appear in *New International* are also available in Spanish in *Nueva Internacional,* in French in *Nouvelle Internationale,* and in Swedish in *Ny International.*